Introduction to Psychoanalysis

The psychoanalytic movement has expanded and diversified in many directions over its one hundred year history. *Introduction to Psychoanalysis: Contemporary Theory and Practice* examines the contributions made by the various schools of thought, explaining the similarities and differences between Contemporary Freudian, Independent, Kleinian, Object Relations, Interpersonal, Self Psychological and Lacanian analysis. The authors address crucial questions about the role of psychoanalysis in psychiatry and look ahead to the future.

The book is divided into two parts covering theory and practice. The first part considers theories of psychological development, transference and countertransference, dreams, defence mechanisms, and the various models of the mind. The second part is a practical introduction to psychoanalytic technique with specific chapters on psychoanalytic research and the application of psychoanalytic ideas and methods to treating psychiatric illness.

Well referenced and illustrated throughout with vivid clinical examples, this will be an invaluable text for undergraduate and postgraduate courses in psychoanalysis and psychoanaltytic psychotherapy, and an excellent source of reference for students and professionals in psychiatry, psychology, social work, and mental health nursing.

Anthony Bateman is Consultant Psychotherapist, St Ann's Hospital, London and a member of the British Psychoanalytical Society. **Jeremy Holmes** is Consultant Psychotherapist and Psychiatrist, North Devon.

D0508569

Introduction to Psychoanalysis

Contemporary theory and practice

Anthony Bateman and
Jeremy Holmes

London and New York

First published 1995
by Routledge
11 New Fetter Lane, London EC4P 4EE

Simultaneously published in the USA and Canada
by Routledge
29 West 35th Street, New York, NY 10001

Reprinted 1996 and 1999

Typeset in Times by
Ponting-Green Publishing Services, Chesham, Bucks
Printed and bound in Great Britain by
Mackays of Chatham PLC, Chatham, Kent

British Library Cataloguing in Publication Data
A catalogue record for this book is available from the
British Library

Library of Congress Cataloguing in Publication Data
Bateman, Anthony
    Introduction to psychoanalysis: contemporary theory and
    practice / Anthony Bateman and Jeremy Holmes.
    p.   cm.
    Includes bibliographical references and index.
    1. Psychoanalysis. I. Holmes, Jeremy. II. Title.
    [DNLM: 1. Psychoanalysis. 2. Psychoanalytic Theory.
    3. Psychoanalytic Therapy. WM 460 B328i 1995]
    RC504.B295   1995
    616.89´17–dc20
    DNLM/DLC
    for Library of Congress   95–7617
                                                        CIP

ISBN 0–415–10738–5 (hbk)
ISBN 0–415–10739–3 (pbk)

Contents

Preface

Newcomers to psychoanalysis, especially if they wish to avoid confusion, are usually best advised to go straight to Freud – to the lectures on technique (Freud 1912a, b; 1914a), the Introductory Lectures (Freud 1916/17), or the two encyclopedia articles (Freud 1922). This is not just because Freud is the fount from which psychoanalysis has flowed, or because of the clarity of his thought and style, or even because 'going back to Freud' remains a psychoanalytic imperative. It is also because in the early years a single psychoanalytic 'mastertext' (Schafer 1990) was still possible, in a way that has become increasingly problematic as the psychoanalytic movement has both expanded and diversified, but also been challenged by controversy and schism.

There are many excellent introductory or semi-introductory contemporary books about the practice of psychoanalysis. Those that we have found especially useful are starred in the bibliography. Each tends to present a particular perspective on the psychoanalytic process: Kleinian, Independent, Contemporary Freudian, Interpersonal, Kohutian, Lacanian, Ego Psychological. This is partly an inevitable result of the unique centrality of personal analysis in analytic training. Each of the differing psychoanalytic approaches represents not just a theoretical orientation, but a tradition, style, affiliation, and set of common values and assumptions that the analysand will acquire in the course of this training. He or she has to undergo the maturational task of both assimilating all that has been identified with, and at the same time achieving the inner freedom needed to find his or her own analytic voice.

When we were invited by Edwina Welham of Routledge, at Jonathan Pedder's suggestion, to write a companion volume to the *Introduction to Psychotherapy* (Brown and Pedder 1993), we felt that the time was ripe for an attempt to bring together the varying strands of psychoanalytic theory and practice, to highlight their 'common ground' (Wallerstein 1992) as well as their differences. We were encouraged by the idea that despite theoretical divergence, 'clinical theory' (G. Klein 1976) can be unified in a meaningful way. We were determined to anchor our text with many clinical examples, and to try to show how a variety of clinical approaches fit within a common framework. We are aware of the dangers and pitfalls of both sectarianism and eclecticism. Analysts need to be able to draw on the range of different ideas and techniques that are encompassed within the diversity of their profession. At the same time, in order to practise effectively, most need to work within a particular analytic perspective.

Our book is perhaps in the 'critical dictionary' (Rycroft 1972; Hinshelwood 1989) tradition in that it tries to clarify, question and extract what is valuable from each psychoanalytic viewpoint. Wherever possible, we have brought research findings to bear on psychoanalytic concepts and practice, and, within the limitations of the lag between composition and publication, to be as up-to-date as possible with contemporary psychoanalytic thought. We have sub-titled our book 'contemporary theory and practice', drawing a useful, but none the less somewhat artificial, contrast between 'classical' and 'modern' (or 'contemporary') practice and thought. 'Classical' and 'modern', while useful as a shorthand, should not be thought of as oppositional, but rather the one resting on the other. Also, since we work both simultaneously within a public sector psychiatric context as well as private practice, we have angled a fair proportion of what we discuss towards the role of psychoanalytic therapy with quite disturbed patients.

That raises the issues of who *we*, the authors are. One of us (AB) is an analyst with considerable psychiatric experience, the other (JH) also a psychiatrist and psychotherapist with psychoanalytic leanings. We hope that as a team we have enough in common to provide a unified view, and enough difference to add breadth to our exposition. On the whole our collaboration has run smoothly. On occasions one of us has felt that we have been too critical and not 'analytic' enough; the other that we were being too reverential and have failed to locate the analytic approach within a wider context.

And what of *you*, the reader? Our hope was to produce a book that would be useful for students of psychoanalysis and psychoanalytic psychotherapy looking for a single volume that would encompass the main principles and practice of contemporary psychoanalysis, be clinically relevant, and theoretically stimulating. For some, no doubt, much of what we say will be familiar, for others obscure. We hope we have created sufficient transitional space between innocence and experience to be of value.

We are only too aware of the many faults of omission and commission in the book. We have tackled the issues of ethnicity, class and gender in only a very limited way. Apropos of the latter, like many contemporary authors we have been stymied by the problem of pronouns, but, in the end, reluctantly have stayed with the less obtrusive, but patriarchal 'he', despite the fact that statistically, female analysts and patients probably outnumber males. Our psychoanalytic approach is almost exclusively 'Freudian', and we have undoubtedly failed to do justice to the scope of Jungian psychoanalysis. Another notable omission is any serious consideration of child psychoanalysis, which is outwith both our competences. Lacking space rather than enthusiasm, we have failed to follow the important cultural ramifications of psychoanalysis into the fields of literary theory, psychohistory and sociology. The text is illustrated with many examples. We are deeply aware of the ethical difficulties in using case material in print. In some instances we have asked our patients for permission to publish such material. In others this has not been possible, but we have in every case disguised and fictionalised biographical details.

Books should not necessarily be read from start to finish. Each chapter is complete in itself, and we have used extensive cross-referencing between them, since some topics – transference, projective identification, mutative interpretations, transitional space, for example – inevitably emerge again and again. There is a dialectic between theory and practice in the learning of any craft or skill, and psychoanalysis is no exception. We are aware of a marked shift of tone between the first, theoretical part, and the second, more clinical and practical part. The first aims to convey an up-to-date account of contemporary psychoanalytic theory, and will, we hope be of interest to advanced practitioners as well as beginners. The second part is inevitably more introductory. This divergence between the sophistication and diversity of theory, and a common strand of practice has become an increasing focus for debate with psychoanalysis (Tuckett 1994).

Acknowledgements

A book such as this owes an incalculable debt to the teachers, analysts, colleagues, students, patients, supervisors, and friends (many of whom fall into several of these categories) who have influenced and helped the authors. We would like especially to thank John Adey, Mark Aveline, Rosemarie Bateman, Harold Blum, Patrick Gallwey, Fiona Gardner, Isabelle Grey, Stephen Grosz, Ros Holmes, Matthew Holmes, Jane Milton, Jonathan Pedder, Rosine Perelberg, Glenn Roberts, Charles Rycroft, and Mark Solms, who have generously and time-consumingly read part or all of the manuscript, and have made many helpful suggestions and corrections. Alison Housley, chief librarian at North Devon District Hospital, Jill Duncan, chief librarian at the Institute of Psycho-Analysis, and Eleanor MacKenzie, chief librarian at St Ann's Hospital, Haringey Healthcare have tolerated our requests for references with amazing cheerfulness and efficiency. Finally, thanks to our families for their support and forbearance.

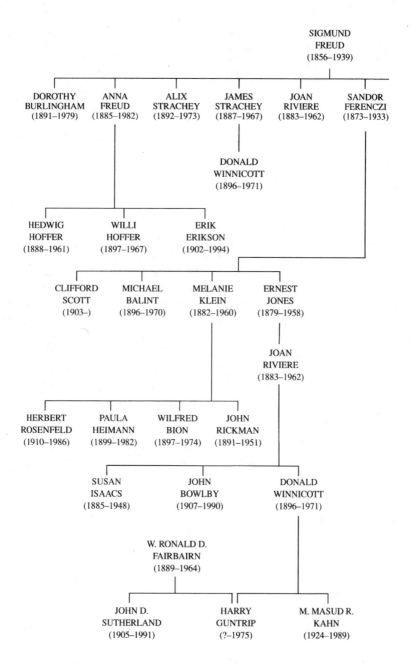

Figure 1 Who analysed whom; the transmission of psychoanalytic culture.

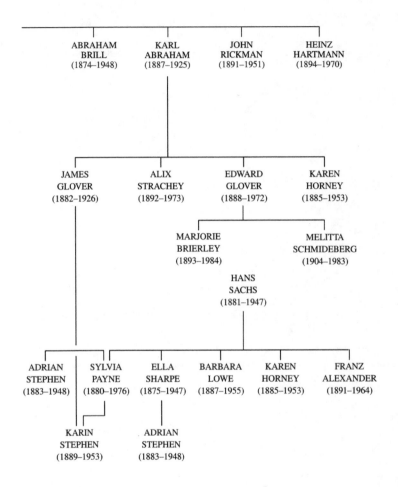

Part I

Theory

Chapter 1

Introduction: history and controversy

> The best way of understanding psycho-analysis is still by tracing its origin and development.
>
> (Freud 1922: 235)

During its hundred-year existence psychoanalysis has grown from modest central European beginnings into a worldwide therapeutic and cultural presence. Freud is one of the half dozen thinkers whose ideas have shaped the twentieth century, and whose influence seems likely to continue into the next. Yet psychoanalysis has from the start been beset with controversy and doubt, both from within its own ranks and from without. Indeed, the universality of conflict, and the possibility but difficulty of its resolution, are central to the psychoanalytic message.

Contemporary political, religious and social uncertainties seem to have created an almost insatiable hunger for psychological knowledge. Training and treatment in psychotherapy and counselling are currently in great demand, especially in liberal and middle-class circles. Psychiatry and medicine, while still ambivalent, are increasingly turning to psychotherapy and counselling to complement their powerful but narrow scientific approach. And yet, at the epicentre of this turmoil, psychoanalysis itself is in crisis. Partly a victim of its own success, it struggles to differentiate itself from psychoanalytic psychotherapy and its other offspring. With the death of Freud's immediate followers, the apostolic era is over and there is a search for new forms of leadership. Economic recession threatens the economic base of psychoanalysis. Historians, not all of them biased, question Freud's personal and scientific integrity. The philosophical credentials of psychoanalysis continue to come under increasingly sophisticated scrutiny. As psychoanalysis diversifies there is an urgent search for unity and common ground.

It is beyond the scope and competence of this 'introduction' to tackle these sweeping issues head on. Our aim is to present the core features of contemporary psychoanalytic theory and practice, a bedrock which might then form the basis for a wider discussion about the nature and role of psychoanalysis within psychiatry, psychotherapy and society. However we shall in this introductory chapter try to point the reader towards some of the key issues of debate and controversy which preoccupy present-day psychoanalysis. In order to put these discussions into context, as well as being a backdrop to the whole book, we start with a simplified account of the history and evolution of the psychoanalytic movement.

HISTORY OF THE PSYCHOANALYTIC MOVEMENT

Freud liked to compare the adult personality with an archaeological site which contained layer upon layer of civilisation, each based upon, and retaining some features of the one which it replaced. He saw the ego as a 'precipitate of abandoned object cathexes', constructed from the important figures from the past with whom each individual has identified. Both metaphors could be applied to psychoanalysis itself, which, if approached historically, reveals how new ideas often emerge from, but do not entirely replace, previous ones, and where the personality of a thinker is sometimes as important as the content of his or her contribution. The story of psychoanalysis is a mixture of history, geography, and charismatic influence. (See Fig. 1 for a 'family tree' of psychoanalysis.)

Freud (1914b,1927) described several phases in the evolution of psychoanalysis.

1885–1897: the 'pre-analytic' phase

Psychoanalysis comprises three interrelated strands: a set of specific psychotherapeutic techniques such as free association and interpretation; a model of psychological development; and a 'metapsychology', speculative hypotheses about the nature and structure of the mind. In this book we approach psychoanalysis as primarily a craft; it is consistent with this viewpoint that Freud was first propelled towards the invention of his 'new science' for quite mundane and practical reasons.

In 1886, at the age of 30, Freud married. He realised that he would need to provide for his wife and what was within a few years to become a large and growing family. Although he was already well known as a distinguished neurologist and neuroanatomist, the opportunities either for advancement in a university rife with anti-semitism, or for private neurological practice, were slight. At the same time he was aware of the many patients with hysterical symptoms and what he was later to call psychoneurotic disorders who thronged physicians' consulting rooms. He had visited Paris and been impressed by Charcot's demonstration of the extent of hysterical phenomena, and by accounts of Janet's successful hypnotic treatment of hysteria. He therefore determined to build his practice around the treatment of these patients.

Here he was helped by one of the several important friendships that contributed to the gestation and birth of psychoanalysis. Freud's friend Breuer, a general practitioner, had been experimenting with the use of hypnosis in the treatment of a young girl (the famous 'Anna O') suffering from paralyses and episodes of mental confusion. Breuer had found that by putting her into a hypnotic trance and asking her to speak freely about whatever was troubling her, the symptoms were temporarily relieved. Freud began to work with Breuer, a collaboration which they wrote up as *Studies in Hysteria* (Breuer and Freud 1895), based on thirteen such cases. Their 'cathartic' approach centred on the idea that neuroses resulted from the 'damming up' of painful affect, and that, like the lancing of a boil, if mental distress could be released via its verbal expression ('abreaction') under hypnosis, relief would follow.

At this point we encounter one of the features of Freud's character which has shaped the course of the history of psycho-analysis: his capacity to confront and theorise about a difficulty (or 'resistance') and turn it to advantage. He came up against a number of problems with hypnosis. First, he found that there were patients whom he was unable to hypnotise. Second, he began to be suspicious of the idea of hypnotic 'suggestion', feeling that it overemphasised the role of the physician and compromised the patient's autonomy. Third, he observed at first hand the phenomenon of transference when Breuer's patient, on waking from a trance, flung her arms passionately around her physician. Finally, searching for a traumatic explanation for the patient's difficulties he discovered, or thought that he had discovered, that they sprung from sexual trauma in childhood, a view that was repellent to the more prudish and timorous Breuer.

1897–1908: psychoanalysis proper: Freud's wilderness years

The next few years were a period of intellectual ferment and emotional crisis for Freud, during which, with the help of his friend Fleiss, with whom he maintained an intense correspondence, he established the practical and theoretical foundations of psychoanalysis which have lasted to this day.

He abandoned hypnosis, and devised the method of free association, aided at first by light pressure of the analyst's hand on the patient's forehead. He began to see neurosis not simply in terms of actual trauma, although this still played a part, nor as Janet had believed as the result of 'weakness' of the nervous system (an idea that was in a sense revived with the 'deficit' models of Kohut and Winnicott, see Chapter 2), but as the result of unconscious *conflict*. At the core of this conflict were instinct-driven *phantasies* (see p. 39) concerning sexuality: the male child's oedipal wish to possess his mother, in conflict with the fear of his father's possessive retribution. The *Three Essays on the Theory of Sexuality* (1905) emphasised the central importance of infantile sexuality and the role of bodily experience in the early development of the personality, which has become one of the pillars of psychoanalytic thinking.

Freud's move from 'seduction theory' to the idea of unconscious phantasy has provoked huge controversy among historians, especially in the light of contemporary knowledge of the extent of childhood sexual abuse. The idea of wish-fulfilment and phantasy are central to psychoanalysis. Freud realised that his patient's accounts of seductions reflected the wish-based, pleasure principle-driven nature of the inner world, and this was a vital step forward. Nevertheless he also continued to acknowledge the role of outer reality: 'seduction during childhood retained a certain share, though a lesser one, in the aetiology of the neuroses' (Freud 1927).

Implicit in conflict was *resistance* to the analyst's attempts to penetrate the defensive structures of neurosis, as a first step towards change. Freud initially saw transference as a resistance, impeding the smooth flow of free association, but as he came to realise that transference phantasies were an *in vivo* re-enactment of the patient's core difficulties, it became the centrepiece of the psychoanalytic method. The culmination of this period was *The Interpretation of Dreams*, which Freud always considered to be his finest work (see Chapter 6). Here Freud drew on his own personal struggles – his sibling rivalry, ambivalent reactions to his father's death in 1896, sense of being his mother's favourite, pride and humiliation in his Jewishness, and professional isolation and ambition – to develop a theory not just of dreams but of the mind itself.

1907/8–1920: the beginnings of the psychoanalytic movement

As the first decade of the century progressed, so Freud's ideas began to take hold among a group of progressive physicians and intellectuals who became the first psychoanalytic circle: Jung, Adler, Stekel, Abraham, Ferenczi, Jones and Rank – the original 'ring bearers' for whom Freud had special rings made, as he did for all of his favoured disciples. In 1908 the first psychoanalytic congress was held in Salzburg and a journal inaugurated. Jung, the first non-Jew to join the ranks of psychoanalysis soon became Freud's 'crown prince', and with the influential Bleuler, his chief at the Burgholzli, formed a psychoanalytic nucleus in Switzerland. Freud and Jung were invited to the USA in 1910, where Freud gave the prestigious Clark lectures. The two men diverted themselves on the Atlantic crossing by analysing each other's dreams. Perhaps this intimacy was too much: by 1913 Jung had split from Freud, protesting about Freud's insistence on the centrality of sex, his suspicion of religion, and authoritarian methods. Adler, too, had left in 1911 to set up his own school of psychotherapy, which emphasised aggression and the 'inferiority complex', rather than Freud's libido and oedipus, as central determinants of character.

Jung and Adler's defections were by no means the last that psychoanalysis was to suffer (Stekel had also left in 1911) but the psychoanalytical movement continued to grow, with clinics established in Budapest, Berlin and London, the latter thanks to Ernest Jones's combination of energy, intellectual gifts and absolute devotion to Freud.

The 1914–18 war had a major impact on the evolution of psychoanalysis in Europe. Freud, now aged 60, his fame fully established, continued to work prodigiously, producing the great metapsychological papers *On Narcissism* and *Mourning and Melancholia*, as well as the *Introductory Lectures in Psychoanalysis* (delivered, by established psychoanalytic tradition, extempore) during this period. The carnage of the world war turned his thoughts to the darker side of human psychology and Freud began to emphasise aggression more than before, ideas that would culminate in the 1920s with the notion of thanatos, the death instinct.

In Britain the war had a positive impact on the spread of psychoanalytic methods and ideas. Large numbers of soldiers returned from the front with battle fatigue or shell shock (forerunners of the contemporary diagnosis of Post-Traumatic Stress Disorder). Conventional psychiatry at that time had little to offer, leaving the way open for psychoanalytic methods at such centres as the Brunswick Square Clinic headed by James Glover, which became a breeding ground for British psychoanalysis, employing James's brother Edward Glover, Sylvia Payne, Ella Sharpe, Susan Isaacs and Marjorie Brierly, all later to become prominent psychoanalysts. The Cassel Hospital was founded in the immediate aftermath of the war as an in-patient unit for psychoanalytic treatment of war casualties.

1920 to Freud's death in 1939

Freud's powers as a theoretician remained undiminished to the end of his life. In 1923 he saw the publication of *The Ego and the Id*, his major revision of the 'topographical' model (which had divided the mind into the unconscious, preconscious and conscious parts), proposing instead the 'structural' or tripartite model of id, ego and superego (see pp. 35–7). In 1926 he produced a revised theory of anxiety, which he now saw as signalling a threat to the self, rather than being a manifestation of surplus erotic energy or 'libido'. A short but highly influential paper on fetishism (Freud 1927) introduced the idea of splitting of the ego, which remains central to contemporary psychoanalysis. Throughout the 1930s Freud continued with his speculations about religion, as well as struggling with ideas about female sexuality, stimulated no doubt by the increasing numbers of distinguished female analysts.

Freud's daughter Anna pioneered the psychoanalytic treatment of children, and, after her mother's death, cared for her father – Antigone to his Oedipus. When the Nazis arrived in Austria in 1938, Freud was allowed to leave for England, whence many analysts had already fled. With Anna, he settled at Maresfield Gardens in Hampstead. He died a year later in 1939, just before the outbreak of war.

Psychoanalysis in Britain

The politics of the psychoanalytic movement has been characterised from the start by a tension between the need to defend the faith –

including the expulsion of heretics if necessary – and the wish to extend its boundaries and to accommodate new ideas. Psycho-analytic ideas had an important impact on intellectual life in Britain in the 1920s, influencing progressive psychiatrists and medical practitioners as well as members of the Bloomsbury Group, among whom Karin and James Strachey began medical training specifically in order to become psychoanalysts (Pines 1991). Ernest Jones was determined to preserve psychoanalytic identity from dilution by psychotherapeutic fellow travellers and hangers on. However, unlike his American counterparts, he was generally in favour of recognition and equal status for 'lay' (i.e. non-medical) analysts, for which he had Freud's full support (Freud 1926). When Alix and James Strachey organised a British lecture tour for the young Berlin-based psychoanalyst Melanie Klein, Jones took to her at once and invited her to come to settle in London, as well as arranging for his children to be analysed by her. Unattached – she was a divorced woman whose children were nearly grown up – she accepted, a fateful move for the history of psychoanalysis.

Klein, who had been analysed by Ferenczi and Abraham, had devised a method of play therapy derived from dream interpretation which she claimed enabled her to understand the minds of infants and small children. As her work developed she applied these findings to analytic work with disturbed adult patients, focusing on the mother–infant relationship, and claiming that oedipal conflicts could be found in the first year of life – much earlier than Freud had thought. Later, especially after the death of her beloved son in a climbing accident (Grosskurth 1986), she emphasised the role of aggression and envy in infantile life, and extended her own analyst Abraham's classification of developmental stages with the idea of an early 'paranoid–schizoid position' to be superseded in the mature child by the 'depressive position' (see pp. 38–9).

Freud was suspicious of Klein, especially as her ideas conflicted with those of his daughter Anna, also a child psychoanalyst, who doubted the validity of Klein's speculations about the mental life of infants, and who felt that a more supportive technique was needed in treating children. As refugee psychoanalysts started to arrive in London in the 1930s, tension built up between the Viennese immigrants and the followers of Klein, who included Riviere, Rickman, Isaacs and, as students, Winnicott, Bion and Bowlby. After Freud's death in 1939 rivalries heightened, and by 1944 two distinct camps had emerged, clustered around Klein and Anna Freud. The atmosphere was electric and there was grave danger of the British Society splitting apart. A series of talks were organised, 'the controversial discussions' (King and Steiner 1990) and a compromise emerged, the 'gentlemen's agreement' (arranged by three women, Klein, Anna Freud and the mediator Sylvia Payne). This established two separate groups within the Society, roughly corresponding with the Kleinians and Anna Freudians, each with its own training programme and quotas on committees. Later a third group, the Independents or 'middle group', emerged.

There followed a period of great creativity within the British Society. Klein became a dominant figure and her ideas were extended by Bion, Segal, Winnicott, Rosenfeld, Joseph and others. The British 'object relations' perspective was a significant move away from Freud's drive-based developmental schema to one in which the infant–mother relationship was of central importance. They drew partly on Kleinian ideas of an inner world populated by representations of early childhood relationships distorted by phantasy, and partly on the work of Independents such as Michael Balint who postulated a primary relatedness separate from the drives for food and sex. Bion and Winnicott, in very different ways, emphasised the role of the maternal environment, or 'breast', in providing favourable or unfavourable conditions for psychological growth and integration. Although John Bowlby was himself gradually estranged from the Society, his linking of ethology with psychoanalysis provided scientific support for object relations ideas. Fairbairn, despite working in isolation in Edinburgh, was also an important contributor, as was his pupil Sutherland who became first post-war director of the Tavistock Clinic.

The three groupings remain a key feature of the contemporary British Society, but, as we shall see, they have become somewhat less rigid with some overlap and cross-fertilisation. Differences do not always harden into ideological positions to be defended almost to the death, but rather variations in style and emphasis. For example, among the 'Contemporary Freudians', Sandler et al. (1992) has helped clarify key psychoanalytic concepts and, in the distinction between the 'present unconscious' (i.e. that which is currently active in the analytic situation) and the past unconscious, have revived the 'topographical model' (Sandler and Sandler 1994b). Fonagy (Fonagy et al. 1995) is vigorously applying experimental methods to problems of child development. Among prominent Kleinian authors, Spillius (1994) has discussed how Segal (1986, 1991), Joseph

(1989), and Hinshelwood (1989, 1994) have carefully clarified the meanings and clinical implications of Kleinian concepts, while Steiner (1993) has consolidated the Kleinian approach to 'borderline' conditions based on projective identification. From the Independent group Symington (1986) and Coltart (1993) have written useful and highly individual introductory texts, while Kohon (1986) and Rayner (1991) have brought together the key thinkers in the group. Casement (1985) and Bollas (1989, 1993) have in different ways extended Winnicott's ideas about transitional phenomena and countertransference in exquisitely detailed accounts of the interpersonal context of the psychoanalytic relationship.

Psychoanalysis in the Americas

In 1925, 22 per cent of the members of the International Psychoanalytic Association were from North America; by 1952 the figure had risen to 64 per cent, mainly as a result of emigration from Europe, but also because of the fertile soil for new ideas typical of the USA. In contrast to its marginal impact on the medical profession in Britain, psychoanalysis became a dominant force within American psychiatry in the 1950s and 1960s. The pre-eminent paradigm was Hartmann's (1939) ego psychology, which emphasised the adaptive function of the ego, and its capacity for creating a 'conflict-free zone' in contrast to the *sturm und drang* of Freud's seething cauldron of the unconscious. Just as immigrants often retain traditional features of their parent culture more fervently than natives, so North American psychoanalysis was far more conservative than its European counterparts. Drive theory and the structural model (see pp. 35–7) reigned supreme. Non-medical analysts were excluded from the American Psychoanalytic Association – a ruling which persisted until the late 1980s when, following a challenge through the courts from a psychologist claiming unfair discrimination, other professions were finally admitted as candidates.

The sheer size of the USA, with many separately operating psychoanalytic groupings, led to a profusion of ideas and approaches. Erikson's eight-stage (1965) developmental schema, emphasising cultural as well as intrapsychic factors, has been very influential (see p. 50). Mahler *et al.* (1975) used direct observations of children in their account of psychological development, later to be modified and put on a more strictly scientific basis by Stern (1985) and Emde (1981). Fromm (1973), one of the so-called 'neo-Freudians', discussed the political role of psychoanalysis in society, laying the foundations for Lasch's later critique (1975) of cultural narcissism. Horney was one of the pioneers of the feminist response to psychoanalysis, later built on by such contemporary writers as Chodorow (1978) and Benjamin (1990). Sullivan (1953) founded the Interpersonal school, which has many similarities to British object relations, emphasising relatedness and the here-and-now, in contrast to 'classical' therapy based on identification of repressed sexual and aggressive drives and reconstruction of a putative past. His theories were influential in the work at Chesnut Lodge, where Fromm-Reichmann (1959) and Searles (1965) also used a Winnicottian 'holding' model, and emphasised the importance of countertransference, in the treatment of severely ill and borderline patients. More recently Mitchell (1988; Greenberg and Mitchell 1983) has developed the interpersonal perspective, showing how it relates to Berlin's notion of 'positive liberty' – freedom *to* develop one's potential, in contrast with classical drive-based 'negative liberty' or freedom *from* conflict and external interference.

The most significant contemporary challenge to American 'classical' psychoanalysis has been the rise of Kohut's (1977) self-psychology, which emphasises deficit rather than conflict at the core of many modern ills, sees healthy narcissism as the foundation of good object relations rather than their antithesis, and highlights empathy and attunement rather than interpretation and insight as the curative factors in successful treatment. Self-psychology struck a chord in the psychological world and fierce debate took place as to whether this was, or was not, 'true' psychoanalysis. In defence of his active empathic method, which he contrasted (possibly in an inaccurate caricature) with the impassivity and silence of the classical analyst, Kohut made the sociological point that Freud's original patients were victims of enmeshed and intrusive family situations, and needed an unintrusive analyst if they were to find their autonomy, while today's patients are products of parental neglect and family breakdown and so need to feel actively held and valued if analysis is to help.

Another challenge to mainstream psychoanalysis in the USA has come from a group of authors, many of them pupils of Rapaport (1951), who have questioned the whole Freudian metapsychological superstructure, calling for a 'theorectomy' (G. Klein 1976) which would leave behind a healthy set of *clinical* ideas and techniques (Wallerstein 1992). In a related vein, Schafer (1976) and Spence

(1982) picked up on Habermas and Ricoeur's suggestion that psychoanalysis is best seen as a linguistic or hermeneutic discipline rather than a strictly scientific one, concerned more with meaning than mechanism, an approach that also arose independently in Britain through the work of Home (1966) and Rycroft (1985).

This tension between conservatism and innovation has meant that the past decade has been one of uncertainty for American psychoanalysis. In addition, thanks to advances in neurochemistry, genetics and brain imaging, the 'decade of the brain' has toppled psychoanalysis from its dominance within American psychiatry (Gabbard 1992). The development of other forms of psychotherapy, together with an economic recession, have also threatened its economic base. A positive result of these changes has been a much greater openness to new ideas – for example, from the British object relations school (Greenberg and Mitchell 1982) and infant observation (Stern 1985) – a *rapprochement* between the warring factions (Wallerstein 1992) and a willingness to subject psychoanalysis to scientific scrutiny (Weiss and Sampson *et al.* 1986; Luborsky *et al.* 1988; see pp. 253–6).

In Latin America, Racker's (1968) contribution to the understanding of countertransference is now widely accepted (see p. 111), and Etchegoyen (1992) has extended it with his massive synthesis of Kleinian and Lacanian thought in relation to the day-to-day practise of psychoanalysis. Psychoanalysts in Latin America have also played an important part in bringing their ideas to bear on the processes of political upheaval (Hoggett 1992), and to the special technical skill and courage needed to continue working psychoanalytically in a culture in which death threats and 'disappearances' are endemic. Australia also has a thriving psychoanalytic culture (see Symington 1993; Meares and Coombes 1994).

Psychoanalysis in continental Europe

With its emphasis on finding and facing the truth, and the goals of autonomy and personal freedom, psychoanalysis and totalitarianism are incompatible. Fascism obliterated psychoanalysis in Germany for at least a generation, and, with Pavlovian behaviourism the official party line in psychology, Stalinism similarly prevented the growth of psychoanalytic ideas throughout Eastern Europe. Vygotsky and Bahktar (Leiman 1994) were notable exceptions, remnants of the flowering of ideas in the years immediately following the Russian

Revolution. With the fall of communism, there has been an upsurge of interest in psychoanalysis and the psychotherapies generally in the post-communist world.

Post-war reconstruction in West Germany led to the re-establishment of a vigorous psychoanalytic culture, often based around departments of psychosomatic medicine, out-patient clinics for patients with neurotic disorders run along psychoanalytic lines, separate from traditional mental hospitals. Economic conditions are favourable since, as in Canada, the national health insurance system funds up to 200 hours of psychoanalysis without cost to the patient. Among others, the Ulm psychoanalytic group has produced an outstanding modern textbook of psychoanalysis (Thoma and Kachele 1987, 1992), based around the 'Ulm model' which sees treatment as following a shifting focus, similar to Malan's (1979) picture of brief psychotherapy. The same group has also established a centre of excellence in psychoanalytic research (Dahl et al. 1988).

France was, through Freud's contact with Charcot and Janet, a vital seedbed for psychoanalysis. The central place held by philosophy in French thought meant that the 'isms' – Existentialism, Marxism and, later, Structuralism – all influenced the shape taken by psychoanalytic thinking, as well as representing rival philosophical systems. Sartre (1957) mounted a powerful attack on what he believed to be the implicit determinism of psychoanalysis, arguing that the concept of the unconscious legitimised 'bad faith', a disowning of responsibility to one's freedom to choose.

French psychoanalysis, like French politics, is strongly factionalised, with many rival groupings and 'groupuscules' (Turkle 1978). The dominant figure – a focus for admiration or disagreement – has been Lacan (1966), who, in his tantalising and gnomic texts, has synthesised Saussurian linguistics with psychoanalysis (see pp. 65–6). In his view, the oedipal child enters a world of 'signs' which convey to him the meanings of self, gender and the body, just as he is similarly confronted by language and grammar which he must assimilate in order to become part of the linguistic community. Lacan was critical of Hartmannian ego psychology with its emphasis on adaptation – perhaps an example of a more general resistance among French intellectuals to what they see as American cultural imperialism. Lacan called for a 'return to Freud' – i.e. to pre-'structural model' Freud (see pp. 30–4). He described three developmental stages: first, a primordial period of unconscious infantile 'desire'; then the world of 'the imaginary' emerging from the 'mirror stage', in which the child first confronts his image and narcissistic-ally and therefore incorrectly, assumes this to be his true self; and finally the 'symbolic order', arising through the contact with language, the 'no(m) du père', a linguistic expression of Freud's picture of the father's combined role as necessary separator of child and mother, ego ideal, and potential castrator. Successful therapy depends on the exploration of desire through the symbolic order of language, and consequent disentanglement from the world of the imaginary.

Within mainstream psychoanalysis in France, Laplanche and Pontalis (1973) have produced the definitive dictionary of Freudian concepts. Green (1975) has developed a variant of the Winnicottian notion of 'space' – the space between the analyst and patient where creativity and growth can occur, but also a location for despair and non-existence. McDougall (1990), a New Zealander living in Paris, has written influentially about the psychoanalytic treatment of psychosomatic disorders. Chasseguet-Smirguel (1985) is an important figure in feminist psychoanalysis, postulating a fundamental male fear of the all-encompassing female, and seeing the phallic response to this in the oedipal child through the development of a 'faecal' or pseudo-penis. She is able to analyse a wide range of clinical and cultural phenomena, including perversions and some aspects of revolutionary politics – a focal point for enthusiasm or reaction in the French imagination – in terms of this 'excremental vision'.

Psychoanalysis is a significant cultural presence in Italy, with a strong Kleinian tradition. There is also a flourishing psychoanalytic culture in northern Europe, perhaps with an 'Independent' flavour, extending from the Netherlands to Scandinavia, where there has been a pioneering emphasis on the psychoanalytically informed treatment of psychotic disorders (Alanen *et al.* 1994).

CURRENT PSYCHOANALYTIC DILEMMAS AND CONTROVERSIES

> We do not even require of our *patients* that they should bring a conviction of the truth of psychoanalysis into the treatment or be adherents of it. Such an attitude often raises our suspicions. The attitude that we find the most desirable in them is a benevolent scepticism.
>
> (Freud 1916/17: 244; *italics* are Freud's)

This brief historical and geographical survey gives, we hope, some feeling of the diversity and vigour of the psychoanalytic movement. It may also convey some of the controversy and debate that are continuing features of the psychoanalytic movement. There is an inherent tension in psychoanalysis between the need for creative uncertainty – Keat's 'negative capability' – in order not to do violence to psychological reality, and the search for safe footholds in the uncharted terrain of the mind. The former can all too easily degenerate into muddle and mystery, the latter into dogmatism: both tendencies are to be found in the psychoanalytic literature. The remainder of this chapter is devoted to a consideration of some of the contentious issues with which contemporary psychoanalysis is struggling.

What is psychoanalysis?

It is hard to produce a satisfactory definition of psychoanalysis that clearly differentiates it from the many forms of psychoanalytic psychotherapy it has spawned. Many of the psychoanalytic therapies can be looked upon as the children of psychoanalysis, with all the inevitable parent–child conflicts involved. The growing child and young adult strive for autonomy and independence from their parents, while valuing what they continue to provide in the form of friendship and support. The parents, on the other hand, have to face the conflict between encouraging the growth and independence of new ideas and methods while being anxious that all they have believed in will be discarded in an adolescent crisis or dismissed as irrelevant ravings of senescence. These boundaries are the stuff of controversy: the Psychodynamic Psychotherapy section of the UK Council for Psychotherapy (UKCP) lists over thirty different organ- isations and training schemes. In order not to be confused or contaminated with these, the British Psycho-Analytical Society has, with the Jungian analytical psychologists and selected psycho- analytic psychotherapy organisations, split off from the UKCP to form its own separate confederation – the British Confederation of Psychotherapists (BCP). Some organisations have remained in both.

For Freud (1914b) the defining features of psychoanalysis as a treatment were the centrality of transference and resistance. But most psychoanalytic psychotherapists would also claim these were central to their work, and, conversely, there is no certainty that what is *called* psychoanalysis accords with Freud's criteria. Indeed, empirical studies of psychoanalysis (see Chapter 11) have failed to show a convincing relationship between the 'development of an analytic process' (i.e. the creation and dissolution of a transference neurosis) and positive outcome of treatment. Good outcomes are possible where the analysis of transference appears to play quite a minor part, and patients can do badly despite heroic efforts at transference interpretation. In view of this, a pragmatic approach is needed. As an academic subject, psychoanalysis can be defined as that branch of psychology initiated by Freud that is concerned with three distinct areas of study: the development of the mind and the influence of early experience on adult mental states; the nature and role of unconscious mental phenomena; and the theory and practice of psychoanalytic treatment, particularly transference and countertransference.

This definition is by no means entirely satisfactory. By tying itself indissolubly to Freud, psychoanalysis runs the risk of confirming Whitehead's warning: 'a science that hesitates to forget its founders is doomed' – and yet Freud remains a colossus, 'the father who does not die' (Wallerstein 1992). More significantly, it contains a potential circularity in that psychoanalysis is defined at least in part as the study of psychoanalytic treatment. At this point the discussion usually moves to the easier, but equally tautologous definition of a psychoanaly*st* – i.e. someone who has undergone training at one of the organisations recognised by the International Psychoanalytical Association. However theoretically unsatisfactory this may be, the pragmatic demarcation line between psychoanalysis and psycho-analytic psychotherapy concerns the frequency, intensity and dur-ation of therapy. Put simply: more than three times a week – psychoanalysis; three times or less – everything else.

While accepting this distinction, several caveats must be con-sidered. First, the emphasis on 'how many times a week?' produces a bias in contemporary psychoanalysis, certainly not present in Freud's early work, towards the primitive anxieties which emerge during the regression evoked by such intensity. Second, even the more-than/less-than three times a week boundary is not watertight, since some French and Latin American societies accept three times a week training analyses. More research is needed to establish the effects and indications of different treatment intensities. In conclu-sion we take a provisional view, seeing psychoanalytic therapy as a *spectrum* from 'full' psychoanalysis to psychoanalytic psycho-therapy, from the use of methods that are expressive to those that are supportive, from interpretation to 'holding'.

One psychoanalysis or many?

Questions of boundaries are not confined to that between psychoanalysis and the rest of the psychotherapies. Psychoanalysts have
worried about whether the many different varieties of psychoanalysis
– Freudian, Kleinian, Kohutian, Interpersonal, Lacanian, Object
Relational, Independent – can all meaningfully stay together as
secure bedfellows. The 'gentlemen's agreement' worked well in
Britain in 1948, and kept the society from falling apart, but is it
applicable, for example, to North America and to the fight between
the Kohutians and the others, and will it serve into the twenty-first
century?

Wallerstein (1992) has been a strong proponent of the 'common
ground' position, claiming that all the different theoretical
approaches have, in clinical practice, much in common. One way to
approach the problem is to compare the responses of analysts with
different perspectives to the same clinical material.

Example: an unscheduled analytic break
Wallerstein discusses Kohut's (1984) account of a discussion with
a Latin American Colleague about a patient who withdrew into
silence in response to the announcement of an unplanned cancellation of a session. The Kleinian analyst had interpreted this in terms
of a shift from the patient's perception of the analyst as a warm
feeding breast to a cold withholding one, retaliating in kind by
'biting back' the rejecting words she felt welling up inside her.
Kohut claimed to be surprised to learn that this interpretation –
delivered in a warm empathic way – elicited a favourable response
from the patient. In his view it was 'farfetched', and what the
analyst *should* have interpreted was her feeling of losing a
sustaining self-object with consequent inner deadness and emptiness. Wallerstein himself offers a third possible interpretation
along the lines of oedipal exclusion from the parental bedroom.

Wallerstein argues that the differences between these interpretations
are more apparent than real: what really matters is that the patient
has reacted unhappily to the planned cancellation and that the analyst
has picked upon this – i.e. the 'present transference' (Sandler and
Sandler 1984) and explored it with the patient. Following Rapaport
(1951) and George Klein (1976), he distinguishes *clinical* theory
from *general* theory. He sees a common ground of clinical theory,
concerning empathy, holding, interpretation, defence, analysis of

transference and resistance, all of which are observable, testable and researchable. In contrast he sees metapsychology as reflecting the different traditions, styles and historical contexts of psychoanalysis: 'pluralistic psychoanalytic articles of faith', 'metaphors we live by', more akin to political and religious affiliations than to scientific postulates. While at a political level Wallerstein's efforts have done much to reconcile warring factions within psychoanalysis, real intellectual differences remain, and doubtless the debates will continue. Pine's (1990) eclecticism takes a different slant. Like the story of the men examining an elephant and taking their own part for the whole, he sees Drive, Ego, Self and Object as each referring to a different segment of reality, each with its appropriate metapsychology and set of technical procedures. The task of the therapist is to focus on whichever is relevant at any particular time in the evolution of the analysis.

These attempts at synthesis run the risk of glossing over real differences and inhibiting creative conflict and debate. Sandler (1983) notes the *elasticity* of psychoanalytic concepts which enables the theoretical contortions to occur. New ideas, rather than superseding old ones, tend to be grafted on to them, so that notions such as transference or projective identification simply expand to accommodate conceptual innovations, thereby becoming increasingly baggy and unwieldy (and confusing for the student!). Greenberg and Mitchell (1982) see the contrast between drive theory and object relations as irreconcilable, reflecting fundamentally differing philosophical viewpoints. Schafer (1990) regrets the search for a 'single master text for psychoanalysis', and celebrates the battles and disputes within psychoanalysis, arguing that 'sublimated aggression does have its uses'. No doubt psychodynamic factors affect the adoption of a pluralistic or sectarian position. The importance of theorists as well as their theories means that espousing or opposing a particular school of psychoanalysis – Kleinian or Kohutian, say – may reflect an individual's unconscious responses to the gestalt presented by the leader. There is, of course, an arbitrary or accidental aspect too: just as our attitudes and fundamental beliefs are affected by the family in which we grow up, so analysands other than the outstanding pioneers tend to stick to the tradition represented by their training analyst. Both pluralism and sectarianism have their defensive aspects. The pluralist may be fearful of the aggression inherent in choosing *this* viewpoint in preference to *that*. Conversely, the champion of one particular sect may be splitting off unwanted parts of the self in a manic and triumphal way in order to avoid the inherent difficulties of the 'impossible profession' (Freud 1927). Our position is one of qualified eclecticism. Real and important differences exist between differing psychoanalytic perspectives. The capacity to see and respect the other's point of view, while remaining true to one's own, is not easy. Our approach is close to Wallerstein's in that we try throughout to remain near to clinical reality, and wherever possible to bring scientific findings to bear on psychoanalytic thinking. Where different languages are describing the same phenomenon we try to point that out; where perspectives are irreconcilable, that too is noted.

The scientific status of psychoanalysis

A central controversy in psychoanalysis concerns the question of whether, as Freud hoped and expected, it is classified as one of the sciences – the science of the mind – or whether it belongs with the arts-based, historical, hermeneutic (i.e. interpretive) disciplines. This debate has itself to be set in context, since we inhabit a society which values (and funds!) science above all else, and takes the 'hard' physical sciences as benchmarks against which 'soft' subjects like psychoanalysis are measured and found wanting.

The issue of the scientific status of psychoanalysis was initiated by the positivist critique which saw psychoanalysis as an ideological closed belief system, lacking falsifiable postulates or a sound empirical basis. Insofar as analysts are prepared to listen at all to this attack, rather than dismiss it as an illustration of resistance or envy, it leads to two kinds of response. One is to concede that *so far* empirical evidence for psychoanalytic propositions is flimsy, and intensify the attempt to find scientific ways to study the phenomena in question. We have devoted the whole of Chapter 11 to this tack. Others claim that the search for a scientific basis for psychoanalysis is inherently misguided, arguing that it is a linguistic discipline concerned with meaning and interpretation rather than mechanism and explanation (Home 1966; Rycroft 1985). Habermas (1968) and Spence (1982) go further. Habermas argues that the causation of mental phenomena is different in kind to those that exist in the physical world. Spence dispenses with the question of the truth or otherwise of psychoanalysts' claims about the impact of childhood events on adult neurosis by his assertion that psychoanalysis is concerned with *narrative* rather than historical truth. What matters, according to this argument, is not whether psychoanalytic constructions correspond to reality, but rather whether they are internally consistent and satisfying.

Here the debate exemplifies the philosophical struggle between the *coherence* and *correspondence* theories of truth (Cavell 1994), i.e. depending upon how robust and internally consistent a theory is, or how much it appears to correspond with the 'facts' of external reality (coherence-theorists argue that what we call a 'fact' is in fact a construction and therefore also subject to coherence criteria). Rorty (1989) argues that philosophical pluralism is all one can hope for, but there is an inherent flaw in this retreat into hermeneutics: if all that matters is coherence, how does one distinguish between the veridicity of different narratives? Is the psychoanalytic account – or the Lacanian or Kleinian version of it – no more or less true than a homeopathic or astrological account of a patient's difficulties? Grunbaum (1984), in contrast to Habermas, argues that, although perhaps more difficult to study than in the physical sciences, cause–effect principles apply just as strongly in psychology as in physics. He also shows that many psychoanalytical postulates *are* falsifiable, and that Freud was in fact quite capable of modifying or even abandoning his ideas if the facts demanded it. Using a rather simplistic and outmoded model of psychoanalytic change, he believes that Freud's 'tally argument' (that patients get better if the analyst's interpretations 'tally' with historical fact) is unproven.

Eagle (1984) claims that the hermeneutic position would suggest that psychoanalysis could only change or evolve 'in the sense that fiction has evolved, say, since Fielding'. While there may be some truth in this, conceptual clarification, technical innovation and empirical testing of psychoanalytic ideas have also produced real advances in our understanding, for example of primitive mental states (see Chapter 4), and of the minutiae of patient–analyst interactions (see Chapter 8).

Several contemporary developments have changed the terms of the debate on the scientific status of psychoanalysis. First, the advent of cognitive science (Bruner 1990), stimulated by the computer revolution, means that the mind is no longer seen as out of bounds for hard-headed scientists. Many interesting parallels can be found between the findings of cognitive science and those of psychoanalysis (for example, Teesdale 1993). Psychoanalysis no longer needs to remain in splendid isolation from its sister disciplines (Gabbard 1992;

Holmes 1994a). Second, recent findings in developmental psychology have made the distinction between narrative and historical truth look less clear-cut (Holmes 1994b). The Adult Attachment Interview (Main 1991; Fonagy *et al.* 1995) – a psychodynamic interview that can be reliably rated – indicates that there is a link between the kinds of stories people tell about themselves and their lives, and patterns of attachment in infancy and childhood. Third, Grunbaum's claim that the efficacy of psychoanalysis may be the result of 'non-specific' factors such as attention, interest, regularity and reliability, rather than, as he claims psychoanalysts believe, the accuracy of their interpretations, can be linked with findings suggesting that empathy and attunement in infancy lead to secure attachment, and that similar development-enhancing qualities may produce change in psychoanalysis (Shane and Shane 1986; Holmes 1993).

Our position is, once more, a compromise. We do not see coherence and correspondence when applied to psychoanalysis as mutually incompatible. Theories and technical practices need to be coherent if they are to be robust enough to stand up to conceptual or clinical challenge, but also to correspond with reality: their adherents must be prepared to modify them in the face of empirical evidence. Parts of psychoanalysis – unconscious awareness, repression, internalisation and identification – are scientifically established; others represent metapsychological superstructures which may eventually be dismantled, amalgamated or modified. Meanwhile the clinical practice of psychoanalysis *is* concerned with stories, meanings, interpretations and these will continue to be the lifeblood of psychoanalytic work. Scientific investigation of these phenomena will inevitably come from the 'third term' (to use Lewin's phrase for the sibling or father watching the mother feeding an infant in the 'oral triad', Wright 1991) of scientific observation.

How does psychoanalysis cure?

Kohut asked this question in trying to differentiate his own approach, based on empathy and the establishment of nurturing self-objects, from the 'classical' view of interpretation and insight as the sole vehicle of cure. Kohut's notion is not so far removed from Grunbaum's suggestion that 'non-specific' factors might explain good outcomes in analysis. Following Freud's characterisation of psychoanalysis as 'transference plus resistance', three main positions on the mode of action of psychoanalysis can be identified (Steiner 1989), each of which implictly has a view about what constitutes psychological health.

1 *Classical/conflict model.* Here the ego has repressed 'problematic experience' (Stiles *et al.* 1995) in order to maintain coherence. This maladaptive solution or compromise, in which satisfaction is sacrificed for the sake of security, is reproduced in the transference: the patient feels angry or amorous or wants to be looked after by the analyst, but resists the expression of these feelings. The aim of treatment is to help the patient gain insight into these processes, and use this awareness to respond more fully to his experience: 'where id was, there ego shall be' (Freud 1923).

2 *Kleinian-object relations/conflict model.* Here there is a conflict between love and hate, between the need for dependency and the fear of loss. The self is depleted through processes of projective identification (see pp. 82–7), which also leads to misperception (a term used equally by Kleinians (Segal 1994) and cognitive therapists) and therefore distortion of reality. Transference is characterised by these processes of projective identification and misperception. The task of the therapist is to contain these projections and to return them when the patient is able to accept them (Bion 1962). Resistance centres around the difficulty in acknowledging dependency on an analyst who will then be an object of envy and potential loss. Analysis moves the patient from the splitting of the paranoid–schizoid position to the wholeness of the depressive position.

3 *Interpersonal-object relations/deficit model.* Here the focus is on the 'present transference' – the living unconscious interplay between analyst and patient. Resistance is not seen in terms of conflict, but as a manifestation of deficit: the patient is developmentally unable to react differently. Under the regressive pull of treatment the patient clings to old maladaptive patterns because he or she knows no other way ('better a bad object than none at all', Fairbairn 1958). Treatment produces change by offering a new experience of empathy and attention, from which the patient can build a secure sense of self in relation to another.

In summary, these models see analytic cure as resulting from *insight*, *containment* and *new experience* respectively. Most analyses contain elements of all three, and none can be reduced to a singular approach. Thus 'Kleinian' therapy centres around insight and containment, 'Kohutian' on containment and new experience, Contemporary

Freudian on insight and new experience, and so on. Here, in line with Wallerstein's 'common ground' viewpoint, the nearer one approaches clinical reality the more the distinctions look blurred, the further one 'zooms out' to metapsychological positions, the more sharply focused become the differences.

Training

If psychoanalysis is one of the 'impossible professions' (i.e. one in which it is impossible to predict outcome with certainty), psychoanalytic training poses insoluble dilemmas. In keeping with the plurality of psychoanalysis, the problem of definition, the divergent views on the process of cure and change, the elasticity of concepts and cultural differences, psychoanalytic trainings around the world are diverse both in their form and content. Variations occur in how candidates are admitted for training, how training analysts are selected and their role in the candidate's training, the number of treatment sessions per week, the content of supervision and seminars, the importance attached to infant observation, the length of training, and the process of qualification. Even the method of payment for personal analysis varies – in some European institutes, candidates are not allowed to reclaim sessional fees even if their insurance company accepts the claim, illustrating the austerity faced by many candidates engaged in psychoanalytic training. In Britain the candidate's analyst writes reports to the training organisation on his progress in analysis, supervision is on an individual basis and regular reports are furnished, and analysis is five times a week; in one society in France the candidate's analysis is separate from his training, some supervision is on a group basis, analysis is three times a week; in the USA and many other countries analysis is four times a week.

Ideally the *process* of training should educate but not indoctrinate, and encourage freedom of thought within a psychoanalytic framework without espousing any one variety of psychoanalysis. The *organisation* of training reflects the need to regulate the expression of powerful transference and countertransference reactions within the training process. Transferences between the candidate and his analyst, the candidate and his patient, the candidate and his supervisor, the supervisor and the analyst, and the analyst and the institution are ubiquitous. A 'good enough' distance between these dyads and between the training analysis, supervision and the institution provides the right conditions for learning and development; an intrusive system leads to fear of self-expression and, at worst, the development of analytic clones created in their analyst's image. Each candidate needs to identify, disidentify, separate and gain independence. There is an interesting symbiosis between psychoanalytic theory and practice. As the length of training analyses has increased so has the duration of analyses of patients. Candidates whose training involves personal therapy three times a week often see their patients three times a week, those trained in five times a week treatment, see patients five times and so on. Freud's hope that candidates will become proficient in theory, patient care and research, and also develop an independence of mind, has yet to be realised.

Psychoanalytic values

In Auden's (1952) obituary poem he wrote: 'Freud is no more a person now but a whole climate of opinion.' Although the focus of this book is almost entirely clinical it is important also to acknowledge the moral and cultural significance of psychoanalysis. Freud (1927) – and, in a different way, Jung – saw society as a thin veneer of civilisation, not unlike the ego in relation to the id, resting on a sea of primitive eroticism and aggression. His advocacy of balance and courage in the face of destructiveness – his 'tragic vision' (Schafer 1976) – and of the power of sublimation of baser drives into cultural achievement, make Freud as much a moralist (Rieff 1959) as a scientist.

Freud's cultural and moral critique is to be found in the concerns of contemporary psychoanalytic writers, many of whom emphasise the ambiguity of the psychoanalytic vision which exposes, but to some extent also legitimises and therapeutically strengthens, the very society it criticises (Frosh 1991). This is nowhere more evident than within feminist psychoanalysis which has moved from its hostility to Freud's phallocentrism to an appreciation of how psychoanalysis can help understand the development of gender, how the notion of bisexuality suggests the cultural relativism of patriarchy, and how psychoanalysis as a therapy can help women find their true selves rather than necessarily producing pressure to conform to male values and visions (Benjamin 1990; Sayers 1995). Even Lacan, with his insistence that paternal law is unavoidable, has been welcomed for the liberating distinctions between creativity, narcissism and symbolism, which shows how alienated selves can be found through the discovery of discourse – therapeutically through finding one's own voice.

Klein-influenced cultural critics (e.g. Young 1994) emphasise how psychotic processes of projection, splitting, perverse destructiveness, hatred and sexual violence lurk not far from the surface of domestic and political life. Others have tried to tease out the moral values implicit in psychoanalysis, in an attempt to link its critique of the micro-society of the family to wider social issues. The moral stance of psychoanalysis includes a number of concerns central to social and political debate. First, there is an overriding valuation of the truth, of the need to face reality however painful, rather than turn a blind eye (Steiner 1993). This leads to scepticism about simplistic solutions in which evil is driven out by love – a balance between the two is a more realistic possibility. Second, the work of Bowlby and the Independent analysts emphasise the link between nurturance and the search for a good society: if we neglect childhood, society will inevitably suffer (Rustin 1992; Holmes 1993). Thus Winnicott (1971; Meares and Coombes 1994) sees psychoanalysis as a process of 'learning to play' – the 'right to play' would appear on any psychoanalytic political manifesto. Third, psychoanalysis values autonomy as a good in its own right, independent of freedom from want, a view that is central to the liberal tradition, and demonstrates how the cradle of autonomy is sensitive parenting, the lack of which can, with luck, be remedied by psychoanalysis (Holmes and Lindley 1989, 1994).

Such diverse ideas spring from the metapsychological super-structure of psychoanalysis, but, if psychoanalytic thinking is to have any validity and if it is to be based on more than myths or wishes, it must rest on firm foundations of clinical theory and practice – the exposition of which forms the rationale and purpose of this book.

Chapter 2

Models of the mind

> Such ideas as these are part of a speculative superstructure of psychoanalysis, any portion of which can be abandoned or changed without loss or regret the moment its inadequacy has been proved.
>
> (Freud 1925a: 32)

Freud's archaeological metaphor (see Chapter 1), in which new ideas are built upon earlier foundations, can be applied to psychoanalytic theory itself. Some ideas are fully covered over, while others are retained in almost their original form. Freud himself continually reworked his theoretical models and he was not afraid to change them radically when the need arose. His successors have happily followed his example and psychoanalytic models of the mind have undergone many developmental changes. All are mixed models, not necessarily building a coherent whole but forming a complex matrix of ideas containing concepts at different levels of abstraction. Contradictory formulations sometimes sit uncomfortably side-by-side. This mixing of models not only has arisen from a continual process of replacement and cross-fertilisation but also from the constant interaction of different *levels* of theory.

Waelder (1962) identified a number of such levels of psychoanalytic theory:

1 The level of individual clinical interpretation – which is a theory about particular patients.
2 The level of clinical generalisation in which theoretical ideas relate to specific groups of patients, e.g. 'narcissistic organisations' (q.v. p. 79).
3 The level of clinical theory containing general psychoanalytic concepts such as defence mechanisms or transference – the level

with which we shall be primarily concerned in this chapter.
4 The level of abstract explanatory concepts such as life and death
   instincts.

Underlying different theories are different fundamental assumptions
about the world: how much experience is determined by the environment, and how much it is innate; whether a basically optimistic
or pessimistic viewpoint is adopted; whether a mechanistic or
humanistic view of the mind is taken; on the balance between
determinism and freedom; on the emphasis on mental forces as
opposed to meanings and language; whether a position of mentalism
or realism is adopted.

All these issues have been discussed by philosophical and
cultural observers of psychoanalysis (see, for example, Rieff 1960;
Wollheim and Hopkins 1982; Greenberg and Mitchell 1982;
Holmes and Lindley 1989; and Cavell 1994). From the clinical
perspective of this book two dimensions stand out. First, the
balance between environmental or intrapsychic factors in the
development of the personality; second, whether the emphasis is
on causation and mechanism in approaching mental phenomena, or
on understanding and meaning. Freud found himself on both sides
of these conflicts. Initially he placed the emphasis more on
environmental factors, especially traumatic external events like
childhood seduction, and suggested they led to the formation of
symptoms in adult life. In the later drive-structural model Freud
saw the internal world as primary. External events were triggers
releasing inherent patterns such as the oedipus complex. This
difference of emphasis continues to this day: models may be
classified as intrapsychic, interpersonal or mixed. Similarly, although Freud set out to produce a mechanistic picture of abnormal
mental life, as his work evolved he became more and more
concerned with meaning, narrative and communication.

The dilemma faced by clinicians is that in order to practise
effectively, especially at the outset of one's career, a firm theoretical
framework is essential; at the same time it is unlikely that any one
model holds the key to the workings of the human mind and human
motivation. In practise, most analysts draw on a mixture of different
theories, even if their basic allegiance is to a particular school. This
chapter contains a schematic overview of the main psychoanalytic
concepts and models, all of which will be elaborated in the course
of the book.

The unconscious

The concept of the unconscious is central to psychoanalytic theory. Although Freud did not 'discover' the unconscious (Ellenberger 1970), he was the first to explore systematically its role in normal and abnormal mental life. From a contemporary perspective the unconscious is seen within psychoanalysis in one of four basic ways.

The unconscious as a 'thing in itself'

Freud initially saw the unconscious as part of the 'mental apparatus' (Laplanche 1989), a Kantian entity that could not be directly apprehended but explained in a deterministic way irrational mental phenomena such as dreams, neurotic symptoms and slips of the tongue. He postulated that unacceptable memories, phantasies, wishes, thoughts, ideas and aspects of painful events were pushed back by repression into the unconscious, along with their associated emotions. In Freud's unpublished 'Project' he hoped to produce a neurobiological account of the role of the unconscious, based on the flow, binding, and discharge of psychic energy, or libido. Although this 'hydraulic' model has largely been superseded, modern neuropsychology has confirmed, via subliminal perception and 'preconscious processing', that many aspects of mental life vital to survival take place outside of awareness (Dixon and Henley 1991).

The unconscious as reservoir of latent meaning

With the shift in contemporary psychoanalysis away from mechanism towards meaning, 'the unconscious' becomes a metaphor for the affective meanings of which the patient is unaware, and which emerge through the relationship with the analyst. 'Unconscious' becomes an adjective rather than a noun: 'unconscious processes', rather that 'the unconscious'. This links psychoanalysis with the 'post-modern' notion of polysemy or multiple meanings which are to be found in any cultural phenomenon or 'text'. The analyst's task, rather than being an anatomist of the mental apparatus, is collaboratively to explore these latent meanings.

The mystery of the unconscious

Jung (1943) emphasised a less tangible quasi-mystical aspect of the unconscious. He was particularly interested in religious and spiritual aspects of human experience and introduced the concept of the collective unconscious. He thought this was innate, common to all mankind, and existed at a deeper layer of the mind than the personal unconscious described by Freud. He based this view on the finding that the beliefs, symbols and mythology of widely different religions and cultures have had a great deal in common throughout the ages and in different parts of the world.

Past unconscious and present unconscious

Sandler and Sandler (1984) made a clinically useful distinction between the 'past unconscious' and the 'present unconscious'. The past unconscious of the adult is the 'child within' that continues in an unmodified form to have a powerful role in determining the adult's responses, wishes and needs as if childhood were still operating. More akin to the preconscious (see below, p. 32), the present unconscious modifies the past unconscious by the use of mechanisms of defence, allowing the past unconscious phantasies some expression, albeit in an attenuated form. The Sandlers argue that, in treatment, the analyst should always work from present unconscious to past unconscious, to attend to the here-and-now of the analytic interaction before proceeding to reconstructions of past traumata.

FREUD'S MODELS

Freud's picture of the mind went through three main phases, which Sandler *et al.* (1972) have called the affect-trauma model, the topographical model and the structural model. We shall consider each in turn.

Affect-trauma model

Freud's earliest psychoanalytic ideas were influenced by experiences with casualties from the Franco-Prussian war in which hysterical paralyses seemed to be related to traumatic experiences at the battle front, relieved once the sufferer was able to speak about (abreact) the terrifying events he had gone through. Once Freud had noted what he took to be the frequency of childhood sexual abuse among his hysterical patients, he speculated that, by analogy with battle trauma, painful external events such as childhood seduction could overwhelm the 'mental apparatus', leaving it unable to deal with the resulting affects. He tried to differentiate between the 'actual neuroses' (neurasthenia and anxiety neurosis) which he believed were caused by current trauma, and the 'psychoneuroses' (hysteria and obsessional neurosis), which he saw as the result of childhood trauma. This distinction is now obsolete (*q.v.* p. 212), although current trauma, such as a recent accident or bereavement, may lead to symptoms of Post Traumatic Stress Disorder.

The idea of the release of 'dammed up' affects (i.e. feelings), threatening psychic equilibrium and potentially leading to symptoms, has been called the 'affect-trauma' frame of reference forming part of the first phase of Freud's metapsychology. Affect-trauma plays an important part in contemporary psychoanalytic thinking, especially since the reality of childhood abuse, physical, emotional and sexual, has become apparent. The *nature* of infantile trauma is viewed differently by different authors, some emphasising intrapsychic factors, others stressing environmental influences. From an intrapsychic perspective, Klein and Kernberg see the intensity of childhood hatred, aggression and envy as inherently traumatic and speculate that potential borderline personality disorder sufferers may experience an excess of such unassimilable negative emotions, leading in turn to excessive splitting and projection (*q.v.* pp. 81–7). In contrast, for Kohut the primal trauma is interpersonal: a failure of parental empathy, leading to disruption of a coherent sense of self and the emergence of 'disintegration products' in later life such as aggression, or attempts at self-soothing through addiction, compulive sexuality and even self-injury.

In both accounts trauma leads to painful affect which, in turn, provides the motivational force behind pathological reactions. The potency of affect as an organiser of mental functioning has received some support from Bower (1981) who found that the recall of memories is affect-dependent. Some memories can only be recalled when the same mood state is present as when they were laid down. The recovery of buried memories of trauma in the transference also enables them to be reworked in a less overwhelming way: loss can be grieved, and anger expressed, leading sometimes to acceptance or even forgiveness.

The topographical model

The term 'topographical' implies a spatial model in which different psychological functions are localised in different places. The division of the mind into the unconscious, the preconscious and conscious systems (Freud 1900), the so-called topographical model, ushered in the second phase of Freud's work (1897–1923), still containing echoes of cerebral localisation, a reminder of Freud's previous career as a neurologist. Contemporary psychoanalysis still uses topographical concepts but has divested itself of their anatomical overtones, just as Freud did, by talking about each part of the mind as a 'system' – the 'system unconscious', the 'system preconscious', etc. This enables a smooth transition to the 'structural model' (see below), which is primarily concerned with the functions of the different parts of the mind.

The 'two principles'

A fundamental idea that comes out of this phase of Freud's theoretical development is his contrast between the 'two principles of mental functioning' (Freud 1911a), which he called the primary and secondary processes. Secondary process thinking is rational and follows the ordinary laws of logic, time and space. Primary process thinking is typical of dreaming, phantasy, and infantile life in which the laws of time and space and the distinction between opposites do not apply; the distinction between past, present and future no longer holds and different events may occur simultaneously and in the same place; one symbol may represent a number of different objects, or have several different and even contradictory meanings.

Unconscious and preconscious

Freud realised that many psychological processes are unconscious in a descriptive sense and the individual is not aware of them, but they are easily brought to mind, and therefore are neither subject to repression nor operating under the sway of the primary processes. These unconscious but non-repressed phenomena he attributed to 'the system preconscious', whose role in the topographical model is both as a reservoir of accessible thoughts and memories, and as a censor capable of modifying instinctual wishes of the system unconscious and so render them acceptable to the system conscious.

Instinct theory

The change from the affect–trauma frame of reference to the topographical model represented a significant shift in the evolution of psychoanalytic theory. The spotlight moved from a focus on external reality and its impact on psychological processes to the internal world itself. For most of his life, Freud saw the internal world as dominated by man's struggle with his instincts or drives.

Instinct or drive theory was put forward by Freud to explain human motivation. Confusion has arisen because the term 'instinct' was used to translate both 'Instinkt' and 'Trieb' from the German. Instinkt refers more to *innate behaviour patterns and responses* while Trieb implies a pressure or *push* towards a general goal, such as survival. Unfortunately Freud's translators used both words interchangeably, perhaps reflecting the continuing struggle within psychoanalysis between biological and psychological concepts. Freud considered instincts as basic developmental needs constituted from phantasies which had a peremptory quality and required expression and gratification.

Freud was always an 'obstinate dualist' (Jones 1953). In his initial formulation of instincts Freud (1905a) emphasised the sexual drives both in normal development and in the origins of psychological illness; later he emphasised the aggressive and destructive drives or death instinct (Freud 1920, 1930). This became known as the dual-instinct theory, although Freud had earlier stressed the self-preservative (i.e. death-defying) instincts as well as the sexual. The individual was at the mercy of these drives, or instinctual wishes, with adult symptoms arising from the psychological defences mobilised to deal with their infantile demands. Each instinctual wish forms a component of the system unconscious and has an innate need for 'discharge'. In order to achieve its aim it becomes connected during development to an object.

In this classical schema instinctual wishes have a *source* and an *aim* as well as an *object*. Their infantile source or origin is in the body and may be an 'erogenous zone' such as the mouth, anus or genital; sensations in these bodily areas develop levels of tension which aim towards discharge. The infant experiencing hunger pains starts to suck. Gradually his activity increases until the object of the instinctual wish – the mother's breast – is provided and hunger is satiated. The presence of the object and its quality is remembered and the next time the infant feels hungry the memory of the breast is revived and the phantasy is once again enacted. The source, the aim and the object begin to mesh together into a complex inter-actional phantasy, part of which is represented in the system unconscious.

Although, in this example, the experience and revived memory derive from a real event – the knitting together of an instinctual wish – its need for expression and subsequent satisfaction can also develop from an imagined occurrence. If an infantile, wish-fulfilling daydream is 'lived' within the self and later repressed, the system unconscious will treat the imagined events according to the principles of primary process and, therefore, as if they were real. The distinction between the recovery of a traumatic memory and the revival of a wish-fulfilling fantasy, both of which have been repressed, is difficult to make in the clinical situation. This also means that reports by patients of their earlier experiences cannot necessarily be taken at face value. Recent accounts of the 'false memory syndrome', in which imagined traumatic events are experienced as real, may, for example, illustrate this principle.

Limitations of the topographical model

Clinical experience led Freud to acknowledge an increasing number of inconsistencies in the topographical model. Foremost among these was the realisation that there was no place within his map of the mind for ideals, values and conscience. Moreover, he recognised that the influence of the external world on mental structures and the unconscious nature of defence both needed more exploration. For example, anxiety had initially been seen as a result of the accumulation of repressed 'somatic sexual excitement', or libido (see Chapter 1, p. 8), which was transformed from a sexual wish into an unpleasant feeling; that is, as arising entirely from within. But it became clear that anxiety also arises in response to threat, either directly, or as part of a psychological conflict induced by the threat. For example, a child who feels anger towards a neglectful parent, may be fearful of expressing this anger for fear of losing the parent altogether. The internalisation of this parent–child relationship was hard to reconcile with the topographical model.

Similarly, in his papers 'On narcissism' (1914a) and 'Mourning and melancholia' (1917), Freud had begun to stress the interaction between the internal world and external events, especially in his discussion of introjection, internalisation and identification. He began to wonder how an experience of, say, a harsh or punitive parent, comes to form a structural part of an individual's internal world. The advent of the structural model (Freud 1923) was Freud's attempt to answer these questions, heralding the third and final phase of his theorising (1923–39).

Structural theory

In the structural model Freud (1923) proposed three parts or 'structural components' of the human personality: translated, or according to Bettleheim (1985) mistranslated, as the familiar id, superego and ego. As with topographical theory, these are nowadays best thought of as *functions*, rather than as structural entities, as metaphors for psychological configurations showing a slow rate of change and reactive stability (Rapaport 1967; Friedman 1978). The structural model remains firmly embedded within instinct theory. The term 'id', for example, refers to the basic inborn drives and the sexual and aggressive impulses. But the structural model is equally concerned with how the individual's personality structure adapts to the demands of these instinctual wishes and it places a greater emphasis on external reality than does the topographical model.

Superego

The earlier notion of the 'ego ideal' (Freud 1914a), an internal model to which the individual aspires or attempts to conform, was subsumed by the wider concept of the superego. The term 'superego' is used to describe conscience and ideals; like the ego ideal these are derived through internalisation of parental or other authority figures, and cultural influences from childhood onwards. From an object relations perspective (see below) the superego represents not so much an internalised parent as a *relationship* with a parent. The internalised parent of the superego may therefore be a representation of a parent into whom has been projected much of the individual's own aggression and punitiveness.

The internalised parental and other figures of the superego are thus formed from phantasy as well as reality and, as such, contain significant components of externalisations and projections of aspects of the self. The whole structure therefore functions according to these modified internal objects, which explains why clinically, for example, a parent who is experienced as harsh may in reality appear to have been relatively benign. The superego is involved in the experience of guilt, perfectionism, indecision, preoccupation with what is the right or wrong thing to do, and hence plays an important role in the aetiology of some forms of depression, obsessional disorders and sexual problems.

Some effects of the functioning of the superego are descriptively conscious whereas others are descriptively unconscious. For example some individuals may be quite clear that what they wish to do goes against accepted values or indeed against their own upbringing; in others there is an unconscious sense of guilt (Freud 1923) – a patient tormented by obsessive–compulsive acts may have no conscious idea of why he is compelled to do something and feels excessively guilty if it is not done.

Ego

The term 'ego' is used to describe the more rational, reality-oriented and executive aspects of the personality, and once again is partly conscious and partly unconscious. The ego's task, as seen by Freud, was to control the more primitive id impulses and to adapt these to outer reality in accordance with the reality principle, as well as to mollify the requirements of the superego: 'the poor ego. . . serves three masters and does what it can to bring their claims and demands into harmony with one another. . . . Its three tyrannical masters are the external world, the superego and the id' (Freud 1933).

The structural model cannot easily be superimposed on the topo-graphical theory. The system unconscious and the id are equivalent, functioning according to primary process thinking, but the system conscious and the ego are not equivalent, since part of the ego may be unconscious. Equally, preconscious and superego cannot be equated. The key issue clinically is not just whether the patient is conscious or unconscious of some aspect of himself, but what part of the mind holds sway: is the patient behaving and thinking according to the primary processes; under the dictates of conscience, or adaptively?

Conflict and adaptation

Implicit in the idea of an inner world is that of *delay*. A wish is shaped, influenced, modified, held back, diverted or disguised by the 'pale cast of thought'. Instinctual wishes cannot obtain direct expression: within the topographical model they have to traverse the preconscious before they reach consciousness; in structural theory the superego and ego hold them back. By the time they reach consciousness they have been modified to such an extent that they can only be pieced together through dreams, parapraxes and, in the clinical situation, transference. Modification of instinctual wishes is effected through the use of the mechanisms of defence (see pp.

81–93), which are mobilised as a result of internal conflict. Conflict occurs between the instinctual wishes under the sway of the *'pleasure principle'* (Freud 1920) and the demands of reality – in simple terms, between past and present, or between the inner child and the functioning adult. In the structural model, conflict is seen as occurring between the three structures themselves and between each one of them and the external world. Through the impingement of reality, gratification of the instinctual wishes is delayed or modified if they threaten the self-preservation of the individual, or contravene his moral and ethical beliefs, or oppose the demands of his social and cultural environment. The introduction of the *reality principle* by Freud (1911a) heralded the move from a primary focus on the internal world rather than on the external environment to an increasing emphasis on the relationship between the two.

POST-FREUDIAN MODELS

In the classical model, psychoanalysis tends to see the personality as a battlefield: central themes are those of innate division and conflict, internal tension and adaptation. Throughout development a struggle occurs between internal demands and external reality, with internal needs taking a primary motivational role. Repression is viewed as the primary mechanism of defence, ensuring that incompatible wishes remain unconscious or disguised, but because of the intrinsic tendency of the repressed wishes and impulses to return to consciousness, tension remains an innate part of the system.

Ego psychology

Heinz Hartmann (1939, 1964), the founder of ego psychology, questioned this view, stressing instead the non-defensive aspects of the ego (and was himself much criticised by Lacan, see pp. 65–6). Instead of the ego simply being a mediator between the demands of the id and the external world, Hartmann conceived of the ego as, in part, outside this area of conflict and thus able to interact with the external world free from internal influences. This 'conflict-free sphere of the ego' develops independently, and flourishes unimpeded by conflict if environmental influences are reasonably favourable. It contains such functions as thinking, perception, language, learning, memory, and rational planning. Development of these aspects of the personality may influence the experience of pleasure and satisfaction.

Freud had moved the focus from the external world to an emphasis on the internal workings of the mind within the topographical theory, and back again in the structural model. Hartmann moved things a little further towards reality by suggesting that the experience of pleasure did not arise simply from satisfaction of instinctual wishes but also depended on what good experiences the external world was in reality able to provide.

A further contribution of the ego psychologists was their distinction between Freud's view of the ego as a structure, and a more modernist concept of the ego as a representation of the self – a view that was developed by Kohut in self-psychology. Anna Freud (1936) also re-emphasised the importance of the relationship of the ego to the external world and the normal and adaptive aspects of the personality. She considered defence mechanisms as not only responding to the dangers of the internal world but also – for example, in 'identification with the aggressor' (see pp. 88–9) – to those of the external world. However her approach was less rigorous in its adherence to the structural model than that of the ego psychologists, and she continued to emphasise the usefulness of the topographical model. Jacobson (1964) developed these ideas further, but ego psychology in general has recently become more integrated with object relations theory, for example in the work of Kernberg (1976, 1980), Arlow (1991), Gill and Hoffman (1982) and Sandler (1987).

The Klein–Bion model

Although primarily a clinician rather than a theory-builder, it is generally agreed that Melanie Klein was one of the most original and challenging thinkers in the history of psychoanalysis. Klein saw that for all its advantages, something had been lost in the move from the topographical to the structural model, especially the notion of unconscious phantasy within intrapsychic life. By focusing on early pre-oedipal experiences Klein hoped to reconcile the apparent opposition between those that emphasised phantasy on the one hand, and drive theory on the other.

The Kleinian 'positions'

Klein is perhaps best known for her account of the two basic 'positions' of mental life, the 'paranoid–schizoid' and the 'depressive', and for her notion of 'projective identification' (see p. 82).

In essence the Kleinian 'positions' are constellations of phantasies, anxieties and defences which are mobilised to protect the individual from internal destructiveness. In the earlier, paranoid–schizoid position the focus of the anxiety is on threats of annihilation and disintegration, and the infant attempts to organise these experiences by the use of splitting and projection (see p. 81). Bad experiences are split off and projected into the object which is then felt to be persecuting and dangerous and especially threatening to the good experiences. In order to protect the good experiences, they too may be projected into the object which then becomes idealised. In the later depressive position, anxiety is not so much about the survival of the self but the survival of the object upon whom one depends. The individual realises that the frustrating and hated object is also the one that satisfies and is loved. Recognition that they are one and the same leads to ambivalence and guilt. Although the positions are set out schematically there is a constant oscillation between the two, and a third 'borderline' position has also been described (see p. 226).

Phantasies and drives

For Freud, libido and aggression were structureless phenomena whose form was dictated by developmental bodily stages as well as by drive gratification or frustration. But for Klein the instincts are inherently attached to objects, as preformed 'primary phantasies' (the 'ph' differentiating them from 'fantasies' in the everyday sense of daydreams or conscious wishes). The basic unit of mental life therefore becomes object-related unconscious phantasy itself, rather than instinctual wishes that seek expression through 'self-created' objects.

There is a continuing psychoanalytic debate about the degree of innate knowledge possessed by the infant and the extent to which it is formed throughout development. For Klein destructiveness and unconscious phantasy are innate and 'primary', but for Freud they arise out of frustration, and are therefore 'secondary'. Klein believed that the infant's mind contained complex preformed images of the object. For example, in 'Envy and gratitude' (1957) she states that 'the infant has an innate unconscious awareness of the existence of the mother' and that this forms 'the instinctual knowledge that is the basis of the infant's primal relation to the mother'. Thus for Klein the unconscious has specific contents right from the start of mental life, namely unconscious phantasies, which are the mental corollaries or the psychic representations of instincts. An instinctual wish can only be *experienced* (as opposed to theorised about by psychoanalysts) as an unconscious phantasy (Isaacs 1943). This concept of a preprogrammed thinking infant, more sophisticated than Freud's *tabula rasa*, has received some confirmation from developmental psychology, although Stern's (1985) picture of happy infant–mother attunement is a far cry from Klein's model of primary envy and hatred (cf. Chapter 3).

Bion and containment

In Freud's early writings 'the object' only appears as the provider or withholder of gratification. By the time the oedipal stage is reached, objects are fully formed; how they became so is unclear. Klein tried to reconcile drive theory with object-finding in her notion of the primary object, but it was Bion, her analysand, who moved Kleinian theory decisively away from drives and towards relationships. In his concept of 'the container and the contained', Bion (1962) extended the idea of projective identification (see p. 82) and suggested that the mother acts as a container for the infant's projected feelings, such as pain, fear of death, envy and hatred. These feelings are 'detoxified' by the nurturing (or in the case of analysis, 'listening') breast, and then returned in such a way that the infant gets back good feelings of being held and understood rather than the original bad projections. In this way the infant makes sense of his experiences, and introjects an object that is capable of bearing and allaying anxiety. There is thus an explicitly stated interactional component, even though the 'death instinct' remains as the organising force for the projections.

Object relations theory

Although Bion moved Kleinian thinking into the realm of object relations, Fairbairn (1952) and Guntrip (1961) are usually seen as the fathers of present-day object relations theory. We have already suggested that models of the mind may be divided into those that focus primarily on the internal world (Freud's structural model – Klein), those that focus more on the external world (the 'Neo-Freudians' – Sullivan, Fromm, Horney, Erikson and Bowlby, see below) and those that lie somewhere between the two (Winnicott, Bion, Kohut – Freud's affect-trauma model). A further distinction may be made between those object relations models that incorporate drive theory and those that do not. Fairbairn and Guntrip made no such attempt and neither did Sullivan, whereas Mahler (see pp. 60–1), Klein, Kernberg and Kohut tried to do so, although the latter, as we shall see, downplayed aggressive drives. Most of the British writers, such as Winnicott and Balint, have had no difficulty in combining the two, especially in their clinical formulations; and more recently Sandler (1981) has proposed a mixed model. Despite their differences, Fairbairn, Guntrip, Winnicott and Balint have been lumped together as the British object relations theorists (Sutherland 1980; Greenberg and Mitchell 1983; Phillips 1988). Although their theories take a variety of forms they share a number of pivotal assumptions (Westen 1990).

Object seeking

Central to the theory of object relations is the belief that a person's primary motivational drive is to seek a relationship with others. Humans are primarily object seeking rather than pleasure seeking, and the end goal is the relationship with another person. The infant's early activity is directed towards contact with the mother, and later others: 'pleasure is a signpost to the object, rather than vice versa' (Fairbairn 1952). The method of object seeking varies according to the stage of development: initially it is through feeding (including mutual gazing, Wright 1991) and later through the sharing of activities and interests. This does not completely overthrow the concept of pleasure seeking, since, as Balint (1957) sensibly says, the individual is both object and pleasure seeking. The compulsive quest for pleasure may of course also be a pathological response when object relationships fail.

The representational world

The core notion of object relations theory is that of an internal world populated by the self, its objects and the relationships between them. This is Sandler's 'representational world', which he likened to a proscenium stage upon which the scenes and dramas of inner life are enacted. The relationships between these internal objects act as templates for subsequent relationships, especially when the primary processes are operative. Intimate relationships with partners and with the analyst will be profoundly influenced by the valencies of the internal world. In contrast to Klein's idea of primary object phantasies, Fairbairn (1952) conceived of internal objects and the phantasies associated with them arising as a consequence of the inevitable failure of external objects. For Fairbairn this leads to a split at the heart of the psyche between the 'libidinal object' which gratifies and the 'anti-libidinal object' which frustrates. These objects are associated with corresponding libidinal and anti-libidinal self-representations. Like Freud, he suggested that the internal world developed as a substitute and compensation for unsatisfying experiences in external relationships, with aggression as an organising factor, secondary to these frustrations. He also stressed that what is internalised is not an object as such but a relationship. This point is often overlooked.

Transitional space

Guntrip was analysed first by Fairbairn, a fairly dour Scot (Sutherland 1989) and then by the benign Devonian, Winnicott (Phillips 1988). The latter, as already described, took a much more positive view of human relationships, seeing creativity and the internal world as natural results of a good-enough mother–infant relationship. Winnicott insisted that object relations theory had to understand not just internal and external objects but their mutual interplay. This he located in a 'potential space' which is experienced as being neither inside nor outside but in between.

Transitional phenomena are the missing link between Freud's pleasure principle and the reality principle. Through his notion of 'transitional space', Winnicott (1965) attempted to reconcile drive theory with an interpersonal perspective. He believed the drive-driven child conjures up in his mind an object suited to his needs, especially when excited. If, at this precise moment, the 'good-enough' mother presents him with just such a suitable object, complementary to his wish, a moment of 'illusion' is created in the baby, who feels that he has 'made' the object himself. The repetition of these 'hallucinatory' wishes and their embodiment ('realisation') by the mother leads the infant to believe he creates his own world. This omnipotence leads to healthy development of a creative and playful self. Only once this 'true self' has been established can omnipotence be abrogated and the reality of pain and loss be faced. Where the mother is not 'good enough', a compliant 'false self' arises, concealing frustrated and sequestered instinctual drives.

Gradually the developing infant comes to differentiate between internal and external and reality and illusion, realising that there is an outside reality that is not simply the result of one's own projections. This results in an experience of contacting other minds and a greater sense of oneself. Guntrip believed that this process could be recreated in analysis through contacting the 'regressed ego', a helpless and vulnerable aspect of an unloved self, defended against by compulsive object seeking, and curable through regression into transitional space within the analytic relationship. Balint also emphasised the importance of regression as a therapeutic tool in the analysis of disturbed or 'basic fault' patients (i.e. those with borderline pathology).

Hate

Just as Winnicott was able to reconcile libido with relationships in his notion of transitional phenomena, so in his concept of positive hatred he tried to relationalise the death instinct. In his paper 'The use of the object' he distinguishes between two types of experience which he calls 'relating to the object' and 'using the object'. Initially the object is related to part of one's own mind and not necessarily experienced as real or separate from the self. Later in development, when the object is experienced as real and independent, a different type of relationship can be entered into in which there is an exchange of a shared reality. Winnicott called this 'using the object' and linked it to the individual's struggle to recognise and be recognised by the other. The driving force behind this struggle was 'hatred': for the object to be recognised and experienced as outside the person's control it has to be destroyed in phantasy but then experienced as surviving in reality. Here destruction becomes not so much a dangerous damaging force, but part of the separation–individuation process.

Winnicott's creative synthesis of the drive-based and relational models did much to prevent an ossification of theoretical views within the British Psycho-Analytic Society. However, in the USA, many psychoanalysts began to chafe at the rigidity of ego psychology, seeing its exclusive emphasis on the oedipal situation and instinct as limited and limiting. Furthermore, in the 1960s there was a cultural shift leading to an interest in the self, both as a positive arena of personal liberation, and negatively as a withdrawal from relationships into self-aggrandisement and self-gratification. Within psychoanalysis these two factors crystallised in Heinz Kohut's self-psychology. According to Lasch (1979) and Schafer (1977) this represented a shift from thwarted instinctual gratification to a concern for self-fulfilment, a move from guilty, oedipal man suffering from internal conflicts within a cohesive self, to tragic man struggling with problems of cohesion and the very integrity of the self. In addition to its reaction against the orthodoxies of ego psychology, self-psychology has its roots in the psychoanalytically heretical interpersonal model put forward by Sullivan (1962) which we shall mention first.

The interpersonal model

The interpersonal model, which was developed by the so-called Neo-Freudians – Sullivan (1962, 1964), Horney (1939), Fromm (1973) and Erikson (1965) – takes a radically interpersonal stance; here, to paraphrase Winnicott, 'there is no such thing as an individual'. Sullivan was a psychiatrist who became convinced that the strict Kraepelinian view of schizophrenia in the 1920s was wrong (i.e. in its view of the illness as a biologically determined, irreversible deterioration of the personality leading to complete breakdown of mental and emotional functioning). Well ahead of his time, he realised that much of what was seen as 'schizophrenia' was the result of institutionalisation, rather than disease process. He argued for stimulating human relationships and not just custodial care. It was in this context that Sullivan developed his interpersonal theory.

In common with other psychoanalytic views, the interpersonal model emphasises early mother–child interactions as central to the subsequent development of the personality, but does not see the child's internal world as being the determining influence. Instead, the drive-structure model put forward by Freud is reversed. Anxiety, rather than arising from within as a result of unconscious instinctual wishes pushing for expression and satisfaction, is seen as being stimulated from without, a response to the state of mind of the *other*. The child forms specific mental representations according to the anxiety that is engendered and imagines that a 'Bad Me' elicited anxiety in the (m)other. In the same way a 'Good Me', which alleviates anxiety, is also set up along with a 'Not Me'. The 'Not Me' is a response to severe panic and confusion, akin to Guntrip's vulnerable helpless self at the core of the schizoid mode of being, which is a nucleus for subsequent psychotic fragmentation.

Anxiety experiences are elaborated into stable interpersonal strategies which are manoeuvres designed to establish a sense of security. Such 'security operations' include avoidance, inattentions, tactical misrepresentations and other interpersonal strategies. Although expressed in rather simplistic terms (there are clear links with Sandler's notion of the 'child within'), interpersonal psychonalysis contributed to a significant technical shift away from 'reconstruction' to a focus on the here-and-now in the analytic situation. The interpersonal approach was clearly a reaction to the esotericism of psychoanalytic theory, and encouraged a simple, less theory-laden, more collaborative relationship between patient and analyst, in which the transference was seen primarily as an intensified slice of life, rather than a distortion of the present by complex phantasies about which only the analyst had expert knowledge.

Self-psychology

Kohut (1971, 1977) challenged psychoanalytic orthodoxy in the USA, claiming that a new approach which went beyond oedipal analysis was needed if patients with narcissistic disorders, who were becoming increasingly common, were to be successfully treated. The focus of his theory became the 'self', and the effect that denial, frustration and fulfilment of wishes has on its development. At first Kohut tried to build on both object relations theory and ego psychology and he portrayed the self as arising from mental representations within the ego, an elaboration of the idea of self-representation. Later he came to depict the self as a supraordinate structure with its own developmental line which subsumed instinctual wishes and defences.

Necessary narcissism

Just as Hartmann had postulated a 'conflict-free' zone of the ego, Kohut built on Freud's notion of 'primary narcissism' (*q.v.* pp. 55–6), to suggest that self-love was necessary for psychological health, seeing narcissistic disorders as resulting from defects in the self brought about by parental empathic failures. He postulated first a 'bipolar' self and later a 'tripolar' self in which self-assertive ambitions crystallise at one pole, attained ideals and values at another, and talents and skills at the third. Pathology may arise from a disturbance at each pole and may be compensated for by strength in one of the others.

The idea of the self, or narcissistic developments following a separate developmental pathway, can be seen as an expansion of Freud's view of psychosexual development, and of Anna Freud's (1965) notion of separate developmental lines along drive-, ego-, and object-related pathways. However the view that the self has a supraordinate or unifying, overarching perspective on personality development is more controversial. The main point of contention is Kohut's view that aggressive drives are secondary, arising from an insufficiently consolidated self brought about by empathic failures. Kernberg (1975, 1984) particularly has called attention to this de-emphasis of the aggressive drives. It is also difficult to see in Kohut's schema where the superego fits as an organising focus, if ideals and values are seen as parts of the self.

The central building block of self-psychology is the *self-object*; this is one's subjective sense of a sustaining intimate relationship with another whose security and interest maintains the self. Self-object needs were initially described in the treatment of narcissistic patients, but are now considered to be ubiquitous and enduring and a requirement of the normal psychological functioning of the self. Self-object needs lead to 'self-object transferences' (see pp. 106–7), comprising mirroring, idealising and twinship transferences, each corresponding to a different pole of the tripolar self.

The term 'self-object' has come to be used in a generic fashion to describe the role that others perform for the self in relation to mirroring, idealising and twinship needs. These needs are never outgrown and self-objects are best viewed as aspects of others which are required to gratify the psychological needs of the self, such as engendering security, soothing, admiration and so on. This view-point differs markedly from the drive-structural and object relations views on the importance of separation–individuation, although Bowlby's attachment theory also acknowledges the continuing need for dependency. In self-psychology the focus is on the need for empathic and affirming responses from others throughout life, but with a move from reliance on archaic objects towards mature dependency.

CONCLUSIONS

Each developing analyst has to struggle with the tension between conservatism and innovation within the analytic tradition. At one extreme there is a desire to overthrow parental authority and define an entirely new territory of discourse; at the other there is a determination to preserve what is good in the old. These extreme 'oedipal' reactions, while necessary in exceptional circumstances and for exceptional thinkers, are not part of 'normal science' (Kuhn 1962). The developing analyst is in the position first of an oedipal child who has to negotiate both healthy identification and separation in the course of his intellectual development, and later is in a parental position, having to reconcile, as far as possible, the different voices of the competing analytic factions.

Self-psychology's emphasis on empathy, environmental failure, positive narcissism, and challenge to a drive-based interpretive analytic stance was a necessary counterweight to the excesses of ego psychology. Indeed virtually all the theories discussed in this chapter developed because of dissatisfaction with aspects of a prevailing theory. Most psychoanalytic models are incomplete, as indeed are all models of the mind from whatever perspective. Different psycho-analytic models are relevant to different aspects of a complex whole, usually emphasising one aspect at the expense of another. Psycho-analytic disputes neglect this complexity and miss the point that differing views are often an attempt to remedy weaknesses within another theory rather than to overthrow it.

Freud's language, influenced by the physics of his day, lives on: psychoanalysts still speak of object, drive and their mutual 'dy-namics'. At the same time, in the contemporary search for a unified theory, three themes stand out: *representation*, *affect* and *narrative*. For Sandler (1981) self and object representations are what guide the individual in his relationship with the external world. Sandler suggests that the primary motivational element is the regulation of feeling states to maintain a sense of security, rather than drives. Similarly, Stolorow *et al.* (1987) have argued that the notion of endogenous drives should be abandoned and replaced with *affects* as motivational elements formed within the interaction between self and self-objects.

In affect theory meaning intersects with mechanism. Meanings are a way of organising and 'fixing' problematic emotional experience into coherent narratives which explain the self's relationship to its world (Elliot and Shapiro 1992). The focus of interpretive work is no longer on instinctual conflicts, frustration of wishes, or aggressive drives but on the patient's affective experience, its origins within the analytic relationship, and the translation of that experience into coherent stories or narratives that make sense and act as guides and warnings for future action. Pine's (1981) emphasis on the importance of 'intense moments' during both development and treatment is a good example of this.

However, just as psychoanalysis sees the personality as 'a precipitate of abandoned object cathexes', so changes in theory and practice often have their precursors. For example, a focus on the affective experience of the patient is not new. Fenichel (1941) summarised the problem of resistance as either an intense affect defending against cognitive awareness of unconscious conflict, or the reverse, intellectualisation as a defence against affective experience. Too great a reliance on cognitive *or* affective experiences impoverishes the understanding of the complexity of human motivation and interaction and loses the unity of affect and cognition.

Psychoanalytic models of the mind remain in a state of development and intellectual tension. Some (Rycroft personal communication) have argued the need for a 'new paradigm' in the psychological sciences arising out of, but going beyond, current psychoanalytic thinking. If psychoanalysis is to remain a relevant and living discipline, it must open itself up to findings in related disciplines such as child development, linguistics and cognitive science. Similarities, differences and contradictions both within and without psychoanalysis must be accepted and, where possible, worked through to a new synthesis.

Chapter 3

Origins of the internal world

> To our surprise we find the child and the child's impulses still
> living on . . .

(Freud 1900: 191)

Freud was a Darwinian. He saw in the adult mind vestiges of its
evolutionary and developmental history and believed that psychological illness could best be explained by tracing back neurotic
symptoms to their childhood origins – 'hysterics suffer mainly from
reminiscences' (Breuer and Freud 1895). He was also strongly
influenced by the ideas of the British neurologist Hughlings-Jackson
(Sulloway 1980), who had demonstrated how in illness the nervous
system reverts to more primitive modes of functioning.

For Freud then, as for Wordsworth, 'the child is father of the man'.
The clinical implications of this are twofold. First, it suggests that
many of our fears and phantasies, doubts and difficulties, are relics
of earlier phases of life, no longer relevant to the adult world in
which we find ourselves; and, second, it helps us to be more aware
and tolerant of the 'child within' (Sandler 1992) that lives on in the
unconscious mind and continues to influence our adult thoughts and
actions.

In this chapter we consider psychoanalytical theories about how
the features of healthy adult psychology which we take for granted –
a secure sense of self, stable self-object differentiation, the capacity
for intimacy and aloneness, a regulated and modulated emotional
life, and feelings of safety and self-esteem – emerge from the
undifferentiated state of infancy. We shall also look at how adult
difficulties have their roots in disturbances of early mental life.

We shall do so in a sequential fashion, but first we must discuss some background issues that influence the overall picture of

development adopted by the differing theoretical approaches discussed in the previous chapter.

PRELIMINARIES

'Stages' versus phases

Freud, at least in his early writings (Freud 1905a), saw psychological development as passing through a series of 'stages' – oral, anal, phallic, genital – which individuals traverse on their way to maturity, with pathology arising from 'arrest' at one or another stage. His ideas were based on the embryology of his day in which each part of the organism was thought to be in some way preformed within the embryo, the process of development being an orderly unfolding of these pre-existing parts.

Contemporary psychoanalysis has modified this model in a number of important ways. First, each stage cannot be equated with an organ or 'erotogenic zone' in the simplistic way that was orginally conceived. Observing the handling and mutual gaze of mother and infant is enough to convince us that the world of the newborn infant is as much tactile and visual as it is 'oral'; the preoccupations, aspirations and fears of the 'phallic' three-year-old can only be seen in the most tenuous way as centring around pleasure and pride in the possession of, or fear of losing, his genital. Second, therefore, Freud's 'zones' are perhaps better seen as a shorthand or metaphor for different existential *themes* which preoccupy a child at different stages of his development. Erikson's (1965) stages (see pp. 71–2) – trust vs mistrust, autonomy vs shame, initiative vs guilt, and so on – attempt to capture the fundamental issue that reflect a child's attitude towards the world rather than the predominance of a particular part of the body.

Third, the idea of 'sensitive periods' associated with particular ages is questionable. For instance, the 'anal' phase is often characterised as occurring in the second year of life and to reflect the child's capacity for control and ability to resist parental impositions. But, as Stern (1985) points out, a child can say 'No!' at four months by gaze aversion, at seven months with gestures, at fourteen months by running away, and at two years verbally.

Thus it is perhaps more useful to think not in terms of stages but of Erikson's (1968) concept of 'epigenesis'. This term harks back to the nineteenth-century embryological debate between the preformationists on the one hand, and those who believed that each generation is created 'epigenetically' by the developmental process itself. Epigenesis implies (a) that development is not predetermined but the result of an interaction between the developing individual and his environment; (b) that there are many different possible developmental pathways, only some of which will unfold in any particular environment; (c) that 'stages' are not superseded or arrested at, but rather remain active as phases or 'developmental lines' throughout life which may be activated at times of stress; and (d) that the impact of environmental trauma continues throughout the life cycle – the most obvious example being that of childhood sexual abuse which most commonly occurs in latency or early adolescence – although good experiences in early life have, to some extent, a buffering effect (Westen 1990).

Example: the woman who could not trust
Martha came into therapy when she became deeply distressed on discovering that her husband had been lying to her. He lied not just about his affairs, but a whole tissue of deceit about his past and present activities – 'a compulsive liar', she called him. Formal and correct in her manner, and slightly distant, she recalled a childhood dominated by waiting for her father to return from the war. 'He will soon be back' she was told as she sat at the window waiting and watching, but he never did return. He was dead, and her mother and grandfather who brought her up knew it. This had never been discussed between her mother and herself, even to the very end of her mother's life. Martha's relationships, including that with her analyst, were typified by a mixture of naive trust and emotional withdrawal.

Here we see how a 'relationship theme' – the inability to trust – can permeate a person's life as a developmental line, forming a focus for analytic work. For Martha the links stretched forward from the 'untrustworthy' father who never came home, to the husband and the analyst; and backwards, by inference, to her earliest relationship to a mother who, grief-stricken in her denied and therefore unmourned widowhood, was probably unable to respond sensitively and trustworthily to her baby's needs.

Internal objects (or archetypes) versus tabula rasa

Freud (1915) assumed that the infant had early knowledge of parental intercourse ('the primal scene'), castration and oedipal seduction. Klein and Isaacs extended this idea and claimed that the infant has inherent functional knowledge of the 'breast', 'penis', 'urethra' and so on, which shapes and guides his early and subsequent experiences. For example, the phantasy of the internal object relation 'breast-in-mouth' becomes a prototype for all incorporative activity, whether nutritive, sexual, or the taking in of knowledge. In this view, the nature of the internal object is primarily intrapsychic. This prototype is only gradually modified by the behaviour of the actual object in question – quintessentially 'the breast'. These phantasies continue to influence mental life in adults as well as children, every thought having unconscious as well as conscious ramifications and reverberations.

Example: 'only connect'
Tom was a gifted, but unusual and rather isolated 17-year-old, with a precocious interest in politics. The oldest of ten children, he entered analysis following an episode of hypomania in which he became convinced that he was privy to secret knowledge that a prominent politician was about to 'defect' from one political party to another. He had telephoned various important people and newspapers at all hours with his 'discovery'. In treatment he was argumentative, opinionated and hyper-rational, frequently asking intrusive questions. He stated that he liked to argue 'in order to penetrate other people's minds'. This remark could be understood at several levels: oedipally as an expression of his burgeoning but repressed and uncertain sexuality, but also at a 'pre-oedipal' level as expressing his desperate need to make contact with others, based on a primitive phantasy of penetration and containment. Similarly his preoccupation with 'defection' could have been an oedipal expression of his sense of being, in comparison with his potent father, 'defective' as a male, and also a reproach to his mother for having 'defected' so readily from him into her many subsequent pregnancies.

However, as we discussed in the previous chapter, Freud also realised that internal objects were not just inborn but, by identification and internalisation, representations of the relationships to which an individual was exposed: 'The shadow of the object fell upon the ego' and 'The character of the ego is a precipitate of abandoned object cathexes and it continues the history of those object-choices' (both Freud 1917). His idea of the superego as an internal representative of parental prohibition is the most striking example of this. Following this, the object relations school, especially Fairbairn (1952) and Bowlby (1988), adopt a radically *inter*psychic or transpersonal approach, in which the nature of the internal object (in Bowlby's terminology, the 'internal working model') is a *representation* of the behaviour of the object, which is impressed, as it were, on the blank screen or tabula rasa of the mind of the developing infant. Padel (1991) points out that what is internalised is not an 'object' (a 'mother' or a 'penis') but a *relationship*, and that the individual, via role reversal, may identify with either 'end' of this relationship – thus in the familial intergenerational transmission of abuse, the abused child in one generation becomes the abuser in the next.

Bion (1962, 1970) takes a middle position, giving weight to both intra- and interpsychic factors, envisaging the behaviour of the caregiver rather like an ethological 'releaser' of inherent mental structures. He sees the nurturant function of the 'breast' as having the capacity, not necessarily realised, to turn a potential thought within the infant (in his terminology a 'preconception') into an actual phantasy or internal object (for Bion, a 'conception'). This model can be compared with Chomsky's (1965) view of the development of language in which a 'deep structure' or potential for speech (the Language Acquisition Device or LAD) is transformed into a particular dialect by the prevailing linguistic world which the infant encounters. The growing child could be said to possess a 'Phantasy Acquisition Device' or PAD. The clinical relevance of this would be, in Kleinian terms, a therapist using his 'breast–mind' to elicit previously unrealised conceptions – i.e. phantasies, creative realisations, or unexplored epigenetic pathways – in the mind of the patient.

The nature of memory

Also relevant to this discussion are contemporary ideas derived from cognitive science about memory. These enable a classification of different types of 'reminiscences', which form the raw material of psychoanalytic work. Tulving (1985) distinguishes between (a) 'procedural memory', a non-verbal representation of how we were handled as infants, akin to Klein's (1946) notion of 'memories in feeling', (b) 'semantic memory', the patterns of interactive behaviour or 'scripts' (Byng-Hall 1991) with which we were brought up, and (c) 'episodic memory', actual events which we can recall.

Although few people can remember specific events before they were two years old, early events and relationships influence the way we experience and relate to the world generally (semantic memory). These influences are continuously revealed through transference. Just as, for example, the behavioural manifestations of sexual love contain vestiges of infant behaviour – mutual gazing, touching, sucking, intense separation anxiety, etc. – so phantasy, and thus transference, continues to shape adult mental life, especially at times of emotional intensity. In health this enhances and deepens emotions: pianists may be observed making primitive sucking movements with their lips while playing music of the highest sublimity. In pathology this transference distorts and may even create *apparent* episodic memories. In summary, as Stern (1985) puts it: 'Development is not a succession of events left behind in history. It is a continuing process, constantly updated.' Indeed, this positive 'updating' process is what makes psychoanalysis possible, based on what Freud called 'deferred action' ('nachtraglichkeit') – a kind of reverse transference in which past memories of all three types are revised in the light of present experience.

The 'clinical' infant and the 'observed' infant

It should also be noted that infancy has itself, until recently, been something of a tabula rasa, a blank screen upon which theorists have projected their preoccupations and ideologies. It is only with the emergence of detailed observational studies of early infant–parent interaction that the *observed*, as opposed to the *clinical*, infant (Stern 1985) has been able to 'speak back' to its theorists and to correct some of the misconceptions that have been heaped upon it.

With these preliminaries in mind, we shall now turn to the psycho-analytic account of psychological development, working chrono-logically from birth. Despite the above caveats we shall follow convention, dividing our account into four phases: 'pre-oedipal' or two person; oedipal or three person; adolescence; and adulthood.

THE 'PRE-OEDIPAL' OR TWO-PERSON PHASE

Pre-oedipal or two person?

For Freud (1916/17) the oedipus complex was the 'kernel of the neuroses'. In the early stages of the psychoanalytic movement a belief in the centrality of the oedipus complex was a hallmark of psychoanalysis, a dogma that could not be questioned, so that when Melanie Klein, building on her analyst Abraham's developmental schema, turned her attention to the early months of life it was natural that she should give respectability to her findings by calling them 'pre-oedipal'. As we shall see, she found evidence for the existence of 'oedipal' structures even at the earliest stages of life. Balint (1952), following Rickman, introduced the more neutral terms 'two-' and 'three-person stages'.

This debate has important consequences which extend beyond terminological disagreement. As we saw in the previous chapter, Freud's model was essentially based on *conflict*: neuroses derive from the incompatibility of the demands of civilisation and those of the instincts, and the tension between the desire to love and be loved by one's parents and the fear of inevitable rivalry and the consequences this arouses. For Freud, civilisation was built around the defence against unconscious incest-wishes. Kernberg (1984) and Kleinians such as Segal (1986), extend this conflict model back into infancy where there is still a struggle between the love an infant has for his care-givers and the hate he feels at their absences. For them, the essence of civilisation is the defence not so much against incest but psychosis (Young 1994). Others, notably Kohut (1977) and Winnicott (1965), see the problems arising from infancy, especially those leading to 'borderline' disorders in adult life, as being based on *deficiency* – the lack of vital ingredients needed for healthy development such as maternal empathy and sensitivity. In reality both are probably right (cf. Chapter 10).

The early weeks of life: autism or symbiosis

Freud saw early infancy in terms of an 'egg' model (Hamilton 1982) in which he compared the state of the newborn to that of chick within its shell: 'a psychical system shut off from the stimuli of the external world, and able to satisfy even its nutritional requirements autistically . . .' (Freud 1911a). This led Mahler *et al.* (1975) to describe a stage of 'normal autism', and Freud (1914a) himself to his controversial concept of 'primary narcissism', the necessary self-love which precedes the capacity to love others, based on the blissful self-absorption of the newborn.

Mahler describes the first six months of life as proceeding from 'normal autism' through 'symbiosis' to 'hatching' (continuing the egg metaphor). However, the use of the term 'autism' is questionable (but see Tustin 1986 for a contrary view, later retracted, Tustin 1994). The newborn is certainly self-centred, but research shows that he participates actively in the two-person environment, and, as mentioned, is able to distinguish his mother's voice, smell and face from others from a very early stage. This leads to a picture of mother–infant *symbiosis*, which is fuelled by the infant's intense need to reach out to a nurturing figure, and the responsiveness of the sensitively attuned mother.

For Freud, primitive feelings of 'goodness' were related to 'primary narcissism', the necessary state of self-love which we all need in order to survive, 'autistic' only in the sense that, as Slavin and Kreigman (1992) put it, 'because we are members of a sexually reproducing evolved species, nobody loves us as much as we love ourselves'. Freud (1914a) saw self-love as developmentally prior to relatedness ('anaclitic', or object love, leaning on narcissistic, or self-love), expressing this in his famous 'amoeba metaphor' of

> an original libidinal cathexis of the ego, from which some is later given off to objects, but which fundamentally persists and is related to object cathexes much as the body of an amoeba is related to the pseudopodia which it puts out.
>
> (Freud 1914a: 75)

Freud visualised this primary narcissism persisting into later life in the form of the 'ego ideal', which informs our aims, values and ambitions, later coalescing into the superego; and in the narcissism of parental love which makes one's own children special above all others: 'His majesty the baby . . . parental love which is so moving and at bottom so childish, is nothing but the parent's narcissism born again' (Freud 1914a).

The Klein–Kernberg model of early infancy

For Freud the newborn baby's mind is pure id, lacking an ego with which to relate to the world. Klein disagreed with Freud in that she saw a primitive ego, and therefore primitive object relations, as being present from birth. The infant encounters and introjects two sets of contradictory experiences: 'good', satiating, nurturing feelings associated with successful feeding, warmth and tactile contact with the mother; and 'bad', associated with separation, abandonment, hunger, wetness and cold. These form the nucleus of feelings of love and hate, both to some extent preformed under the influence of eros and thanatos, the life and death instincts.

The primitive ego can only maintain psychic equilibrium by keeping good and bad apart. The infant introjects and identifies with the good 'me' experiences, while splitting off the bad 'not me' feelings and projecting them outwards. 'Bad' is projected into the nurturing parent, whose 'good breast' becomes thereby transformed into a 'bad' persecutory one. Thus the external world is a reflection of the inner world. In this omnipotent and potentially psychotic state all is magically personified: 'everything is the result of the actions of objects' (Etchegoyen 1991). Further anxiety now ensues because in order to get good experiences 'in', the child has to 'cannibalise' (i.e. introject) the parental goodness, but the child now feels he has 'destroyed' the breast and this destructiveness also has to be projected, leading to another spiral of the vicious circle (see pp. 81–7 for further discussion of 'primitive defences').

In this model, 'splitting' is very much a two-edged phenomenon. On the one hand, it is a necessary defence which enables a core sense of self-worth and goodness to hatch, uncontaminated by bad feelings of rage and disappointment. The attuned parent, or receptive breast, allows these bad feelings to lodge safely until they are ready to be reintegrated in the depressive position. On the other hand, splitting can act as a brake on development if this detoxifying function of the breast is unavailable due to neglectful, inconsistent or abusive parenting, and/or if the bad feelings are excessive and cannot be reintegrated. The clinical implications of this mean that the analyst must judge whether splitting needs to be left uninterpreted, at least initially, or whether negative transference must be faced and interpreted from the start. Kernberg (1984) tends to advocate the latter, but Joseph (1989: 76) cautions:

> When analysts ask their patients to face their fears, their yearning, their sadness long before they have the resources and imagination to do so, they may be asking too much.

In the 'paranoid–schizoid position', Klein's child trails clouds, not so much of glory, but of envy, rage and disappointment. Klein envisaged this state as balanced by the 'depressive position' in which good and bad, love and hate, come together when the child realises that the very object which he hates and fears is also the one he loves and depends on, the guilt and 'depression' associated with this realisation being the spur to reparation and creativity. Klein saw the interplay between these two positions as continuing throughout life and underlying the rhythms of all the major crisis-points of psychological development.

Interpersonal models of early infancy

In contrast to the Kleinian model, the interpersonal perspective emphasises the emergence of self and pre-linguistic meanings from the two-person matrix of infant and parent. For Fairbairn the fundamental trauma is maternal indifference: not to be intimately known, which can, for example, arise out of maternal depression. The child deals with this trauma omnipotently by imagining that it is either (a) his love that has destroyed her feelings, a schizoid response, or (b) his hate that has obliterated them, a depressive reaction.

Winnicott (1965) and Stern (1985) see a stable sense of self arising out of parental 'handling' based on maternal sensitivity and attunement. For Winnicott, *holding*, *integration* and *personalisation* (a typically Winnicottian term referring to the development of a sense of self) are the key issues. Holding starts long before the birth with *primary maternal preoccupation*, in which thinking about the baby comes to assume great salience in the mother's conscious and unconscious mind. The child is thus a recipient of parental projection as well as a source of projection. Fraiberg *et al.* (1975) evocatively call these projections 'ghosts in the nursery'. The 'environment mother' (a holding function, in contrast to the 'object mother' from whom the child receives satisfaction of needs) accepts and makes sense of the infant's 'spontaneous gesture', leading to the emergence of a 'true self', and a psychosomatic sense of being a person.

Winnicott (1965) and Kohut (1977) bring an interactive, two-person perspective to the notion of 'primary narcissism'. For Kohut, 'healthy narcissism' arises out of the 'empathic mirroring' of the nurturing parent (or analyst), leading to an internalised 'nurturing self-object' which is not outgrown as object love supersedes self love, but which is required in one form or another throughout life. Self-esteem is based on the mutual absorption and devotion of mother and child. He sees narcissistic disorders – with their defences of role reversal, compliance and 'false self' – arising not from the internal threat to primary narcissism posed by excessive aggression (the Klein–Kernberg model), but on disruptions to this first all-important bond.

In this account the responsiveness of the mother's *face* as a mirror, and later as a symbol of relatedness (Wright 1991), is as important as the much vaunted 'breast'. Winnicott tries to retain the omnipotence of narcissism, but couches it in interactional terms by imagining a transitional space between mother and infant (transitional in the sense that it is neither self nor other, subjective nor objective, inner nor outer) in which the infant's wish is so sensitively responded to by the mother ('his wish is her command') that he has the illusion he has 'created' the object, this being the basis for feelings of self-efficacy and creativity in later life.

These interpersonal authors make a sharper distinction than Klein between normal and abnormal development. For Klein there is always a movement from splitting to integration, from the terrors and precarious security of the paranoid–schizoid position to the sadness but also sanity of the depressive position. The interpersonal authors tend to see these primitive defences not as a normal response to the inevitable unmanageable anxiety of infancy soothed and integrated by adequate parenting, but as a pathological manifestation of the infant's struggle to survive in the face of inept or cumulatively traumatic parenting.

With normal responsive parents, a child can deal with 'bad' experiences – a delayed feed, a cold cot, a respiratory infection, a boring day – by healthy protest which will be accepted and 'transmuted' by the responsive 'breast'. The parent can cope with this healthy hatred, with the infant who says, in effect, 'Hello object, I destroyed you!' (Winnicott 1965). Conversely, the infant can keep an image of the good parent alive long enough for inevitable brief separations to be tolerated without feelings of persecution or abandonment. Healthy aggressive protest is linked to 'metabolising' and so surviving loss. Eventually this 'optimal disillusionment' (Kohut 1977) leads to the acceptance of the reality of loss, which can coexist with a sense of persisting 'ordinary specialness'.

The primitive defences of disturbed adult patients – splitting, projection and projective identification, omnipotent control, narcissistic self-absorption – are not in this interpersonal model regressions or developmental arrests at early 'fixation points', but examples of 'secondary narcissism', that is, a withdrawal into the self in the face of a hostile environment. Kohut calls these 'breakdown products', resulting from failed nurturing.

Example: the 'Oxo mother'

Mark was a young man in his early twenties suffering from schizophrenia. He heard voices telling him how bad he was, and saw visions of terrifying snakes and other monsters. He tended to be attracted to older, motherly, women who at first liked and took pity on him, especially as he was so 'good' and biddable, but then found his possessiveness claustrophobic and so rejected him. A similar pattern characterised his relationship with his analyst. His parents had been 'hippies', both heavy drug users, who had found it hard to care for Mark who had throughout his childhood oscillated between being fostered and living with his mother. His earliest memory was of 'stealing' an Oxo cube from the kitchen cupboard and gnawing it, while he heard his mother and her friends laughing helplessly in the next door room in a drugged state. Mark was desperately seeking nurturance from this 'square' breast in the face of drastic environmental failure.

Although each model starts from an opposing premise – for Klein, 'goodness' comes from without, and 'badness' from within; for the interpersonalists, the innocent child is corrupted by a deficient environment – in practice the two positions are not so far removed. Kleinians envisage good parenting as mitigating inherent splitting tendencies within the infant, while the interpersonalists and the self-psychologists emphasise the effects of bad parenting in engendering splitting and other 'primitive' defences. Since the real world is a mixture of good and bad, and infants can from the start love and hate, both accounts contain valuable insights.

Separation–individuation

So far we have considered the infant and his care-giver on their own. But two people are needed to make a baby, and even before the father becomes important, a third term has already arisen between infant and mother – absence. Conceived oedipally, the absent mother is imagined to be with the father as a 'combined parent'. Certainly, at about seven months' old the child begins to show stranger anxiety and to be much more obviously aware of the mother's comings and goings. This is also the starting point for Mahler *et al.*'s (1975) 'separation–individuation' and the point at which the infant begins to establish internal 'object constancy', the capacity to retain a mental image or memory trace of the absent mother – and by analogy, the analyst absent during weekends and breaks.

Attachment Theory (Bowlby 1988) emphasises that the way separation is handled is the key to secure bonding, and sees the parents providing a 'secure base', both in reality and in the child's mind, from which he can begin to explore the world, and to which he can immediately return when danger threatens. Mahler *et al.* (1975) identify a 'rapprochement subphase' of separation–individuation in which, during a toddler's ecstatic exploration or 'love affair with the world', he will momentarily return to his mother for reassurance, as though frightened that the secure base has abandoned him, perhaps in punishment for what Einstein called 'holy curiosity' (Hamilton 1982), but what might be seen oedipally as forbidden fruit.

Kernberg (1984) sees the replacement of splitting by repression as the main defence against unwanted feelings arising around this time. In normal development there is now a much stronger ego, based on internalisation and identification with a stable nurturant parent. The early superego is also beginning to emerge. The child is thus able to cope with some degree of integration of good and bad, which can therefore relegate unwanted feelings to the id within, rather than having to project them outwards.

As separation proceeds the child begins to conceive of a world of autonomous individuals, each with its own vantage point: as he gathers a sense of his own emergent subjective self, so he begins to be aware that others have selves too. This is the cognitive aspect of the 'depressive position', in which 'good' and 'bad' part-objects coalesce into a whole separate being, a source of both nurturance and frustration. Fonagy (1991) depicts this as the emergence of the child's 'theory of mind'. This concept is especially important in the treatment of abused patients who may have defensively obliterated the horrifying idea that 'care-giving' adults might have minds that could wish to harm or even destroy them. In treatment they can begin gradually to recognise the analyst's mind as a separate 'place' which they can safely inhabit.

THE OEDIPAL OR THREE-PERSON PHASE

Freud's conception of the oedipus complex, first mentioned in a letter to his friend Fliess in 1897 arising out of his self-analysis following the death of his father, has become part of popular folklore. The little boy, like Oedipus, wishes to kill his father and usurp his place in his mother's bed; this wish to possess her arouses fear of retaliatory castration by his all-powerful father – the ultimate punishment of the loss of his genital is symbolically enacted in the ritual of circumcision. The reality of castration is confirmed by the little boy's sexual curiosity, when he discovers that females lack a phallus, and in his mind must therefore have been castrated – a view that is confirmed by the flow of menstrual blood.

Freud seemed to assume that the psychosexual world looked roughly similar to little girls, who therefore love their fathers and wish to replace their mothers, and, lacking the essential organ of power and significance, feel castrated and therefore powerless. Freud saw the oedipus complex as a necessary developmental task to be undergone, or 'resolved', for the boy by identification with the feared father which offers him the promise of true potency in the future, in the little girl by identification with the mother, and by the promise that her lack of a phallus will eventually be compensated by the capacity to attract and so 'have' a man (since she cannot 'be' one) and to produce something much bigger and better than a penis – a baby.

Although contemporary psychoanalysis, strongly influenced by the feminist response to this phallocentric account, departs radically from Freud's original view of psychosexual development, the oedipus complex continues to resonate psychoanalytically in the image of a parental couple which the child both desires and feels cast out from, and in the experience of desire, prohibition and ambivalence which every individual must negotiate on his or her pathway from infancy to adulthood. We shall look at four aspects of the oedipus complex – the Kleinian, and Lacanian perspectives, feminist responses, and the effect of social change, especially the impact of absent or abusive fathers. Bur first let us consider the continuing relevance of Freud's original conceptions. As Mitchell (1989) points out, a central project for Freud's was to understand the psychology of male impotence ('where they love they do not desire, and where they desire they cannot love' (Freud 1916/17). This problem was the starting point for the following case.

Example: his father's son, or his own man?
While not technically 'impotent', Peter's presenting problem was his persistent inability to form stable relationships with women. A businessman in his early 30s, he had had numerous liaisons with 'suitable' women, and in the early stages all went well, but whenever the possibility of commitment threatened, he would begin to panic and eventually, as he later put it, the relationship would 'peter' out. A subsidiary problem was his moodiness and

irritability at work, which, he said, gave him a reputation for being 'an awkward bugger'.

Peter was the eldest of three boys with a very powerful and domineering father who ran the family business in which Peter worked, and with a retiring and compliant mother. It soon became clear that Peter had modelled himself on his father whom he both revered and feared, but that somehow the identity did not quite fit. Secretly he felt that he was 'like' his mother – whom he could talk to and who expected him to come to regular meals with the family even though in theory he was living independently, and with which he complied so as not to offend her. As yet another promising relationship foundered, Peter suddenly saw that the point at which things tended to go wrong was when he introduced girlfriends to his parents, and that seeing his father being charming to them filled him with feelings of inadequacy and envy, which he then projected onto the girls whom he saw as faithless and cheap. Expressing these thoughts in analysis created enormous difficulties for him, since he maintained a rather brusque and 'tough' manner, and tended to dismiss the male analyst's comments with remarks like 'you could be right' or 'I hadn't thought of that', implying that these were the crazy comments of a psychoperson, hardly relevant to a down-to-earth businessman like himself. When his rivalry with the analyst was interpreted he began to recall childhood feelings of misery and utter betrayal around the time his mother was pregnant with his brother, and episodes in which he was humiliated by his father who tried to force him out of his taciturn sulks at meal times. He began to realise how stuck he was in a battle with his father which he felt he could never win, and a secret intimacy with his mother which no girlfriend could ever match, and even that his bachelorhood (which worried her dreadfully) was a reproach to her for her 'faithlessness' in producing two more boys when surely he was good enough? In talking about this he began to cry, and fully expected the analyst to ridicule or attack him. After this session he began to be much more assertive with his father, found a new girlfriend who lived abroad, and, by protesting his need for holidays that did not conform to analytic breaks, became much less overtly compliant with analysis.

From an interpersonal perspective, this case illustrates the importance of parental handling and containment of their child's oedipal feelings: a mother needs to be able to enjoy her son's infatuation with her while, at the same time, not being seductive; the father must be able to accept this infatuation without feeling threatened by it, and be prepared to offer himself as a model, while accepting his son's wish to attack and belittle him: 'a boy needs his father both to protect him from the danger that his mother represents for him, and to protect her from the danger he represents for her' (Horrocks 1994). The case might also be seen as representing the father's failure to provide Peter with a valid initiation into manhood, and so help him overcome his fear of being merged with his mother and, by extension, with his girlfriends (Bly 1988). Peter's 'castration anxiety' embodied this fear, as did his sense of psychic mutilation.

The Kleinian perspective on the oedipus complex

For Klein, the seeds of the oedipus complex are to be found in the earliest stages of infancy (Britton *et al.* 1989). Separation from the mother symbolises the existence of father, and the child's own aggressive phantasies that are aroused by the separation are then projected into the father. This explains the ubiquitous phantasy of the punitive and prohibitive father of the oedipus complex, who seems far removed from the normal reality of contemporary paternal attitudes. For Klein, negotiating the oedipal stage is closely linked with the maturation associated with the movement from paranoid–schizoid to the depressive position. In the latter, good and bad have to be kept separate until the child is able to accept the guilt and sadness associated with the realisation that they are directed at one and the same person. Similarly, the resolution of the oedipus complex requires the child to accept his or her temporary exclusion from the parental couple, to allow mother and father to come together, and to tolerate the phantasy of 'good intercourse' or 'primal scene'. If this can be achieved the child 'loses' the mother, but gains the capacity to think – creative thought requires the bringing together of ideas in new combinations – and to lead his or her own life, having internalised the parental couple. He or she also 'gains' the father as a real object, and not just as an alternative mother. The latter position is encapsulated in Klein's famous equation, 'breast = penis', which can be used to account for the way in which some women are continuously disappointed by men in whom they are seeking the elusive breast, and also some homosexual men's unconscious decision to renounce the unreliable breast in favour of the ever-available penis.

Lacan

Some feminists have seized on Freud's views on female sexuality, as expressed in the oedipus complex, as the ultimate example of patriarchy and male chauvinism. But here again we encounter a paradox. One of the strengths of psychoanalysis is its emphasis on bodily experience and the biological fundamentals of feeding, elimination, sexuality, physical illness and death ('the ego is first and foremost a bodily ego' (Freud 1923)). On the other hand, if taken literally, Freud's idea of females as castrated males, only to achieve fulfilment through producing a 'penis-baby', is absurd, inaccurate and insulting. The importance of Lacan (Lacan 1977; Bowie 1991) was his notion that Freud's ideas are best seen as metaphors rather than scientific facts, and if couched in the terms of linguistics and anthropology constitute a devastatingly perceptive account of the psychological structures of a patriarchal society. To describe is not necessarily to condone.

Lacan sees a crisis in development around the age of two when the child begins to acquire self-awareness and language. The primitive pre-oedipal unity of mother and child is shattered by the advent of the 'no(m) du père' – the name of the father (as opposed to the 'maternal' 'Christian' name), and also the 'no', the prohibition placed like the archangel's sword at the gates of paradise by the jealous father. Language (a 'mother-tongue', but policed by patriarchy) is the reality to which the child must accommodate his primeval experience of the world; sensory impressions coalesce into objects, named and classified by the power of society, and the most potent symbol of these is the phallus, the father's penis. It is not so much, as Freud implied, that because females lack power because they lack a penis, but, rather, because they lack power they believe they must submit to the rule of the phallus.

Just as a child's experience at the oedipal stage is shaped and potentially alienated by language, so his self-perception begins to estrange him from his original self, a moment which is epitomised in what Lacan calls the 'mirror-stage' (Lacan 1966). If a coloured dot is crayoned on a child's forehead and he is shown himself in the mirror he will, up to the age of about two, try to touch the dot in the mirror, but after two years will touch his own forehead, suggesting that self-awareness arises at around that age. Unlike Freud and Klein who see the origins of narcissism in the pre-oedipal phase, Lacan contrasts the child's inchoate self-experience with the perfection of the image in the glass. The 'mirror stage' can also be understood in oedipal terms of the 'I' (eye) seeing 'me', an objectification of the self that depends on the 'third term' (i.e. the father), a new vantage point outside the mother–infant couple, creating a triangle with the possibilities of feelings of exclusion and envy, but also freedom of movement and abstract thought.

Lacan's conception of the mirror stage is thus very different from Winnicott's emphasis on mirroring. For Lacan the mirror epitomises the insertion of the father into the child's blissful pre-oedipal life: alienation and self-estrangement start here. For Winnicott, mirroring is a quintessentially maternal function, helping to build up the infant's sense of self and contributing to healthy narcissism.

Feminism and oedipus

The early women analysts – Klein, Horney, Brunswick – responded to Freud's patriarchal bias not so much by challenging him directly but by moving away from the role of the father to a focus on the early mother–child relationship (Chodorow 1978; Sayers 1992). In place of 'penis envy' in women (and oedipal boys who never grow up) arose the spectre of the all-powerful, all-giving maternal breast, which males respond to by denigration and distancing, and into which females get sucked and sometimes depressively stuck. For Chasseguet-Smirgel (1985) the essence of the oedipal stage is the discovery and working through of the 'double difference' – the difference between the sexes and the difference between the genera-tions. She sees perversity – at an individual and social level – as based on a denial of this difference, the oedipal boy building his perverse and false potency out of a 'faecal penis' composed of hatred and fear. Similarly 'penis envy' is based on a woman's devaluation of the power and generativity of her own body, deriving from a failure of identification with her mother.

Chodorow (1978), Mitchell (1989) and Benjamin (1990) have brought a feminist perspective to bear on contemporary psycho-analytic thought. The latter emphasises Freud's notion (borrowed from Fleiss) of the inherent bisexuality of the human psyche. Benjamin visualises an early oedipal stage before gender identity is fixed, at which activity and receptiveness, exploration and passivity, inner space and outer space, assertion and submission are available to both sexes and emerge in children's play as much in little boys as in little girls. She sees the role of the father not just as representing prohibition and power, but as vital at this stage in offering excitement for the child and recuperative space for the mother. She proposes a non-oedipal (i.e. non-conflictual) *identificatory love* (Benjamin 1995) in which boys and girls alike 'contain' the attributes of the 'other' parent. In the conventional family this means for boys the security and innerness of the mother, for girls the difference and exploratory possibilities of the father. Like Temperley (1993), she is critical of the overemphasis in the Freudian–Lacanian account of power and domination, stressing instead the need to recognise and value playfulness and 'inner space' in a child who, in Winnicott's terms, is not just 'alone in the presence of the mother' but can also tolerate the parents' separate relationship without anxiety. As Benjamin (1990: 163) puts it:

> In the oedipal experience of losing the inner continuity with the mother and encountering instead the idealised, acutely desirable object outside, the image of the female as the dangerous regressive siren is born. The counterpart of this image is the wholy idealised, masterful subject who can withstand and conquer her . . . As we give greater value to the pre-oedipal world, to a more flexible acceptance of difference, we can see that difference is only truly established when it exists in tension with likeness, when we are able to recognise the other in ourselves.

The reality of the modern family: absent and abusive fathers

Benjamin's perspective contrasts a real relationship with an actual father with the distortions that occur in the all too common single parent families of Western societies. 'Masculinity' becomes idealised and invested with dominance and unwarranted power, or is projected into a 'phallic mother', who is unattainably desirable and terrifying, creating what Lasch (1979) has called a 'culture of narcissism' in which the individual has to rely on self-love as the only means of survival in an objectless world.

Several authors (e.g. Young 1994) have pointed out that Oedipus was himself an abused child, left to die by his father Laius, who feared the oracle's prediction that he would be killed by his own son.

This perspective on the myth opens out an interpersonal, inter-generational viewpoint that fits with the realities of the modern family. The abusive father, or, more often, step-father, with a mother who fails to protect or even turns a blind eye, represents for the little girl the nightmare version of the oedipal myth in its modern form. Both abused and abuser are trying to escape from this cold oedipal world of separation to a pre-oedipal state of fusion and obliteration of difference. What is 'traumatic' and psychologically damaging in trauma is the piercing of the normal barrier between oedipal phantasy and reality (Garland 1991): that which the child so desperately wants in phantasy becomes overwhelming in reality. The regressive trans-ferences seen in patients who have been abused reflect both the search for a secure and responsive mother who will protect, and the need for a father who can allow closeness while still respecting separateness.

Example: oedipal themes in the transference of an abused patient
Ella, a 50-year-old divorced teacher with a grown-up daughter, who suffered from depression in the context of borderline symp-toms, had been systematically humiliated and mentally, physically and sexually abused by her father throughout her early childhood, until her parents' separation when she was 11. Her mother was herself intimidated, exhausted and neglectful. Ella's earliest memory was of being hurled across the room at the age of three when she had asked her father to play with her, not long after he had returned from the war. She was hypervigilant in her sessions, sensitive to the slightest lapse of concentration from the analyst. She was the antithesis of Winnicott's (1971) notion of being 'alone in the presence of another', finding it almost impossible to relax enough in analysis to explore her own inner world without worrying about what her analyst would think of her or want her to be saying. Just as her father had abused his paternal role by his invasiveness while her mother was unavailable, so the analyst's countertransference swung between feeling detached and sleepy, and uncomfortably intruded upon.

On one occasion, just before a break, Ella brought a set of pocket chess into the session, inviting the analyst to play with her. He was torn and confused between the wish not to make her feel rejected, while resisting vigorously this invitation to a mutual 'acting in' (see Chapter 9). After a while, when Ella evidently had felt humiliated by his refusal to join in, he interpreted this along the lines of her terror of intimacy, heightened by the impending break, and her imperative need to control at all times. He indicated that he saw the wish to play as positive, but suggesting that the idea of a board game was a reflection of her despair at being unable to 'play' spontaneously on the couch. The 'good' oedipal parent, which Ella felt so cut off from, is simply 'there' (Balint 1993), neither present nor absent, not too close nor too far away: like Goldilocks' three bears, neither too hot nor too cold, too hard nor too soft, but a 'transformational object' (q.v. pp. 74–5) grounded in reality, able to be incorporated into phantasy.

Summary

The oedipal period is seen as arising out of the two-person phase which preceded it. The main issues of the pre-oedipal period are: (a) the forming of affectional bonds with a nurturing parent and hence the achievement of a secure base from which exploration of the inner and outer world can occur; (b) learning to tolerate separation and absence and to respond with healthy protest, rather than split-off hatred and envy, when appropriate; (c) learning to think and to feel, via the sensitivity of the nurturing environment which turns a preconception into a conception, and modulates affect so that it becomes manageable; and (d) the emergence of a stable sense of self and others, able to survive separation and angry attacks.

In the oedipal phase the themes of intimacy and separation, of similarity and difference, are projected onto the three-dimensional screen of two parents and child. Children learn how to be close enough to their parents so as to feel special and loveable, but not so close as to be engulfed; how to respect limits and boundaries without feeling unbearably excluded; how to tolerate envy without being overwhelmed by it, or using it to destroy.

Compared with its emphasis on the early years of life, psychoanalysis has tended to have less to say about the later phases of the life cycle. Space allows us to touch only lightly on these important topics. However, epigenesis continues to apply. Developmental pathways are never fixed, and later good experiences (including psychoanalytic treatment) can compensate for earlier environmental failure, leading an individual away from the vicious circle of neurosis towards the benign cycles of psychic health.

ADOLESCENCE

After the dramas of the oedipal phase and before their continuation in adolescence, there follows a period of comparative quiet. 'Latency' provides respite, a period in which psychosexual development and emotional maturation continue in a much more muted vein, and in which the acquisition of cognitive and motor skills, and the capacity to go beyond the family into a world of peer relationships, are the predominant developmental tasks.

Just as the ways in which attachment and loss have been handled and felt in the pre-oedipal phase will affect the oedipal stage, so too a child's oedipal experiences will equip him for good or ill during the turbulence of adolescence. Each phase is both a continuation of the past and offers opportunities for new beginnings. The adolescent faces the twin tasks of separation from his family of origin, and preparing himself for the intimacies of his family of generation – putting the developmental trajectory of the first two decades into reverse by moving from loss to bonding. Two central issues here are *the body* (Laufer and Laufer 1984) and *identity* (Erikson 1968). The adolescent no longer relies on the parent to regulate and modulate his bodily affective states, but has to undertake this task for himself. The anorexic who does not know when she is hungry, or when she has had enough, is struggling with this issue. At the same time the adolescent has to learn how to entrust the other with his anger and sexuality, and not to feel that they will be destructive or rejected. He has to know who he is so as to make choices and begin to create a world of his own. In place of parents come ideas, systems, role models, fashions, aspirations. Their purpose is to contain and define the self whose lineaments are beginning to solidify. A negative identity built around protest and a preoccupation with what one is *not*, or a conformism based on compliance with parental aspirations may equally conceal an inner sense of emptiness and lack of connection. Psychoanalysis with adolescents (cf. p. 200) is difficult, since it represents their worst fears of being odd or abnormal, but also can offer a 'moratorium' or 'Speilraum' (Erikson 1968) within which adaptive regression can occur.

Example: oedipal inhibitions
David was a pleasant 19-year-old presenting with panic attacks which had temporarily crippled him, making him unable to leave the house alone or to study effectively for his exams. His movements were tentative, as though he did not quite inhabit his

adult body; his hair and voice slightly soft and child-like. A middle child, he had a successful older brother and a much adored younger sister. The family was supportive, but tense. David's father, a builder, suffered from severe asthma which had kept him off work for long periods. The family was in financial difficulties and there was pressure on David to leave school and earn his living. David was very close to his mother, sympathising with her worries about his father's health, but he resented her pushing and domineering manner, and he envied her more straightforward relationship with his sister, feelings he expressed by sulky withdrawal. During his sessions David was polite but wary, communicating a sense of helplessness and a passive wish that the analyst should instruct him how to live without his fears. He felt guilty about following his own interests, rather than helping in the home where he felt he was needed. At times he felt his life was empty and meaningless. He had a girlfriend – of whom his parents did not entirely approve – with whom he slept, but did not make love. Interpretations focused on the possible connection between his presenting anxiety and the oedipal fears of breaking the bond with his mother if he made a sexual relationship with his girlfriend, and of triumphing over his damaged father if he was successful in his exams and achieved sexual potency, linking this with his cautious and deferential attitude towards the analyst. David was at first outraged at this 'ridiculous' suggestion, insisting that he and his father were the best of friends, but he then admitted that he did resent the way he felt that his father favoured his elder brother. This open conflict with the analyst seemed to shift things. By the end of David's time-limited treatment he was feeling better, had been to two school dances, had made love enjoyably with his girlfriend, and his exams had gone reasonably well.

ADULTHOOD

Psychological development does not come to an end once physical growth is complete. It takes a lifetime to learn to love and to work. The two motors of psychological development, biological change and the vicissitudes of attachment and separation, continue throughout the life cycle. Erikson (1968) schematically saw the task of young adulthood in terms of relatedness versus self-absorption; the task of the middle years as generativity versus stagnation; and the task of old age as integrity versus despair.

A somewhat arbitrary, and no doubt culturally biased, list of the developmental 'tasks' of adult life would include: the acquisition of skills and the capacity to submit to tutelage but to challenge it when necessary; the capacity to love a partner 'in sickness and in health'; tolerance of the transition from romantic to conjugal love in a long-term relationship; capacity to love and to hate without fear (Skynner 1976); ability to hold the balance between immersion and detachment as a parent; ability to achieve stability and security while still being ready to explore new territory (Bowlby 1988); being able to come to terms with loss and to grieve appropriately; acceptance of the inevitability of one's limitations and eventual death (Jaques 1965); acceptance of loneliness (Nemiroff and Colarusso 1990); being able to detach onself from one's children, occupation at retirement, and, in the end, life itself (Porter 1991); retaining appropriate optimism and not being overwhelmed by despair.

From a psychoanalytic perspective an individual brings the history of his early relationships to these 'tasks'. Being a parent reawakens oedipal phantasies, so that through our children we look back upon our own childhood, and are made aware of the limits of our abilities and lifespan. Awareness of the reality of death in middle life forces a reworking of the paranoid–schizoid/depressive interface as an individual moves towards acceptance or violent repudiation of his limitations (Jaques 1965). Psychoanalysis examines the interplay between the three basic polarities of (a) connection and separation, (b) destruction and reparation and (c) self-love and other-love, which are played out on the broader canvas of adulthood. The way someone responds to 'slings and arrows of outrageous fortune' is shaped by the mental structures that derive from childhood. While it is not possible to survey the whole field, we shall touch briefly on three psychoanalytically central topics: mourning, marriage and maturation.

Mourning

The idea that suppressed mourning leads to psychological difficulties and, conversely, that facing loss and expressing grief are curative, is central to much psychoanalytic work. Following Abraham's suggestion, Freud (1917) drew attention to the parallels between depression and normal grief. He saw that in depression the sufferer is struggling not just with himself, but, often unaware, with a *relationship*: 'the shadow of the object falls on the ego'. The work of mourning involves the paradox that in acknowledging what is lost, the bereaved person is at the same time reclaiming it. Based on her own mourning for her son who died in a climbing accident, Klein (1940) realised that what was at stake in loss was the integrity of the whole inner world. She therefore linked loss with internalisation. The bereaved:

> 'through the work of mourning is reinstating all his loved internal objects which he feels he has lost'. . . . Every advance in the process of mourning results in a deepening of the individual's relation to his inner objects, in the happiness of regaining them when they were felt to be lost.

> (Klein 1940: 356)

Many of the tasks and transitions of adult life involve loss. Klein is sensitive to the feeling that with one loss 'all' feels lost, and to the continuities between the handling of loss in childhood and adult responses to separation. Where loss can be mourned (including by healthy protest) then the lost object is 'reinstated' internally. This leads to an enrichment of the inner world which can balance the sadness about what has gone; where it cannot, depletion and depression may follow. Much of the work of analysis centres around this regaining and reinstatement of lost objects, especially as the analysis itself becomes an object that, between sessions and at breaks, is constantly lost and found, so that finally, at successful termination, the patient will have internalised a therapeutic function, even though the relationship with the therapist has come to an end.

Marriage

The psychoanalytic literature specifically devoted to marriage is surprisingly scant (but see Dicks 1967; Clulow 1985; Ruszczynski 1993). Perhaps this is because the majority of people seeking psychoanalysis are so obviously suffering from the problems of 'relationships', or the lack of them, that much of the psychoanalytic project is a treatise on relationships. Falling in love, and the search for the physical, emotional, intellectual and moral intimacy of marriage, requires a retracing of the history of the inner world and its mutual alignment with the partner – an inner process that parallels the way in which lovers exchange their 'external' life stories and incorporate one another into their respective families.

Marriage is therefore the most potent and fertile source of 'transference' outside the psychoanalytic relationship. The partner is a 'transformational object' (Bollas 1987), a vehicle for projection, a receptacle for unwanted aspects of the self, a source of delight and terror, bringing one into touch with one's deepest desires and disappointments. The potential for transformation or destruction suggests that health is not an escape from transference, but integral to it. Transference is, in Slavin and Kreigman's (1992) terms, a 'retranscribing of the relational environment', a 'probe' based on past affective experience embodied in 'semantic memory', which, when marriage (or therapy) goes well, leads to the mutual emergence of new patterns of maturity.

Maturation

Implicit in the developmental perspective of psychoanalysis is the idea of maturation. For Freud, this meant becoming more reality-oriented, as he expressed in his Zuider Zee metaphor of the reclamation of the unconscious by the conscious, his view of neurosis as a 'turning away from reality', and his famous aphorism 'where id was there ego shall be'. Implicit in Freud's work is also the notion of the coherence of an inner world illuminated by self-knowledge, and the acceptance of the different aspects of oneself. Mahler *et al.* (1975) combine both a Jungian and Freudian perspective in their concept of 'separation–individuation'. Some psychoanalytic writers emphasise the outgrowing of childish preoccupations, stressing a painful but heroic autonomy as the goal of treatment and as an ideal state of emotional health. This viewpoint has been criticised by authors such as Bowlby and Fairbairn who see dependency as integral to the human condition and autonomy as the false goal of a consumerist society intent on producing 'normosis' (Bollas 1987), not health. Fairbairn (1952) described maturation as a movement from immature to mature dependence, and Kohut (1977) insisted on the need for the persistence of 'self-objects' – i.e. 'narcissistic' and 'special' relationships with spouse, children and parents as well as ideas, places, pets, mementoes, etc. – throughout life. These authors see development as a dynamic system, an equilibrium balancing past and present, and maturational and regressive tendencies. Klein saw a shifting balance between paranoid and depressive positions continuing throughout life. This perspective explains the way in which an overwhelming trauma can bring out 'primitive' responses in the most mature of individuals (Garland 1991), and how psychoanalysis, like life itself, is always an 'unfinished journey'.

CONCLUSION

The developmental perspective of psychoanalysis provides a rich source of clinical metaphor for understanding the affective interactional matrix between patient and analyst. Analysts constantly search for the 'child' in the adult patient and try to reconstruct from the transference and countertransference the developmental situation in which the patient is ensnared. But the search for the 'inner child' is not just a metaphor: it connects the hermeneutic project of psychoanalysis – the construction of meaning through a life narrative stretching back to infancy – with the empirical world of developmental science. The mind has a developmental history no less than the body, and the evidence linking coherent or incoherent narrative styles in adulthood with patterns of secure or insecure attachment in infancy and childhood (Bruner 1990; Fonagy 1991; Holmes 1993) provides striking support for this view (see p. 255).

Chapter 4

Mechanisms of defence

The ego makes use of various procedures for fulfilling its task, which, to put it in general terms, is to avoid danger, anxiety and unpleasure. We call these procedures 'mechanisms of defence'.

(Freud 1937: 235)

We saw in Chapter 2 how models of the mind may be divided into those that are predominantly intrapsychic, interpersonal or mixed. Similarly, the concept of defence, and even the individual defence mechanisms themselves, may also be viewed from an intrapsychic, interpersonal/relational or mixed point of view. Some defences refer primarily to internal life (for example, repression), others to interactional or interpersonal phenomena (for example, projective identification, splitting), and yet others to both, such as denial.

THE CONCEPT OF DEFENCE

Classical psychoanalysis views defences primarily from an intrapsychic perspective, placing *conflict* at the heart of psychic life. First, conflict occurs between wishes and external reality which produces inner tension and anxiety. Second, conflict develops between the different agencies of the mind. Adaptation is made possible by *defences*. These are psychological configurations operating outside the realm of consciousness which minimise conflict, reduce tension, maintain intrapsychic equilibrium, regulate self-esteem and play a central role in dealing with anxiety whether it arises from internal or external sources.

Repression

Repression, the pushing back of unacceptable wishes from consciousness, is the classical primary mechanism of defence. Repression ensures that wishes which are incompatible with reality, superego demands, or other impulses, remain unconscious or disguised. The inherent tendency of repressed wishes and impulses to return to consciousness – the 'return of the repressed' – means that tension and anxiety remain, and that an array of further defences are mobilised to alleviate the resulting conflict, reduce tension and stabilise the personality. But all this occurs at the cost of distorting internal reality.

Example: a happy abandonment?
A borderline patient told her analyst that she was pleased to have a break from treatment when he told her that he had to cancel a session. Her mood changed from one of generalised anxiety and depression to overt happiness, accompanied by curt comments. Her apparent happiness at the cancelled session was clearly a defence against feelings of abandonment. On the missing day she came, expecting her session, and, on finding no one present, she became acutely anxious, feeling that her existence was meaningless. She was admitted to hospital, complaining that the analyst had discarded her because he preferred to see his family. The cancelled session had reawakened previously repressed feelings of abandonment by her mother, who had sent her away to stay with her aunt when her younger brother was born.

Further clinical work led to an understanding of her repressed wish never to be left, the consequent rage towards her mother and its displacement onto the analyst, and the denial of the emotional impact of the cancellation of the session.

In contrast to this classical picture, relational models see defence mechanisms as a protective shield within which the authentic self is held: defences form part of the attempt to facilitate the development of a 'true' (Winnicott 1965) or 'nuclear' (Kohut 1984) self in the face of a defective relational environment. Alvarez (1992), in keeping with Freud, has taken this point further and considers some uses of defence as developmentally necessary. The boasting of the little boy becomes a powerful force in overcoming inferiority and attaining manhood; omnipotent and paranoid defences, rather than avoiding inherent destructiveness or innate division and conflict, are desperate attempts to overcome and recover from states of terror and despair resulting from environmental failure.

Bowlby reframed defences in interpersonal terms, basing his view on attachment theory (Hamilton 1985; Holmes 1993). Secure attachment provides a positive primary defence while secondary or pathological defences retain closeness to rejecting or unreliable attachment figures. In 'avoidant attachment', both neediness and aggression are split off and the individual has no conscious knowledge of the need to be near the attachment figure, appearing aloof and distant; in 'ambivalent attachment', omnipotence and denial of autonomy lead to clinging and uncontrolled demands (cf. p. 256).

Coping mechanisms

A markedly different view of defence is put forward by experimental and social psychologists who conceptualise defences as 'coping mechanisms' (Lazarus *et al.* 1974), primarily aimed at dealing with problems in the external world. In contrast to the unconscious nature of defence mechanisms, *coping mechanisms* are supposedly (a) conscious and (b) mobilised to deal with external rather than internal threat. This distinction has also been questioned (Murphy 1962; Haan 1963). First, a number of everyday coping activities occur automatically, much like a reflex, while a refusal to listen to something or a denial of particular feelings may be conscious. Second, changes in the external world may evoke unacceptable affects which are then dealt with through the mobilisation of the mechanisms of defence. Third, the perceived danger of an external threat requires internal assessment, which is itself dependent on unconscious antecedents, and so there can be no clear distinction between internal and external conflict, with the two interacting in a complex way (Bond 1992).

Coping strategies can be taught and further developed into cognitive-behavioural strategies, which can be operationally defined for research purposes. Horowitz *et al.* (1990) have attempted to conceptualise mechanisms of defence within cognitive psychology; they see defences as the outcome of cognitive control processes which sequence ideas and join meanings together. Thus, defence and coping mechanisms are related phenomena, being both adaptive *and* potential sources of pathology.

Anna Freud

The adaptive aspect of defence was elaborated by Anna Freud (1936). She showed how phantasy and intellectual activity can be used defensively and how defences can be directed against external situations, superego demands, cultural requirements, etc. She contrasted dynamic defences with permanent or character defence phenomena such as those described by Wilhelm Reich (1928, 1933) as 'Charakterpanzerung' (character-armour). At the same time Hartmann (1939), the founder of ego psychology, placed special emphasis on 'conflict-free spheres' of the ego which were not solely associated with defence and conflict, and this led to greater emphasis on normal aspects of the personality.

Klein

By contrast, Klein (1946) emphasises a new array of defences, including splitting of the object (a different use of the term from Freud), projective identification, omnipotent control over objects, idealisation and devaluation (see p. 219). Her followers have developed these ideas further, and now consider defences not so much as transient psychological processes brought into play when necessary, but psychological configurations that coalesce to form a rigid and inflexible system. These defence *systems* of the personality have been variously known as narcissistic organisations (Rosenfeld 1964), defence organisations (O'Shaughnessy 1981) and pathological organisations (Steiner 1982). They are associated with powerful, controlling internal objects (*q.v.* pp. 222–7). Meltzer (1968) described a patient dominated by a 'foxy part' of the self that continually persuaded him of the attractions of grandiose and destructive aspects of relationships. Rosenfeld (1971) identified an internal 'mafia gang' that demanded emotional 'protection money' from the good parts of the personality, which were then forced to collude with the 'gang's' idealisation of destructiveness and devaluation of love and truth. Sohn (1985) writes of the omnipotent self created by identification with an external object, the weak and needy parts having been discarded, to form an arrogant 'identificate', which then takes over the whole personality (cf. p. 220).

This 'structuralisation' of defence systems has been applied to such complex areas as social systems and groups (Bion 1961; Pines 1985) which may themselves be under the sway of destructive interactions, or driven by the equivalent of 'foxy' parts and 'mafia gangs'. Such understanding forms a major aspect of psychoanalytically informed intervention into organisations (Jaques 1955, Trist and Bamforth 1951, Menzies-Lyth 1988, Hinshelwood 1987, 1993, 1994b). Implicit in all the formulations is the fact that defence may become maladaptive in certain circumstances and lead to the formation of symptoms. This is especially likely if *primitive* methods of defence are reawakened through regression or remain active through developmental arrests at early 'fixation points'. Such ideas stem from Freud (1894, 1896, 1926) and there is now empirical evidence to suggest a relationship between psychological adjustment and maturity. Vaillant (1971, 1977) has shown that there is a continuum of defences from normal or mature through to pathological, and that the use of more mature defences is correlated with successful life adjustments in work, relationships and medical history.

The differentiation of defences into (a) psychotic/immature or primitive, (b) neurotic and (c) mature, links specific aspects of childhood psychological functioning to emotional difficulties in adulthood. However, the use of primitive mechanisms is not in itself pathological: as mentioned, they emerge in psychologically healthy individuals exposed to extreme stress (Garland 1991); it is their persistent use that is maladaptive.

Summary

In summary, the main features of defences are as follows:

- They may be normal and adaptive as well as pathological.
- They are a function of the ego.
- They are usually unconscious.
- They are dynamic and everchanging but may coalesce into rigid, fixed systems in pathological states and in character formation.
- Different defences are associated with different psychological states, e.g. repression in hysteria, isolation and undoing in obsessional neurosis.
- They are associated with levels of development, with some defences being seen as primitive and others as mature.

We shall now consider some of the individual defences in more detail, starting with the psychotic/immature or primitive mechanisms, and then move on through some of the neurotic defences to those of maturity. A list of defences is given in Table 4.1.

Table 4.1 Mechanisms of Defence

Primitive/Immature	Neurotic	Mature
Autistic phantasy	Condensation	Humour
Devaluation	Denial	Sublimation
Idealisation	Displacement	
Passive-aggression	Dissociation	
Projection	Externalisation	
Projective identification	Identification with aggressor	
Splitting	Intellectualisation	
	Isolation	
	Rationalisation	
	Reaction formation	
	Regression	
	Repression	
	Reversal	
	Somatisation	
	Undoing	

PRIMITIVE MECHANISMS

Splitting

Following Klein, contemporary psychoanalysts use the term 'splitting' to refer to a division of an object into 'good' and 'bad'. A child, in his mind, will split his mother into two separate persons: the bad, frustrating mother whom he hates and the good, idealised mother whom he loves. By mentally keeping the good and bad mother strictly separate, the ambivalent conflict between loving and hating a mother who is, in reality, one and the same person, and a mixture of good and bad, can be avoided.

Example: the envied siblings
A depressed patient who was one of four children continually complained that her mother had neglected her and favoured her siblings. She repeated stories of her mother's favouritism and unceasing concern for her sisters and brothers, from whom she was now estranged. In between sessions she began to feel that the analyst was kinder and more helpful to his other patients. She envied them and started to wait outside his consulting room, asking them whether he saw them more often than he saw her. In the sessions themselves she felt better and couldn't understand why outside the sessions she accused the analyst of hating her and of cruelly withholding help that he willingly gave to others.

As a result of the patient's ambivalence, her internal representation of the analyst had become split. Outside the sessions she could only see him as someone who was cruel and neglectful. Within the sessions she experienced him as ideal, caring and thoughtful. Thus the 'good' analyst was protected from her envious attacks.

Klein also recognised that, since internal and external objects are intrinsically related to the ego, a split in the ego may also occur. This was in keeping with Freud's original use of the term 'splitting'. He referred to a splitting of the ego in fetishism, allowing a quasi-psychotic simultaneous holding of contradictory ideas (Freud 1927). The split coincided with the contradiction between a wishful fantasy and a reality, rather than between object representations – 'the instinct is allowed to retain its satisfaction *and* proper respect is shown to reality' (Freud 1940, our *italics*). This descriptive use of the term is compatible with Bleuler's (1924) account of the loosening of associations in schizophrenia. However, splitting is now viewed, especially by Kleinian analysts, as a primary phenomenon of mental life in infancy potentially leading to the development of borderline and psychotic disorders later in life (Kernberg 1975). In these cases splitting is extreme and leads to a distortion of perception, a diminution in the capacity to think, and fragmentation of objects.

As mentioned in Chapter 3, splitting can be benign as well as pathological. The ordering of the internal world relies on splitting. Its success is, therefore, a precondition of later integration and the basis of the faculty of judgement. Splitting is also used to pay attention, to suspend one's emotional distress in order to come to a decision, to make moral choices, or form an intellectual judgement (Segal 1973). In this aspect it has similarities to Freud's (1909) concept of negation (see p. 189). The widespread tendency to split the world into good and bad, right and wrong, black and white, or heaven and hell persists throughout life and profoundly affects our attitudes not only to individuals but also to social institutions and political, religious and other organisations.

Projection, identification and projective identification

A recent enthusiast compared the significance of Klein's 'discovery' of projective identification in psychoanalysis with the discovery of gravity or the mechanism of evolution (Young 1994). Projective identification is undoubtedly an important but complex subject, partly because of its inherent difficulty, partly perhaps because its name is misleading, and partly because, as one of the fundamentals of Kleinian psychoanalysis, it provokes political controversy disproportionate to its clinical role and relevance.

The notion of *projection* is relatively straightforward, and has entered the vernacular of 'folk psychology' (Bruner 1990). The depressed young man lying on a beach who stated 'everyone on this beach looks utterly miserable' was clearly attributing to others his own affective state. We commonly attribute our more difficult and unacceptable feelings to others – for example, blaming those that are close to us for our own shortcomings. Externalisation, the outward limb of projection, allows us to disown responsibility and to feel an illusory sense of mastery over our impulses. If our unwanted impulses and feelings are reflected, like a boomerang, resulting in a feeling of being under constant attack, the projection has gone full circle and leads to anxiety or, if extreme, paranoid delusions.

Identification, similarly, is relatively straightforward, referring to the process by which self-representations are built up and modified during development, as distinct from the conscious copying of imitation. The little boy who shuffles around in his father's shoes is simply imitating, but as his internal image of himself is influenced and later transformed into a personality characteristic, identification has occurred, especially if he eventually 'steps into his father's shoes' and takes over the family business. Piaget's (1954) concepts of 'assimilation' and 'accommodation' are similar although referring to the development of cognitive ability rather than self-representation. Piaget suggests the young infant has internal 'schemas' of only actions and perceptions, but later the child represents one thing by another through the use of words and symbols. New experiences are 'assimilated' into existing schemas, and may be distorted by them, much as the external world is introjected and modified by unconscious phantasy within a psychoanalytic model. Schemas are modified, extended, and combined to meet new situations through 'accommodation'. Similarly, self-representations are modified and built-on through new identifications.

As Klein (1946) originally conceived it, *projective identification* combines these two notions in a highly specific way. She described projective identification as a phantasy in which bad parts of the infantile self are split off from the rest of the self and projected into the mother or her breast. As a result, the infant feels that his mother has 'become' the bad parts of himself. Of particular importance is, first, that the projection is 'into' rather than 'onto' the object – prototypically the mother or the analyst, and, second, that what is projected is not so much a feeling or an attitude, but the self, or part of it. Klein imagined that in the paranoid–schizoid position the infant might project 'bad' sadistic parts of himself into the mother's body in order to control and injure her from within. If these are then reintrojected – 'introjective identification' – the individual contains a 'bad' identificate, a potential source of low self-esteem or self-hatred. In contrast, 'good' parts of the self may also be projected and reintrojected, increasing self-esteem and enhancing good object relations if not carried to excess.

In this original formulation, projective identification was defensive, intrapsychic, and solipsistic, a mental transaction involving the self and a perception, but not the participation, of the other. How then does projective identification differ, if at all, from projection? Klein, herself, was clear about this. Projection is the mental mechanism underpinning the process and projective identification is the specific phantasy expressing it. Spillius (1988) suggests that projective identification adds depth to Freud's original concept of projection by emphasising the fact that a phantasy of projection is only possible if accompanied by a projection of parts of the self. She comments that British authors rarely consider the distinction between projection and projective identification to be of particular importance. In contrast, many American writers have devoted a great deal of discussion to the topic (Malin and Grotstein 1966, Langs 1978, Ogden 1979), often distinguishing projection and projective identification by whether or not the recipient of the projections is emotionally affected or not by the phantasy. In projection the target of the projections may be blissfully unaware of his role – as no doubt were the holidaymakers on the beach in the example above. The paranoid person projects malevolent intentions onto politicians, pop stars, Freemasons, etc., with whom he never comes in contact, or indeed onto inanimate objects. This distinction has arisen from developments of Klein's original idea of projective identification emphasising its *communicative* aspect.

The communicative aspect of projective identification, as opposed to its defensive nature, means that it can be used to describe three distinct processes. First, if projective identification is seen as an interactive phenomenon, then the recipient of the projection may be induced to feel or act in ways that originate with the projector. This accounts for the realisation by Heimann (1950), Grinberg (1962) and Racker (1968) that countertransferential feelings evoked in the analyst can reflect aspects of the patient's inner world. Ogden (1979) argues that identification occurs within both projector *and* recipient, while Grotstein (1981) and Kernberg (1987) both feel that the term should be confined to identification within the projector. These ideas, often in a diluted form, have become widely accepted in psychodynamic circles: if the analyst is feeling bored or irritable or sad, these feelings may, via projective identification, originate with the patient. Here the 'identification' is occurring within the target of the projective identification rather than, as Klein first saw it, within the projector (i.e. a 'misperception').

Second, by extension, projective identification becomes a mutual process in which projector and recipient interact with one another at an unconscious level. The analyst who is unaware of the feelings induced in him by projective identification may *enact* them by, for example, being rejecting or sluggish in the session – feelings which may, in turn, be picked up by the patient. Spillius (1994) suggests the term 'evocatory projective identification' to describe this pressure put onto the analyst to conform to the patient's phantasy. Sandler (1976a, 1976b) and Sandler and Sandler (1978) see this aspect of projective identification in terms of 'actualisation' and 'role responsiveness' in which the analyst has to be flexible enough to respond slightly to the role in which he is cast by the patient's projective identification, and must also remain sufficiently centred in himself to observe and interpret this process as it happens.

The ramifications of the communicative aspects of projective identification are so great that it can eventually cover almost all that happens in the analytic situation. However, it is clinically mistaken to assume that everything that the analyst experiences is a result of what the patient is 'putting into' him. It is important to distinguish between 'patient-derived countertransference' and 'analyst-derived countertransference' (see p. 111), however difficult in practice this may be (Money-Kyrle 1956). The former is based on projective identification, while the latter most definitely is not.

The third extension of projective identification derives from Bion (1962, 1963). Klein saw projective identification primarily in negative terms: the projection of sadistic feelings as part of the paranoid–schizoid position. Bion realised that there was also a 'positive' form of projective identification underlying empathy, and the processes by which the mother contains projected painful and hostile feelings, 'detoxifies' them, and returns them to the infant in a more benign form at a phase-appropriate moment. However, some of Bion's clinical uses of the idea of projective identification have been controversial. He advocated speaking to psychotic patients in concrete ways; thus he might say 'You are pushing your fear of murdering me into my insides'. While this kind of interpretation may occasionally be successful, in inexperienced hands it can be at best incomprehensible, at worst dangerous, and as a standard technique has been much criticised (Sandler 1987). It is rarely used now.

Many authors, including Bion (1955), have stressed the importance of projective identification as a method of control of the object and of unmanageable feelings. In this aspect of projective identification, whole aspects of the ego are split off and projected into another person, animal or inanimate object, who then represents and becomes identified with the split-off parts; attempts are then made to control these split-off parts of the self by asserting control over the other person (Sandler 1987).

Example: the controlling teacher
A man in his late twenties was working as a probationary teacher and was put in charge of a class of adolescent boys; he soon began to resent any boy who was disobedient, rude or otherwise badly behaved so much so that he became frightened before each lesson lest he would be unable to control the class. Indeed, the class was becoming increasingly badly behaved. He began to hate these pupils and feared that he might himself lose control and hit one or other of the boys. During analysis it emerged that throughout his own adolescence he had been a good boy, obedient, hardworking and never causing trouble either at school or at home. He had split off all those destructive and rebellious aspects of himself which, as a result of his upbringing, he considered to be evil, dangerous and unacceptable. By means of projective identification he was now projecting all these unacceptable aspects of himself into his adolescent pupils. They had become identified with his own split-off rebellious parts. He hated these unwanted aspects of himself and desperately but unsuccessfully tried to control them by trying to control and punish his pupils. He suddenly understood this during a session and then reported that as a boy he used to collect and play with toy animals, such as tigers and crocodiles, making them attack and devour other animals and human beings. These

toy animals had at that time also become identified with the
projected aggressive parts of himself. By projecting all these parts
into them he had, however, lost any inner sense of being strong
enough to stand up for himself and to fight other boys and, later,
adults who might insult or oppose him.

Good aspects of the self can also be projected into others. Projective
identification can thus leave an individual feeling deprived of
essential aspects of his own personality. A central task of analysis is
to help the patient recover these lost aspects of the self (see p. 178).

Example: the worthless woman and her worthy friend
A young woman who had always tended to regard herself as
unattractive, and unlovable became dependent on and envious of
a slightly older woman friend whom she regarded as very compet-
ent, beautiful and successful in all her relationships with men.
During analysis it became clear that she had projected all her own
positive qualities of which she felt unworthy, and hence unable to
contain inside herself, into this other woman, who thus became
identified with all her own assets. This made her feel even less
attractive and less worthy of being loved so that she felt impoverished inside herself. She made constant demands on her friend, as
only in her presence and with her backing did she feel able to do
anything worthwhile. When her friend married and moved away
she became depressed, feeling her friend had taken away with her
everything good that she no longer contained within herself.

Projective identification is therefore important because it tackles the
lifeblood of psychoanalysis, the interplay of phantasy in intimate
relationships. It is both defensive and communicative and the
response of the analyst may be the primary factor in determining
which aspect is uppermost (Joseph 1987). It is 'difficult' because the
concept originates in a rather casual definition given by Klein (1952)
and retains a title that does not really capture post-Kleinian exten-
sions. Although 'communicative projection', or 'projective interaction' may be preferable expressions, Spillius (1988) suggests that
projective identification should be retained as a general term within
which various subtypes can be differentiated. The many motives
behind the process – to control the object, to acquire its attributes,
to evacuate a bad quality, to protect a good quality, to avoid
separation, to communicate – may be useful starting points to
identify subtypes.

NEUROTIC MECHANISMS

Repression, denial and disavowal

Repression has already been mentioned as *the* primary mechanism of defence during development which enables the child to maintain a balance between internal wishes and the constraints of the external world without excessive psychic pain. However, later in life, when used excessively, it leads to marked dissociation of whole areas of emotional life from consciousness and according to classical theory leads to the formation of symptoms such as the 'belle indifference' associated with hysteria.

> *Example: the deadly memory*
> A clear example of repression was observed in a patient suffering from depression. During analysis, he burst into tears when talking about the death of his mother when he was a child. He became aware that he had 'forgotten' that the cause of her death was an overdose of tablets. Only after having faced the fact that she had killed herself was he able to work through his long delayed grief reaction and recover from his depression.

In contrast to repression, which aims to remove an aspect of internal reality from consciousness, denial or disavowal (Freud 1940) deals with external reality and enables an individual to repudiate or to control affectively his response to a specific aspect of the outside world. Denial involves splitting in which there is cognitive acceptance of a painful event while the associated painful emotions are repudiated. The protective aspect of denial is illustrated by Greer *et al.*'s (1979) finding that women with breast cancer who showed denial (or defiance) when told the diagnosis, had a significantly higher survival rate after mastectomy than women who reacted with hopelessness or depression.

Reaction formation; identification with the aggressor

If an individual adopts a psychological attitude that is diametrically opposed to his conscious wish or desire, it is known as a reaction formation. Reaction formations often appear during latency and act as a bridge to more mature defences such as sublimation. Reaction formations may be highly specific – for example, showing excessive deference to some person one hates, or caring for others when one wishes to be cared for oneself – or more generalised, in which case they form part of a character trait. Conscientiousness, shame and self-distrust may be examples of this when they are associated with obsessional personality and obsessional neurosis. As with all defensive pathologies, reaction formations alter the structure of the ego in a permanent way, so that the defence is used although the danger is no longer present.

Although Freud (1920) had alluded to 'identification with the aggressor', and Ferenczi (1932) had used the term to describe the behaviour of a child towards an adult in which there was a total submission to the adult's aggression and a resulting internalisation of profound feelings of guilt, it was Anna Freud (1936) who described the mechanism in detail and related it to the early formation of the superego. Identification with the aggressor has links with both reaction formation, in that there is a reversal of affects, and identification.

Example: the unassuming lawyer

A quietly spoken and timid patient was frequently threatened, humiliated and beaten during childhood by his father. Prior to being beaten he would run away to his room while his increasingly angry father chased him. After the chase the little boy would suddenly go quiet and bend over and his father would then beat him, while he remained completely silent and entered a dissociated state. At this moment, the boy had dis-identified with his self-representation and identified with his father (the aggressor) who was going to beat his naughty bad body. In adult life, he himself continued the identification with the abusive father by taking illegal drugs and cutting himself, thereby allowing both the abuser and the abused to continue living out their interaction through his mind and body.

This process is particularly important in the intergenerational transmission of child abuse, in which the abused of one generation becomes the abuser in the next.

Isolation and undoing

These mechanisms are part of the psychoanalytic conceptualisation of obsessional disorders. Freud first described isolation as a distinguishing feature separating hysterical conversion and obsessional neurosis. He suggested that if the individual did not 'convert' painful affects through repression into bodily symptoms, then the affect was neutralized by isolation. The affect was rendered unconscious while the idea, stripped of feeling, remained conscious.

This contrasts with repression in which the idea rather than the affect is banished, and also with dissociation, in which the affect and idea both remain conscious but the connection between them is rendered meaningless. In isolation a traumatic memory may be easily retrieved but is denuded of any feeling – patients who have recently taken an overdose or cut themselves often talk about the circumstances leading up to the event with considerable calm and may induce a false sense of ease in the assessing doctor. Fenichel (1946) suggested that the sexual and tender components of male sexuality are often 'isolated', leaving men more able to enjoy sensual feelings towards those whom they do not love, although his point could also be seen as an example of splitting.

Undoing is often referred to as 'doing and undoing' or 'magical undoing' and is well known to anyone who has treated patients with an obsessive–compulsive disorder. Undoing enables the individual to reverse hostile wishes which he believes he has already perpetrated in the 'doing'. In the obsessive–compulsive disorders this is often seen in the behaviour of the sufferer who may have to do things in a specific order only to have to repeat the whole ritual if one component is missed. The attempt to undo has a magical quality and is not just an attempt to make up for some error. It aims to reverse time, attack the reality of the original hostile thought or wish, and recreate the past as though such intentions had never existed.

Internalisation and incorporation

Internalisation is a ubiquitous psychological process that is not necessarily defensive but can form part of adult defensive man-oeuvres such as projective identification (see p. 83) and identi-fication with the aggressor (see p. 83). Internalisation is a supra-ordinate term which subsumes introjection, incorporation and identi-fication (see p. 83) and refers to all those processes by which the individual builds up his inner representational world by taking in and modifying the external world. Introjection is synonymous with internalisation early in development and applies to the formation of memories of perceptions.

When object relationships are well established, introjection does not consist so much of 'taking in' and laying down memories but more of modifying their status in relation to the self – a student, after adolescent battles with his parents, who returns home from his first term at university and expresses surprise at how much his parents have changed, may have identified with his parental introject, or, more correctly, with that part of the introject which, in his rows, he was trying to differentiate himself from, and become more like them. This process is also common when young people become parents for the first time and finally identify with introjected parental attitudes in their approach to their child. Introjection, therefore, has an important role to play in the formation of the superego.

'Identification with the lost object' (Klein 1955) (cf. p. 72–3) is part of the normal mourning process which, along with introjection, may serve to delay the loss of the object. It is also a common feature in abnormal grief reactions:

Example: an internal object

A woman mourning the loss of her granddaughter appeared to have resolved her grief. However, some months later she developed intractable abdominal pain for which no physical cause was found. Her granddaughter had died from intestinal volvulus and the patient's symptoms were a result of an identification with the symptoms of the dead child. She was helped to recognise this during bereavement counselling and this led to the disappearance of her symptoms.

Incorporation is the psychological correlate of eating and refers to the 'swallowing whole' of an identificate (*q.v.* pp. 219–20) without modification or assimilation, and can be part of a psychotic form of internalisation.

Example: psychotic identification

A 45-year-old borderline patient with severe bulimic symptoms repeatedly cut herself and attempted suicide on a number of occasions. She exercised excessively – biking at least 10 miles a day and swimming a kilometre in the evenings. Her fantasy when exercising, cutting and inducing vomiting was that all the 'evil things' were being expurgated, and it was especially relieving to her if the vomit had streaks of blood in it. Indeed, she believed that the only way to find absolute calm and tranquillity, and to be released from everything inside her, was if she stuck a knife into her body to see all the red evil things gush out of her inside. Her mother had always called her a selfish, wicked girl and she had continually prayed that it was not true. This had allowed her to feel less wicked. Her mother's view of her had become a non-assimilated incorporated object. It had never fully resulted in a change in her self-representation which was protected by prayer. Only when she accepted these aspects of herself did her self-destructive acts diminish.

A similar process may occur in globus hystericus in which some 'thing' is experienced as being lodged in the throat.

Intellectualisation and rationalisation

Intellectualisation and rationalisation are common in politics, business and medicine. They bridge the gap between immature mechanisms and those of maturity and often persist into adult life without leading to any overt problems. Intellectualisation covers a range of subdefences, including thinking instead of experiencing, and paying undue attention to the abstract in order to avoid intimacy. It may be associated with isolation, magical doing and undoing as well as rationalisation. The adolescent, fearful of his developing sexuality, may talk intellectually about premarital sex or earnestly discuss the sexual behaviour of young people. Rationalisation similarly offers logical and believable explanations for irrational behaviours that have been prompted by unconscious wishes.

MATURE MECHANISMS

Sublimation and humour were honoured by Freud as mature defence mechanisms for their capacity to allow partial expression of underlying wishes and desires in a socially acceptable way, while simultaneously enriching society. In sublimation, wishes are channelled rather than dammed or diverted: aggressive urges may find expression in games and sport; feelings are acknowledged, modified and directed towards significant goals. Similarly, narcissistic needs might be fulfilled by becoming a successful stage actor.

Example: the paint pot and the palate

A 50-year-old engineer and amateur artist entered analysis suffering from severe depression after he had been made redundant by a firm to which he had devoted the best years of his life. He had never known his father, who had been killed in the war, and had grown up as an exceptionally controlled and 'good' boy who had devoted himself to his widowed mother. When she remarried when he was 7 years old he submitted without murmur to his step-father's harsh discipline. He prided himself on never losing his temper. He had married a subservient wife. On one occasion near the start of his depression, while he was decorating the house, she supplied him with the wrong sort of paint. To his horror he found himself simply upending the entire gallon tin on the floor and walking out of the house, leaving her to clear up the mess. As the analysis progressed he began to get in touch with deeply sup-pressed feelings of longing for closeness and intimacy, and anger that no one realised what he really wanted. Later, to his surprise he returned to painting, but instead of the rather meticulous line drawings he had done in the past, he started to smear paint thickly with the palate knife directly onto the canvas. Thus his aggression and need for emotional expression, which earlier had been a rageful manifestation of depression, were now sublimated into creativity.

Freud saw sublimation as the vehicle by which a society's basest and deepest desires as well as aspirations and ambitions gain expression, through carnival, drama, music, poetry and religious and political aspirations. Humour allows us to share emotion, often aggressive, without discomfort, to regress without embarrassment, to play games with freedom, to laugh with impunity and relax with pleasure; it includes rather than rejects and may at times allow terrible tragedy to become bearable.

Vaillant and Drake (1985) and Vaillant et al. (1986) have confirmed the adaptive value of mature defences. Vaillant's longit-udinal studies of men, followed from graduation over a forty-year period, show that those who use them are consistently happier and more successful and stable occupationally, and in their family lives, than those using less mature defences. Perry and Cooper (1989) similarly found that immature mechanisms of defence are associated with psychological symptoms, personal distress and poor social functioning. Such findings, along with the general usefulness of defence in understanding psychological function, led Sartorius et al.(1990) to suggest that descriptive (i.e. non-psychoanalytic) psy-chiatry's efforts to link clinical symptoms, causal factors, pathogenic models and prognostic types had generally failed. They argue that the return of 'allegedly out-dated Meyerian reaction patterns and Freud-ian defence mechanisms is warranted'. This comment emphasises the continuing importance of psychodynamic contributions to psychiatric diagnosis, and Vaillant (1992) also argues cogently for an 'axis VI' (Defence Mechanisms) to be added to future multi-axial classificatory systems. Reliable measurement of many of the defence mechanisms is now possible (Bond *et al.* 1983; Vaillant *et al.* 1986) and study of their change during psychoanalytic treatment may allow a better understanding of the interventions needed to help overcome neurosis and to achieve psychological health.

Chapter 5

Transference and Countertransference

> It cannot be disputed that controlling the phenomenon of transference presents the psychoanalyst with the greatest difficulties.
>
> (Freud 1912b: 108)

The hallmark of psychoanalysis is the use of transference and countertransference as a guide to understanding the inner world. But what precisely *is* transference, and how does it relate to the different models of the unconscious? Here again we come up against the 'elasticity' of psychoanalytic concepts discussed in the previous chapters. We have seen how variations between psychoanalytic models of the mind, and contrasting theories of development, may affect the analytic approach to the patient. These theoretical differences inevitably also impinge on the concepts of transference and countertransference since both are inseparable from the framework within which they are discussed. To put it schematically, interpersonal approaches are likely to describe transference in terms of a two-person interaction with contributions from both analyst and patient; ego psychology considers transference in terms of the expression of instinctual wishes; and a Kleinian perspective in terms of representation of unconscious phantasy. As has already been mentioned in Chapter 2, some of these are differences of substance; others no more than variations of language. However, no approach is pure and the interpretation of unconscious phantasy is no more the prerogative of a Kleinian position than consideration of instincts is that of ego psychology or a contemporary Freudian approach. There is general agreement about the existence of transference as a phenomenon, but a real debate exists concerning its *content* – i.e. what exactly is 'transferred'. There are also important differences of opinion about the centrality or otherwise of transference interpretation as the only truly effective therapeutic intervention. These clinical aspects are discussed further in Chapter 8 while more theoretical issues are considered here. Although transference and countertransference are inextricably linked, they will be discussed separately in this chapter.

TRANSFERENCE

Breuer and Freud (1895) initially saw transferences as 'contaminating influences' which interfered with or resisted their cathartic method. Freud was worried that transferences were a result of the doctor's undue influence on the patient and that psychoanalysis, if it focused on them, would be seen as a modified form of hypnosis or 'suggestion'. But Freud soon came to realise that transference did *not* arise solely out of suggestion, and that the relationship between the patient and the analyst was of primary importance in understanding the internal world; transference became an expression of a pathological oedipal attachment to the analyst which represented the individual's earlier relationship to parental figures (Freud 1895, 1905c). This led to the idea that there could be a *transference neurosis* (Freud 1914c), comprising positive and negative transferences, paralleling the affects and wishes surrounding the original oedipal situation which was then recreated within the analysis itself. Analysis of all aspects of the transference neurosis, as lived out with the analyst, was a requirement for an effective analytic cure, as it would otherwise act as a resistance to the remembering of repressed phantasies. Thus, at a very early stage, Freud saw a dual aspect to transference: on the one hand, a resistance to verbalised recollection; on the other, a 're-presentation' of infantile conflict in a way that was therapeutically useful.

Freud (1912b) also distinguished between the mechanism of transference which reflects past experience and the dynamics of transference which are aroused in the present situation. The *mechanism* of transference he saw in terms of a 'template', or store of infantile images in the system unconscious, out of which arises the *dynamics* of the patient's current emotional relationship with the analyst. This double aspect of transference continues in the debate among contemporary psychoanalysts between the relative importance of the 'past' and 'present' unconscious (Sandler and Sandler 1984). Some authors see transference as the main route to the reconstruction of childhood trauma; others see exploration of the here-and-now transference as central. Similarly, there is a lively debate between those who take an intrapsychic view of transference and those who emphasise the interpersonal aspects. Whatever view is taken, transference, eventually occupying a pivotal role in Freud's clinical theories, continues to be the central theme of contemporary psychoanalysis.

Transference interpretation: classical and modern

In order to compare different aspects of transference we shall use a somewhat artificial contrast between 'classical' and 'modern' (or 'contemporary') practice and thought. 'Classical' and 'modern', while useful as a shorthand, should not be thought of as conflicting, but rather the one resting on and intermingling with the other. The most straightforward 'classical' definition of the dynamic aspect of transference may be summarised as a process by which the patient transfers onto his analyst past experiences and strong feelings – dependency, love, sexual attraction, jealousy, frustration, hatred – which he previously experienced in relation to significant persons such as his mother, father or siblings earlier in life. The patient is unaware of this false connection, and experiences the feelings not as if they belong to the past but as directly relevant to the present. This viewpoint suggests that interpretation of the transference uncovers and allows the re-experiencing or reconstruction of the past in the present and, once insight into it has been achieved, helps to overcome past trauma; it regards the infantile neurosis as central to the analytic work; it likens the analyst to a neutral screen onto which infantile wishes are projected; it emphasises reconstruction of the past, and accepts transference as a potential resistance (see p. 164).

In contrast, the 'modern' view sees transference not so much as the inexorable manifestation of unconscious mental forces, but rather as the emergence of latent meanings, organised around and evoked by the intensity of the analytic relationship. This involves examining how the detail of present-day wishes, character formations and personal expectations are influenced by the past; it does not accept the idea of infantile neurosis as the only explanation for adult pathology, nor does it see transference neurosis as a simple pathway to cure; hence it de-emphasises reconstruction. Transference has thus become a much wider concept involving the interplay between the patient and the analyst, representing the conflicts of the mind and reflecting the interactions of the internal object representations; it is a medium through which the individual's internal drama is 'played out' with the analyst; a new experience influenced by the past, rather than a repetition of an earlier one (Cooper 1987).

Brenner (1982) believes that the term 'transference neurosis' is redundant and should be dropped. In fact, there is now little discussion of transference neurosis as an entity separate from transference itself. Not all would agree (Wallerstein 1994): there are undoubtedly some patients for whom analysis assumes increasing salience and in whom, as treatment progresses, neurotic difficulties disappear from their outside life, to be contained largely within the therapeutic situation.

The classical and modern views of transference interact in a complex way (see Table 5.1). This will emerge as we discuss three key questions that have preoccupied contemporary theorists:

(a) transference as a distortion of reality, or as a valid representation of a present unconscious situation, coloured by experiences from the past;
(b) transference as a general, or specifically analytic phenomenon;
(c) transference as the whole or only part of the analytic situation.

Distortion or reality?

From a classical point of view psychoanalysis sees transference as a distortion of reality: transference represents the individual's infantile wishes pushing for gratification through present relationships. It is therefore an intrapsychic displacement of the past projected onto a present relationship, leading the relationship to be experienced not as it actually is, but as a mosaic of past and present.

Example: the unappreciative analyst

A young woman complained that her analyst didn't seem to appreciate how hard she worked and didn't seem to care how she was getting on in her job. The analyst responded by suggesting that she felt that he didn't appreciate how hard she worked in the job of analysis or care about how she was progressing. She then described how her mother had had a successful career early in her life but gave up work when the patient was born. The patient's mother was unable to resume her career for many years and the patient felt that her mother resented her academic success and took little interest in her schoolwork, always saying only that she wished she could return to work herself. The analyst interpreted that she believed her success could only lead to envy and resentment in others. She now believed that the analyst was

Table 5.1 Classical and modern views of transference

	Classical	Modern
Definition	Displacement of past onto present shaped by past experience	Organise present experience according to models
Reality	Distortion – objective reality	Subjective reality
Motivation	Aggressive/libidinal drives related to infantile wishes, phantasies, fears	Adaptive; organising perceptual/affective/cognitive experience necessary for cohesive self
Analyst	Neutral/blank screen; objective	Contributes through interaction; Subjective
Intervention	Interpretation of distortion	Reflects patient's construction and how he organises analytic relationship
Change	Decrease in infantile wishes and less distortion	Rigid psychological schemas become flexible; new ones emerge as a result of analytic experience

resentful of her success just as her mother had been and had given up on his work with her.

This example shows the complex mix of classical and modern approaches used in everyday clinical practice. The analyst's first interpretation was 'modern' in that he linked outside material with the transference relationship, finding hidden meaning in the patient's reference to her job as an allusion to the analytic relationship. The second was classical in that her past relationship with her mother was, in a fairly straightforward way, distorting her perception of the analyst. From a classical perspective the emphasis of interpretation is on an understanding of the past as it is 're-presented' in the present. But from a modern point of view the annoyance with the analyst is seen as representing a *present-day* wishful phantasy or expectation – inaccessible to consciousness and therefore needing a transference interpretation to bring it to light – only indirectly linking with earlier failures of the mother. Here the fantasy itself, as enacted with the analyst, becomes the centre of interpretation. In this modern view, the dynamic is in the present, often only remotely influenced by an infantile constellation from the past. Further, transference becomes a positive therapeutic force, not just as a representation of the past which, if interpreted, can lead to insight, but as a probe that will elicit or provoke responses from the analyst required to pursue further developmental needs. Transference is an interactive process by which the patient responds to selected aspects of the analytic situation, sensitised by past experience.

There is no doubt that there is a strong influence from the past driving a patient's perception of the analyst: one patient may see the analyst as caring and understanding while the next sees him as hostile and rejecting. Levenson (1983) emphasises these distorting elements of transference – we see and experience what we expect to see, and transference is a resistance to understanding by repeating and rigidifying relationships. However, patients may also be unconsciously aware of aspects of the analyst's reality based on his behaviour – the way he arranges and decorates his room, runs his practice or his own life. Therapeutic 'reality' is determined by both patient and analyst, with the patient experiencing and reacting to the analyst both as he is *and* as he sees him, and the analyst responding to the patient as he is, as well as being counter-transferentially driven.

An implication of some modern approaches is that there is an underlying knowable truth or internal 'psychic reality' which is accessible through interpretation of the defences or unravelling of distortions. This Platonic view of an underlying truth is shared by those analysts influenced by Klein and Bion who see the inner more 'truthful' state as being organised around psychotic anxieties related to the death instinct rather than, as in Freud's original conception, the infantile neurosis (cf. Chapter 3) which was never fully knowable. Idealising and erotic transferences are seen as part of pathological organisations and interpretation focuses on the idealising transference as a defence against the hostility and destructiveness towards the analyst rather than as a resistance. Schafer (1981), Gill (1982) and Spence (1982), by contrast, have questioned the very concept of a knowable truth. They see the transference relationship more as a personal narrative truth rather than as a distortion of some fundamental aspect of the psychic reality of unconscious phantasy. For them, there is no such thing as a reconstruction, but only a *construction* of the past from the viewpoint of the 'here and now'. Others agree and suggest that what we reconstruct may be helpful and yet may never have happened, and that we should place greater emphasis on how the past is modified by subsequent experience. This debate between the 'correspondence' and 'coherence' models of truth has deep philosophical roots (Cavell 1994, cf. p. 21).

The development of object relations theory has also had an influence on how transference is perceived. The concepts of projective identification and the externalisation of internal objects (see p. 85) are clearly relevant both to transference in the analytic process and in everyday relationships. Kernberg (1987) suggests that analysis of the transference is in effect the analysis in the here-and-now of past internalised object relations as well as the analysis of conflictual elements between different aspects of the psychic structures. He cautions against too simplistic a link between the representation in the present and the actual past and sees the internalised object relationships as being formed from fantasy as well as reality.

All these views are influenced by the classical model of transference as a distortion or misperception which can be ironed out through analysis. This goes back to the idea of transference as a resistance, albeit one essential to progress in analysis. But the modern view of transference as the emergence of latent meanings allows it to be seen more positively. Slavin and Kreigman (1992) argue that it is unlikely that human beings face life hampered by continual misperceptions and distortions and suggest an adaptive view of transference in which it represents the bringing of learned experiences to a new situation so that the previous experiences may be revised in the light of new experiences. Thus transference becomes an 'earlier version' rather than a distortion of the present situation. From an existential perspective, Stolorow *et al.* (1987) suggest that transference is the way in which an individual uses unconscious organising principles to understand life around him. Bollas (1987), in his description of the 'unthought known', sees transference as not merely a reliving of an earlier relationship but a fundamentally new experience in which elements of psychic life which have not been previously 'thought' are now being given time and space. Schafer (1977) similarly sees transference as 'an emotional experiencing of the past as it is now remembered' and not as it actually happened.

General or specific?

At one stage controversy raged as to whether transference arose only in the therapeutic situation (Waelder 1956) and the analytic relationship (Gill and Hoffman 1982) or was part of relationships in general. There is now general agreement that transference is found within all relationships and also within our attitudes to institutions. For example, someone who repetitively reacts to institutional organisations in a combative and aggressive way may be reliving unresolved battles with his father; similarly, patients in hospital may be disappointed by the way they are looked after. Complaints, stimulated by real defects, may resonate with regret or anger that their needs were not met in a way they had wished them to be by earlier important figures in their life. Nevertheless, the analytic situation clearly favours the development and observation of transference phenomena.

All or part?

More difficult is the question of whether all or only part of the analytic process can be understood as transference. There have been as many attempts to tighten the definition of transference as there have been to broaden it. Anna Freud (1936) wanted to confine the concept of transference to three aspects: transference of libidinal impulses, transference of defence, and 'acting in the transference'. These different aspects of the transference all follow the classical approach in which earlier infantile wishes and former defensive manoeuvres or actions are repeated in the present. A useful overall term is 'enactment', which can occur in the session, or outside it. In the case of 'acting in the transference' infantile wishes stimulated by the analytic work are enacted outside the analytic situation. This concept is so similar to acting out (see p. 194) – although acting out is usually seen as a failure to draw a problem into the transference rather than a result of the transference itself – that it has fallen into disuse. It also needs to be distinguished from 'acting in' (*q.v.* pp. 189–94) when a patient acts rather than puts feelings into words in the course of a session.

Strachey (1934) was the first to spell out the interpersonal implications of transference. For him transference is essentially a *misperception* in which the analyst is seen in the distorted light of the superego – idealised, denigrated, seen as harshly punitive or judgemental. In everyday life transferences create the vicious circles of neurosis since others are recruited to behave (by what is now seen as projective identification, *q.v.* pp. 82–7) in ways that confirm the transferential preconceptions – in other words, people actually appear to *be* harsh, inconsistent, rejecting, etc. The task of the analyst is, by a combination of benign neutrality, by spotting transference as it happens and by conveying this understanding in a 'mutative interpretation', to disconfirm these vicious circles, leading to dynamic change based on the internalisation of a modified and less harsh superego.

Klein (1932) similarly saw transference as a representation of unconscious phantasy, reflecting the relationships of the internal world. Given that within this framework the 'internal world' comprises continuing interaction between unconscious phantasy, defences and experiences with reality both in the past and the present (Spillius 1988), it seems as though almost all of mental life is affected by transference in one form or another. Joseph (1986) has put forward the notion of transference as the 'total analytic situation', but others feel that the term is in danger of becoming overinclusive.

Not everything can be transference (Sandler *et al.* 1969): the analyst, as a real person and someone who is engaged in a specific task with the patient, must also be taken into account. Furthermore, if Strachey's views are valid, some interactions with the analyst *correct* earlier responses to actual environmental failures and therefore cannot be transference in the sense of being repetitions.

Greenacre (1954), like Freud and others, distinguished between a 'basic transference' and the analytic transference proper. The basic transference of implicit trust reflects the early infant–mother relationship and allows the development of the therapeutic alliance while the transference proper mirrors later conflictual aspects of development. The basic transference is a prerequisite for effective work within the conflictual transference relationship. For Brenner (1979), however, these are just different aspects of transference and he rejects the concept of the therapeutic alliance altogether, pointing out that it is just as important to analyse the patient's 'alliance' with the analyst as it is to analyse his resistances. There are important implications for technique in these differences, as analysts taking a partial view may endeavour to develop an area of their relationship with the patient that is free from transference distortions, while those taking a total view will not. Interventions by analysts taking a partial view may then include confirming or reality-oriented statements as well as interpretations to correct the distortions of reality by transference.

Example: The waving patient

A 28-year-old woman who had a rejecting and 'workaholic' father continually formed short-lived sado-masochistic relationships with men. She reported that she had seen her analyst on his bike and had waved to him; he had not returned her greeting but had ignored her. She began to berate him in the session and accuse him of being cruel. Since the analyst had not in fact seen her, he commented that although he could understand that she had felt rejected by him in the street, in reality he had not seen her and so could not have acknowledged her. What was important was the way in which past experience had sensitised her to such unintentional rejections.

This reality-oriented statement was an attempt to discourage pathological distortions prior to interpreting the underlying unconscious phantasies. Later in the session, the analyst took up the obvious links to the past as well as the attempt on the part of the patient to form a retaliatory cruel interaction. More importantly, the analyst searched himself to see whether there had been any contributing factors from himself or within his countertransference reaction to her that had contributed to his not seeing her. Was there anything that he did not wish to see within their analytic relationship? (*See* p. 114.)

There is an important debate as to whether it is technically correct to validate or invalidate a patient's perceptions in this way (Hamilton 1993), or whether to focus solely on the meaning to the patient of everything that happens, relying on the interpretive element itself as a source of security. Many analysts believe that this should depend on the developmental level at which the patient is operating. Borderline patients often have a defective grasp on reality and so need to lean on the analyst's 'ego function' in this way, whereas in neurotic patients a more direct confrontation with the inner world – implicit in interpretation devoid of all reassuring reality confirmations – may have a greater impact.

In summary, transference can be understood in a number of different ways:

- It describes the process through which an individual transfers onto his analyst and others, past experiences, attitudes and feelings that he used to experience in relation to important figures earlier in life.
- It describes the externalisation of internalised object relationships within the analytic process and within everyday relationships.
- It encompasses all unconscious aspects of the analytic relationship, including non-verbal communications.
- It subsumes the concepts of the treatment or therapeutic alliance.
- There may be a resistance to the development of the transference, or the transference itself may become the resistance to resolution of underlying conflict.
- It may be a 'probe' of relational reality (Slavin and Kriegman 1992).
- It can be a manifestation of latent meaning, stimulated by the real relationship with the analyst, but shaped and coloured by past experience.

Special forms of transference

Interest in the analytic treatment of patients with severe psychiatric disorders has led to the identification of several different forms of transference. Freud believed that one major difference between psychotic and neurotic patients was their incapacity to develop a transference relationship, but there is no doubt that he was wrong. (This is an interesting example of how even masters can be blinded to reality by theory: Freud saw psychosis as a retreat into narcissism and so, by definition, all relationships including transference, were impossible.) Recent interest in severe personality disorders has also given rise to more detailed descriptions of transference phenomena in psychotic, erotic or erotised, and borderline and narcissistic disorders (see p. 222). There is, of course, considerable overlap between these different forms of transference: erotised transference is itself often psychotic; borderline and narcissistic transferences are themselves often erotised and may at times be psychotic.

Self-object transference

Self-psychology (see p. 45), arising out of the study of narcissistic patients, pays particular attention to the development of the self. It sees the self in terms of three poles. Self-assertive ambitions crystallise at one pole, attained ideals and values at the other, and talents and skills at the third. Each pole gives rise to self-object (see p. 46) needs which themselves lead to self-object transferences. If the pole of ambitions is damaged a mirroring transference will arise, reflecting the grandiose-exhibitionistic elements of the self. Just as the child who is collected from school is picked out by the parent from all the other children as special, eliciting a 'gleam in his mother's eye', so the patient hopes the analyst will see him as special. Failure of mirroring in childhood leads to lack of cohesion in the self, and low self-esteem. In response the child may escalate attempts to be perfect and become a show-off, continually craving approbation and admiration. Kohut argues that, like a good parent, the analyst should act as a mirror to the patient's tentative search for self-esteem, rather than puncturing it with premature interpretations.

The idealising transference reflects the opposite pole, in which the individual experiences the other as perfect, thereby vicariously strengthening his defective self-esteem. Some degree of idealisation and symbiosis is a normal part of an analytic relationship, especially if the patient has had difficulty in sustaining normal idealisation of parents, and, in later life if all his Gods turn out to have feet of clay. Just as for the mirroring transference, Kohut argues that idealisation should be accepted, since premature interpretation can lead to catastrophic disillusionment and feelings of unworthiness.

In the twinship self-object transference (Kohut 1984) the individual feels unsure of his talents and abilities, and turns to a phantasied alter ego in whom his qualities are more securely grounded and who provides an externalised self-object to whom he can resort at times of loneliness and desolation. Here, too, more conventional interpretations of the need for twinship might see it as a defence against dependency on the analyst or implying inadequacy ('castration anxiety'), if real differences between analyst and patient were to become apparent. Kohut's deficit model (cf. p. 227) implies that the analyst should wait patiently, accepting the patient's necessary narcissistic investment in the analytic relationship, and that premature interpretations would reinforce the patient's already defective sense of value and competence.

Psychotic transference

The term 'psychotic transference' (cf. pp. 214–22) has been used in a variety of ways ranging from situations in which the analyst feels out of touch with the patient, to attempts by the patient to force the analyst to think for him (Searles 1963). The analytic literature uses the term 'psychotic' in a loose way, unrelated to its much tighter definition in psychiatry. Analysts often use the word to describe the way in which some patients seem unable to conceive of others as having minds like their own, or to imagine that they could be held in mind by those who care for them – this would be a psychotic transference since the existence of the analyst as a thinking being is obliterated even if the patient would not be considered psychotic by psychiatrists.

Another use of the term 'transference psychosis' is to describe transient psychotic symptoms occurring in the psychoanalytic session in patients who are faced with an intolerably painful situation (Wallerstein 1967). Such patients have often been accepted for psychoanalytic treatment without the severity of the underlying disturbance being recognised.

Example: the poisonous analyst

A depressed female patient in analysis was also seeing a psychiatrist for depression. A trial of anti-depressant medication had made little difference to her mood and so the psychiatrist decided to try another drug. The patient had rapidly formed a strong bond to her analyst, whom she idealised as the person who was going to help her survive, and so she asked her whether she should take the new anti-depressant. The analyst suggested that she should follow the advice of her psychiatrist, and so she took the new anti-depressant but had severe side-effects after two days. In the next session she accused the analyst of poisoning her and read out a written statement to her about trust and betrayal and demanded that she sign it. Her belief led her to write letters about the analyst's professional misconduct, which she withdrew the following day.

Transient psychotic symptoms such as this during an analytic session seem more likely to be related to earlier experience, and in this particular patient they linked with her experience of her mother, whom she felt had abandoned her to her violent, drunken father – just as she now felt her analyst had abandoned her to the poisoning doctor. Such individuals do not usually break down into a full-blown psychotic state, but are more likely to show further features of borderline personality disorder as treatment continues, such as the development of an erotic or erotised transference.

Erotic transference

Anna O unexpectedly developed such a powerful transference imbued with erotic features towards Breuer that he broke off the treatment, and 'fled the house in a cold sweat'. He went on a second honeymoon to Venice with his wife (Jones 1953), and began distancing himself from psychoanalysis. Thus psychoanalysis began with an *erotic transference*. Freud (1915) later recognised the universality of affectionate and erotic feelings in the transference and saw them as valuable aspects of the analysis, with resistances reflecting the patient's core pathology which could be resolved within treatment. The relationship with the analyst becomes imbued with erotic strivings in order to deflect the relationship from its therapeutic endeavours, thereby avoiding the need to face painful experiences. This transference love has infantile roots and can be present in almost every therapeutic contact whatever the gender mix of the analytic dyad (Bolognini 1994); it is recognised by the patient as being unacceptable and may lead to feelings of shame and embarrassment. It is less clear against which painful experiences transference love defends. Joseph (1987) and Steiner (1982) have suggested that the exciting and gratifying aspects of the interplay between the patient and analyst arise from pathological organisations (*q.v.* p. 79) and may coalesce into an erotic transference as a defence against the guilt and pain of the depressive position, or the fragmentation of the paranoid–schizoid position. On the other hand, from an attachment theory point of view, it is a way of forcing the object to respond when one despairs of a caring reaction. Whatever view is taken, erotic, loving and affectionate strivings can propel an analysis forward if treated sensitively within a sufficiently rigorous setting. A particular form, known as the maternal erotic transference, represents a creative attempt to transform the patient–analyst relationship from pre-oedipal to oedipal issues, and from mother–baby boy dependency, to mother as love object. It contains within it the earliest sensual interactions between mother and infant (Wrye and Welles 1989).

In contrast, the *erotised* transference (Rappaport 1956; Blum 1973) may threaten the very existence of the analysis (Etchegoyen 1991). Erotised transference is distinct from erotic transference and transference-love, in that the demand for sexual gratification is extreme and not experienced by the patient as being unrealistic. The persistence of the demands may lead to a breakdown in treatment or, disastrously, acting out on the part of the analyst. Blum reported that patients developing an erotised transference showed a number of common features in their past, such as sexual seduction in childhood, inadequate parental protection from phase-inappropriate activities, and family tolerance of incestuous/homosexual behaviour. The erotised transference seems therefore to represent a repetition and perhaps a desperate attempt to master the earlier sexual traumata. Not surprisingly, the erotised transference causes severe counter-transference and technical problems for the analyst, and the latter are discussed in Chapter 9. Suffice it to say here that the erotised transference requires all the skill and knowledge of the analyst if treatment is to succeed – as Person (1985) has said, and Breuer discovered to his cost, it is 'both a gold-mine and a mine-field'. Now we must turn to some general questions of countertransference which similarly offers both golden and treacherous opportunities.

COUNTERTRANSFERENCE

No psychoanalyst goes further than his own complexes and internal resistances permit.

(Freud 1910: 145)

The term 'countertransference' has undergone a number of radical changes in meaning since it was introduced by Freud (1910). Initially, like transference, it was regarded as a hindrance to analysis (Freud 1912a), representing the need for further analysis on the part of the analyst; today it is a central part of analytic theory and technique. Broadly speaking, the term 'countertransference' now applies to those thoughts and feelings experienced by the analyst which are relevant to the patient's internal world and which may be used by the analyst to understand the meaning of his patient's communications to help rather than hinder treatment, i.e. 'patient-derived countertransference', in contrast to the earlier notion of 'analyst-derived countertransference' (Langs 1976).

Freud and his immediate followers saw themselves as interpreters of the unconscious meaning of their patient's communications and symptoms and, as such, were experts, detached from the hurly-burly of the session itself, invested with authority and arbiters of the normal and the pathological, of what was real or unreal. Counter-transference interfered with accurate listening to unconscious processes, and led to failures in maintaining the recommended analytic position of a mirror-like posture. It was not considered useful in understanding unconscious communications.

Ferenczi (1921) was the first to challenge this technical stance and, in his 'active techniques', advocating much greater involvement between analyst and patient (see pp. 231–2). However, he continued to see countertransference in terms of the analyst's own difficulties in which he might, for example, narcissistically encourage flattery from the patient. This view continued until after Freud's death. The rise of the object relations school in Britain and the interpersonal tradition (Sullivan 1953) in America began to push for a wider definition. The Balints (1939) predicted the widening of the concept of countertransference but it was Winnicott (1949), Heimann (1950) and Little (1951) who produced the most cogent case for a revision of the concept. Not surprisingly, this split the psychoanalytic movement into those who preferred the new approach and those who wished to retain the more restricted definition of unconscious interferences in the analyst's capacity to understand and interpret appropriately (Fleiss 1953; Reich 1951). For the Interpersonalists, such as Sullivan, this sea-change was a confirmation of their view that *relationship* was the important factor in the treatment of the patient's problems and it represented the final blow to what they felt was the authoritarian and rigid stance of earlier analysts. The mantle of authoritarianism had been thrown off, to be replaced by greater equality and a more democratic and humanistic role for the analyst (Abend 1989). For British analysts it was the start of a creative and fertile debate.

Paula Heimann's paper (1950) remains a cornerstone of con-tempory thinking about countertransference. The essential element of the new idea of countertransference was that the analyst's own feelings, attitudes and associations to the patient's communications and behaviour were helpful in understanding the unconscious processes occurring in the patient, even though the analyst may at first not be fully conscious of them, and only recognise them by careful self-scrutiny. However, Heimann went further than this by regarding 'all the feelings the analyst experiences towards his patient' as countertransference, as well as suggesting that countertransference is not just part of the transference–countertransference dynamic within relationships, but that it is 'the patient's creation, it is part of the patient's personality'. Inevitably this further fuelled the controversy, as it became allied to other Kleinian challenges to Freudian orthodoxy such as questioning the centrality of the oedipus complex. Klein herself was wary of this revisionist view of countertransference and expressed caution about its link with projective identification; nevertheless her colleagues pushed on with the idea that the two concepts were inextricably linked, seeing them as almost indistinguishable.

Countertransference, empathy, and projective identification

In projective identification (*q.v.* p. 82) the patient projects disavowed aspects of himself into the analyst, who becomes unconsciously identified with those parts and may begin to feel or behave in accordance with them. The first aspect of this process is clearly allied to transference while the second can be correlated with countertransference in view of its obvious interactional aspects. Racker (1953, 1957, 1968) explicitly linked the two concepts, distinguishing between what he called complementary and concordant countertransferences.

Complementary countertransferences are emotions that arise out of the patient's treatment of the analyst as an object of one of his earlier relationships, and are closely linked to the notion of projective identification. *Concordant* countertransferences are empathic responses, based on the analyst's resonances with his patient and are not solely a result of projective identification. Concordant countertransferences link with affective attunement, empathy, mirroring and a sense that certain aspects of all relationships are based on emotional identifications that are not solely projections. Similarly, Money-Kyrle's (1956) 'normal countertransference' is akin to empathy, and yet it remains unclear as to how empathic responsiveness or the sharing of affective states comes about, even though Money-Kyrle linked it with rapid projective and introjective processes. Stern's (1985) 'affective attunement' between mother and baby, and, by extension, between patient and analyst, is a different way of explaining such interaction, involving as it does the ability of the mother (analyst) to 'read' the patient's behaviour and respond in a complementary manner, which is in turn 'read' by the child (patient). One feeling state has been knowable to another and both sense that the transaction has taken place without the use of language (see Chapter 3). Affective attunement can perhaps be distinguished from empathy, although both share the same stem of emotional resonance (Hoffman 1978). Affective attunement takes place outside consciousness while empathy involves cognitive processes. In empathy, the initial emotional resonance in the analyst is followed by an empathic abstraction using conscious knowledge based on earlier understanding and experience. This leads in turn to an integrated empathic response based on transient role identification with the patient. Affective attunement is a more immediate emotional response, much like one may shout 'aaaagh' and suck one's finger when someone else hits theirs with a hammer.

One may ask whether all these are not simply 'positive' aspects of 'normal', as opposed to pathological, projective identification. As we have seen in Chapter 3, 'projective identification' is sometimes usefully confined to a pathological, albeit widespread process, based on an externalisation and actualisation of an internal object relationship in which the analyst takes on a particular role that is thrust upon him. In empathy, for example, there is no such enforced role and the analyst uses a transient identification process to experience the underlying or expressed affect of the patient. This process is dependent on the analyst's capacity for regression within himself, or 'regression in the service of the ego' (Kris 1952, 1956), while maintaining a hold on his ability to think and reflect.

Casement (1985), following Fliess (1942), uses the term 'trial identification' and suggests that the analyst has to maintain a benign split within himself to allow a constant interplay between thinking and feeling, between himself and the patient, and between his experience and the events the patient is talking about. Sandler (1993) uses the term 'primary identification' for an equivalent process and regards it as similar to automatic mirroring. Thus, if the analyst has a direct emotional reaction to a patient's actions or behaviour, and this reaction is not one into which he is being unconsciously pushed, then this should not be seen as projective identification but recurrent primary identification. He sees primary identification as a mirroring in the analyst of whatever the patient expresses in verbal or non-verbal form, and if this is taken to include unconscious communication, then everything the patient expresses is also fleetingly experienced by the analyst.

Only if such identifications stimulate unresolved unconscious wishes within the analyst will conflict arise, which results in the mobilisation of defences and the formation of blind-spots within the analytic relationship. This concept of primary identification is very close to Grinberg's (1962) idea of projective counteridentification, in which the analyst identifies with and is temporarily taken over by aspects of the patient's unconscious process. However, Grinberg takes the process a stage further, invoking the defensive aspects of the identifications which often take the form of distancing the analytic relationship. For example, feelings of inadequacy engendered in the analyst by the patient may lead to annoyance or overzealous attempts to help the patient.

Bion's (1962) formulation of the container and the contained explicitly linked projective identification with developmental processes and relates to the idea of normal countertransference in which the transference–countertransference dynamic moves along constructively between patient and analyst. In Bion's model, feelings are communicated to the other, digested and returned to the projector in a modified and acceptable form. It is when this process is disrupted by problems of understanding on the part of the analyst, or his inability to communicate, that trouble arises and pathological projective identification emerges. The patient hopes to find better understanding by escalating the projections and makes the analyst feel just as he himself was forced to feel by important others in his past. The analyst may only realise that he has been pulled into such a position after reacting inappropriately in some way. Sandler (1976b) considers this as 'role responsiveness' on the part of the analyst, with the patient attempting to bring about in reality an unconscious wishful phantasy by forcing the analyst to play a particular part while he himself takes another role. There is then a constant interplay between the two roles, and the analyst needs to be both involved and detached, listening to the patient and reflecting on himself to extricate himself from such a role. The cold reflecting mirror is no longer an appropriate metaphor or desirable technique. The clinical emphasis needs to be on those parts of the patient that are projected into the analyst and the extent to which the analyst can 'metabolise' or 'digest' the feelings that are engendered without enacting them with the patient.

Example: Further thoughts on the waving patient (see p. 104)
After accepting that he had not seen his patient waving at him, the analyst began to wonder if there was a blind-spot in himself, if he was not seeing something in the analytic material, or if he was failing to address an aspect of his patient. In searching himself and reflecting on earlier material, the analyst realised that he had been making a large number of empathic remarks in recent sessions. This was unusual. For example, when his patient had been talking about her father's rejections, he had taken up how hurt she had felt and how she must have wished for his love. Beneath this, he had felt increasingly sleepy and unable to think. Perhaps, then, he was being pushed by his patient to feel sleepy to ensure he did not see something in her and, if so, was his feeling arising from the patient's own wish not to awaken something in herself? Utilising his sleepiness as a countertransference response, the analyst interpreted that perhaps she herself was wanting to be seen but something in her was asleep, unable to be roused. It emerged that the patient's tender and loving feelings were hidden and lost in the sessions, hidden beneath her sado-masochistic attacks. Furthermore, the analyst realised that his own tender feelings for his patient were also covered over, lost in his empathic remarks. He had been blind to them. These feelings were, in part, relevant to his patient, and, in part, related to his own anxieties about his feelings towards his female patient. Later in her analysis it was apparent that the analyst's tender feelings for his patient represented the unexpressed feelings that the patient yearned for from her father – part of a complementary countertransference.

Brenman-Pick (1985) has expanded Bion's idea of the containing function of the analyst and emphasises the need for the analyst to be open and receptive to the patient's unconscious communications, which are mostly viewed as projections. She suggests that the analyst has his own primitive functions within his personality which may be in collusion with the projections of the patient, through identification, and until 'disidentification' takes place the projections will not be analysable or even recognisable. This is a return to the classical conception of countertransference, and Reich (1951) put forward a similar idea using the term 'defensive countertransference' for situations in which the analyst is unable to recognise intolerable material. The task of the analyst is an uncoupling of the pathological identifications within himself, so that the desire not to know is transformed into a possibility of knowing – in Bion's terminology 'minus K' becomes 'K'. Only then will the patient be able to face those aspects of himself that he does not wish to accept, and take back his projections in the same way as has the analyst. This view follows the idea that the analyst has symmetrical, or concordant, aspects in his personality with those of his patients, and emphasises greater equality within the relationship.

A further influence on the formulation of countertransference can be detected through the work with borderline and psychotic patients which began in the 1950s and 1960s. Winnicott (1949) coined the term 'objective hate' to describe a natural response in the analyst to the patient's outrageous behaviour, which he believed did not arise from unresolved conflicts in the analyst. It was a normal common-sense reaction to provocative and intolerable behaviour. This was important in that it removed the pejorative, guilt-inducing aspect of countertransference prevalent at the time. Kernberg (1984), in his work with patients suffering from borderline and other severe personality disorders, sees countertransference as a multi-faceted process in which the difficult emotional feelings aroused in the analyst are:

(a) a reaction to the patient's premature and chaotic transferences;
(b) a reflection of the difficulties of withstanding severe psychological stress and anxiety;
(c) related to the projective systems of the patient.

The projected components are considered to stimulate primitive aspects of the analyst's personality, much in the same way as was suggested by Brenman-Pick, allowing him to understand the patient better, to interpret effectively and to empathise appropriately.

Table 5.2 summarises the various meanings associated with the

Table 5.2 Definitions of countertransference

- Affective resonance and empathy (Stern, Winnicott)
- The results of projective identification (Klein, Bion, Steiner, etc.)
- Part of the bipersonal or intersubjective field (Sullivan, Langs)
- The analyst's response, conscious or unconscious, to the patient's transference (Heimann, Sandler)
- The analyst's transference response to the patient, i.e. the patient representing important people from the analyst's past (Freud)
- The analyst's blind-spots or resistances (Freud, Sandler)
- All reactions of the analyst to his patient (Joseph)

concept of countertransference. Once again, countertransference illustrates Sandler's (1983) notion of conceptual 'elasticity'. The different definitions of countertransference depend upon how narrow or broad a boundary is drawn around the term.

The focus in contemporary psychoanalysis is mainly on countertransference as a means by which the patient's mental state is communicated to the analyst. This communication happens in a number of different ways, not all of which are, strictly speaking, countertransferential. First, there are the analyst's capacities for affective resonance, empathy, trial identification and primary identification. Second, the analyst may have an immediate reaction to something about the patient – such as feeling frightened if he is threatened – which may not be a result of the patient's unconscious intent. Third, feelings in the analyst may arise through the process of projective identification in which there is an unconscious requirement for the analyst and the patient to enact something. Fourth, the analyst's intellectual and cognitive abilities and the understanding from his training will enable him to follow the thread of his patient's communications.

The projective identificatory aspects of countertransference have received the most attention from Kleinian analysts. Affective resonance, empathic responses, primary and trial identificatory processes have gained the interest of the ego psychologists and other developmentally oriented analysts. Knowing how and when to use countertransference – the transformation of the analyst's feelings into useful work, his intellectual understanding into affectively relevant interpretation, his direct reaction into understanding, his identification and sympathy into empathic comprehension – are the quintessential skills of the analyst.

Conclusions: the bipersonal field

Overall, the controversy about the definition of countertransference has abated, and there is a broad consensus that it refers to the emotional responses aroused in the analyst by specific aspects of the patient. Langs (1978), in putting forward the concept of the *bipersonal field*, has firmly located countertransference as an interactional phenomenon, and not solely within the realm of either the patient or the analyst. The bipersonal field refers to a temporal–physical field, whose limits are defined by the analytic structure in which the patient and analyst interact, both contributing from their own psychological worlds. If we regard the analytic dyad as two mutually influencing psychological systems, then the intermingling of transference and countertransference becomes a subtle interplay of these systems within a highly charged affective milieu – a four-way matrix between the patient's and the analyst's conscious and unconscious systems. Unconscious phantasy and conscious knowledge of the patient influence those of the analyst and vice versa along a two-way channel in which any combination of influencing processes may occur (Arlow 1993). Money-Kyrle (1956) predicted such developments by suggesting that the emotional task of the analyst is to distinguish his own unconscious phantasies from those of his patient. Failure to do so leads to 'positive countertransference', which takes the form of placating the patient and giving reassurance, or a 'negative counter-transference' in which the patient is attacked. More recently, Baranger (1993) has argued that there is a shared unconscious phantasy rooted in the unconscious of both participants which is the creation of the intersubjective or bipersonal field itself – a concept akin to Bion's idea of a group mind formed in group therapy (Bion 1952). This presupposes an active participation by the psychic processes of the analyst as well as the patient, overthrows the notion of the analyst as a neutral mirror, and moves the analytic encounter from the objective towards the subjective. Transference and counter-transference have become complementary processes which mix together to form a unique pattern in each analysis, and the analysis has its own personal history and culture created by both patient and analyst.

Chapter 6

Dreams, symbols, imagination

Psychical reality is a particular form of existence not to be confused with material reality.

(Freud 1900: 620)

From a psychoanalytic perspective, psychological health depends on a balance between adaptation and innovation, attachment and separation, integration and regression, the inner and outer worlds. We now turn to the uncoupling of inner from outer reality in dreams and imaginative play. As the demands of adaptation are relaxed so a clearer picture of the inner world emerges – a window or 'royal road' (Freud 1900) to the understanding of the unconscious.

Freud considered *The Interpretation of Dreams* his finest as well as his most personal work, laying the foundations for the entire edifice of psychoanalysis. 'Insight such as this falls to one's lot but once in a lifetime', he claimed, explaining how writing it was 'a portion of my own self-analysis' stimulated by 'my reaction to my father's death – that is to say, to the most important event, the most poignant loss, of a man's life' (Freud 1900).

That statement in itself locates its author – historically, ethnically, and by gender. In the century since Freud first started to try to understand his dreams much has changed in the worlds of both neuroscience and of psychoanalysis. In the course of this chapter we shall trace some of those changes; but we begin with an exposition of Freud's model of the mechanism of dream formation and their interpretation.

FREUD'S MODEL

Freud started from two fundamental questions. What is the function of dreaming – why do we dream at all – and how do we account for the strangeness of dreams, their bizarre nature? As we shall see, his answers to both these questions are, in the light of subsequent knowledge, at least partly wrong. We should also note at this stage his wish to link dreams with abnormal mental functioning: 'it is my intention to make use of my present elucidation of dreams as a preliminary step towards solving the more difficult problem of the psychology of the neuroses'.

When, on the night of 24 July 1895, Freud dreamed his famous 'specimen' or 'Irma' dream, his self-analysis led him to believe that he had solved the problem of the purpose of dreaming – he had fulfilled his dream – 'a dream is the fulfilment of a wish'.

Example: Freud's 'specimen' dream
'Irma' was a patient – Emma Eckstein (Schur 1966; Roazen 1979) – about whom Freud was worried; the day before the dream he had met a colleague, 'Otto' (Dr Oscar Rie), who had seen her recently; Freud asked how she was; 'better, but not quite well', came the reply. In the dream, Freud meets her at a party; he sees that she is unwell and worries that he has missed an organic illness; Freud and three other doctors then examine her; she opens her mouth and they find large white patches on what look like turbinate (i.e. nasal) bones; Freud decides that she *is* unwell and that this must be due to an injection of 'trimethylamin' from a dirty syringe given her by Otto. He sees the formula for trimethylamin in front of him printed in heavy type; in the analysis of the dream Freud connects this with the sexual theories of Fliess, who also believed that there was a link between the nose and the genitals and had in fact operated on 'Irma's' nose.

Freed from the constraints of reality, under the sway of the pleasure principle, and in response to some current preoccupation, or *day's residue*, a person's deepest feelings and desires are activated. By blaming his friends and colleagues, the Irma dream acquitted Freud of responsibility for the deterioration in Irma's condition about which he felt so guilty. But these desires, often expressions of infantile sexuality (although, curiously, Freud hardly touches on these aspects – four men examining a female 'cavity', one of them a 'dirty squirter' (Erikson 1954)) are disturbing to the conscious mind, whose awareness of the constraints and prohibitions of reality, although relaxed in sleep, is not wholly in abeyance. The disturbing wishes threaten the peacefully sleeping consciousness, which wants no more than to remain in slumber. The wishes therefore are cleverly disguised in the compromise created by the *dream work*: in their modified form they are relieved of their energy, their cathexis is discharged, without at the same time awakening the sleeper. Thus: 'the dream is the guardian of sleep'. Like a secret code in times of war, a hidden message has been smuggled through hostile enemy lines (the *censor*), without suspicions being aroused by its *manifest* content. The bizarreness of dreams is a consequence of this scrambling of the original, or *latent*, content of the dream.

Interpreting dreams, a primary tool of analysis, means reversing this process of disguise, undoing the dream work to reveal the original wish beneath it, just as the hysteric was to have the underlying impulse behind her symptom uncovered so that she could own her desire and so no longer be in thrall to it. In order to interpret dreams the analyst needs to understand the mechanisms of dream work which turns 'thoughts previously constructed on rational lines' (Freud 1900) into the puzzling imagery and juxtapositions of a dream. Dream analysis, as Freud conceived it, is a triumph of the rational over the irrational.

Freud considered several methods by which, as he saw it, the original dream thoughts are modified on their journey from the unconscious to the manifest narratable dream. In *condensation* different elements are combined or fused into a single image, so that the explication or unpacking of such an image is invariably longer and more complex than the dream itself. To take an unusual but amusing example, Rycroft (1979b) cites the case of a man named Ernest whose dream consisted of the single word *Frank* – who had been tempted into financial deceit, and who needed to remind himself of the importance of being honest.

Example: puns and amalgamations

Another example of condensation occurred in the dream of a highly ambitious and narcissistic man whose mother had been both seductive and inaccessible. He dreamed that he *met a friend on a train whom he hadn't seen for a long time. When he asked him what he was doing these days the man replied that he was appearing in a television programme called 'knockers'*. The 'man' was a condensation of two successful colleagues of the patient whom he imagined, in contrast to his own faltering career, had access to all the girls and the glory which he lacked. The condensed double meaning of 'knockers' contained both his envious tendency to 'knock' worldly success, and a derogatory 'macho' word for the breasts which he enviously imagined the colleagues enjoying.

Displacement resembles the prestidigitation of the magician: the censor's attention is distracted by a shift of emphasis, so that what is important in the dream may appear in the manifest content as insignificant, and vice versa. For example, a young man with anxiety about making love to his girlfriend was initially puzzled by a dream in which he was *swimming in deep water, doing the breast-stroke*, until he suddenly realised in the dream an allusion to his fears of moving from foreplay to penetration.

A central concept in Freud's unravelling of the meaning of dreams is that of associations, or trains, of thought. *Free association* forms the basis of the technique of dream analysis in which the dreamer explores his responses to elements in the dream, following the *fundamental rule* in which no memory or idea is rejected however trivial, embarrassing or irrelevant it may seem. With the help of free association the dreamer gains access to his dream thoughts which have, 'under pressure of the dream-work . . . broken into fragments and jammed together – almost like pack-ice' (Freud 1900). In this process of jamming together, or condensation, the logical connections between ideas – which linguistically take the form of words like 'as' and 'because' and 'if' – have been obliterated, and thoughts are presented in visual rather than verbal form. These processes Freud calls *representation* or *dramatisation*.

In the second and subsequent editions of *The Interpretation of Dreams*, under the influence of his disciple Stekel (whom he subsequently repudiated), Freud included a discussion of *symbolisation* in dreams. The 'Freudian symbol' has become a cliché, but Freud believed that the fundamental biological issues such as birth, death, parenthood, sibling relationships and sexuality were represented in dreams by symbols which tended to be universal and to reflect man's archaic psychic heritage. This idea was later greatly elaborated by Jung, in his notion of 'archetypes'. This view of symbols conflicts somewhat with Freud's critique of the 'dream-book' approach to dream interpretation, and his insistence on the personal meaning of the dream elements, to be illuminated primarily by free association. For example, a woman who had just suffered a miscarriage dreamed of *a small cutting from a plant that was pulled up by its roots and died*. Here displacement becomes a special case of the general phenomenon of symbolisation. Another example warns against facile readings of symbols into dreams:

Example: a Freudian fish

A woman dreamed that she was *holding a large live fish that wriggled frighteningly within her grasp.* 'A fish', she said, 'that's a Freudian symbol – it must be a penis.' But when asked for her associations she remembered that her mother was a piscean, and a fanatical believer in astrology, and the dream led to a discussion of her fear of her mother's disapproval of her being in analysis.

The final phase of the dream work was called by Freud *secondary elaboration* or *secondary revision*. This term refers to the way in which, in remembering and telling the dream, the subject automatically edits and cleans up the text, to give it greater coherence and intelligibility. With his mistrust of the manifest content Freud saw this as a further obfuscation of the dream's true meaning. He pointed out that if the dreamer is asked to repeat his dream, elements that have been left out in the first telling emerge, often with great significance. For example, a woman whose mother had had a puerperal depression after a stillbirth when the patient was 3 years of age, recalled on second telling a dream in which '*I was in a large house, empty and rather gloomy . . . oh, I've just remembered, my mother was there, crying and turned away from me*'?

Although Freud remained loyal to his original conceptions about dreaming – and, by the 1930s, bemoaned their relative neglect by the new generations of analysts (Freud 1932) – he did recognise one outstanding exception to the wish-fulfilment hypothesis. This is the phenomenon of post-traumatic dreams in which the sufferer repeatedly dreams of an undisguised painful or terrifying event. He understood this in terms of the attempt to gain mastery over psychic stimuli which threaten to overwhelm the organism (Freud 1920) – in Bion's terms, to contain the uncontainable (Garland 1991). Here, too, the dream was seen to have a purpose: to 'bind' psychic energy, a necessary precursor to the normal processes of repression and discharge via dreaming. Anzieu (1989, in Flanders 1993) has argued that, rather than being an exception to the wish-fulfilment rule, all dreams can be seen as based on the micro-traumata that comprise the day's residue in need of psychic processing.

POST-FREUDIAN PSYCHOANALYTIC VIEWS OF DREAMING

Each of the different psychoanalytic schools has developed its own slant on dreams. Jung (1974) was the first to dissent from Freud, although his views represent more a shift of emphasis than a radical departure. He saw dreams as openly rather than clandestinely expressive of the inner world: 'a symbol does not disguise, it reveals', and thus paid more attention to the manifest content of the dream than Freud would have recommended. In line with his idea of the repressed bisexual 'shadow' self he saw dreaming as springing from the 'compensation principle' by which dreams 'try to re-establish equilibrium by restoring the images and emotions that express the state of the unconscious'. In this move from drive to self he saw the dream as peopled by aspects of the self that the dreamer had neglected or suppressed, an idea that was to re-emerge in a different guise with the development of self-psychology. Here the dream as a manifestation of the unconscious is not so much 'irrational' as representing a different sort of rationality: in Rorty's (1989) phrase 'it feeds us our best lines'.

The Interpretation of Dreams contains the first comprehensive account of Freud's 'topographical' theory of the mind (see Chapter 2, p. 31). Freud never fully revised his ideas on dreaming in the light of his more mature 'structural' model (Freud 1923). At the end of his life he did concede a synthetic conflict-solving role to the dreaming ego in reconciling the demands of the id and superego (Freud 1940, quoted in Flanders 1993), more akin to the revelatory Jungian model. Ego psychologists have developed this theme by emphasising the importance of the dream's manifest content, seeing the dream as a construction by the ego, based on the attempt to recover repressed affective experience (Brenner 1969, in Flanders 1993). Erikson (1954), in a classic paper, re-analysed the 'Irma' dream and showed how the manifest content reveals an ego struggling with all the doubts and conflicts that beset Freud, especially his wish to become both recognised as a leader and yet remain separate from the gentile medical establishment. The Irma dream is undoubtedly a 'dream from above' (Freud 1925b) – i.e. one stimulated by current conflicts rather than originating 'from below', based primarily on infantile conflicts – given recent historical research which suggests that Freud was preoccupied with his anxieties about the rather dubious nasal operation performed on 'Irma' by Fliess, whom he was about to drop as a mentor (Loewenstein *et al.* 1966).

An important breakthrough in the analytic understanding of dreams occurred with Lewin's (1955) notion of the *dream screen*. With the advent of film in the early decades of the century the cinematic quality of dreams had been noted many times, but Lewin asked, 'What is the "screen" upon which the dream is projected?' He suggested that it is the maternal breast, flattened and invisible, except in 'blank' dreams. As Pontalis (1974, in Flanders 1993) puts it: 'to Freud, the dream was a displaced maternal body . . . he committed incest with the body of his dream'.

Lewin's insight led object relations analysts to realise that the *dream itself is an object*, and that the way a patient relates, and relates to, his dreams is as significant as the content of the dream itself. Thus the patient who overwhelms his analyst with long, tortuous and muddling dreams may be conveying an experience of confusion and psychic entrapment; or he may 'evacuate' his dreams into the passive analyst as a way of ridding himself of hostile and frightening feelings. An obsessional recording of dreams and de-tailed recounting of them in the session may reflect the patient's sense of an inner world that is only just alive so that each creative product has to be preserved and revered, a fear of losing what is good inside himself; there may be a contrast between a dramatic and vivid dream life and the depression and emotional poverty of the patient's waking hours. 'We know too well that patients learn to exploit our interest in dreams by telling us in profuse nocturnal productions what they should struggle and learn to tell us in straight words' (Erikson 1954).

The idea of the dream screen creates a context for the dream: the dreamer and his relationship to the analyst matters as much as the dream. The patient who told her analyst of a dream in which there was a *perfectly harmonious moment of peace in which you lay beside me and put your arm around me, in a non-sexual way* felt anxious and tense throughout most of her sessions and had intense waking phantasies of sexual involvement with him. The 'bliss' dream represented a wish for a moment of maternal reverie – sadly absent in her childhood – but also a reproach to the analyst for failing to provide what she wanted so badly in her waking life.

Once the dream is grasped in a context of relationships it is possible to see dreams, in Freud's terms, as *sleeping thoughts*: 'The dream is fundamentally nothing more than a special *form* of our thinking' (Freud 1900). As Brenner (1969, in Flanders 1993) puts it, 'we are never fully awake *or* asleep'. Bollas (1993) has shown how we unconsciously assemble around us objects, interests and occupations in our waking life that reflect our core unconscious 'preoccupations' (or 'destiny'), just as the dream is furnished with the contents of our inner world. He sees interpretation as a condensation of this ceaseless quotidian activity of phantasy, in which through his interpretative 'stories', 'the analyst dreams his patient' (Bollas 1993).

Self-psychology approaches the dream as an existential statement, continuing Jung's idea of the dream as a manifestation of the inner self or selves, with an equilibrating function based on the 'need to maintain the organisation of experience' (Stolorow *et al.* 1987). Kohut (1983) writes of 'self-state dreams', in which the manifest content is an expression of the patient's current state of being. The young man who dreamed that he was *clinging to his mother telling her he was dead*, was expressing his lack of inner aliveness, his pervasive anxious attachment and was accusing her of robbing him of his liveliness. It is a useful rule of thumb for the analyst to assume that all the 'characters' in a dream represent parts of the patient's self, and that aggression, sexuality, submission, anxiety, persecution, retribution, etc., may be split off from the waking self, but embodied and so potentially recoverable through the analysis of their appearance in dreams.

DREAMS AND MODERN NEUROSCIENCE

There has been a gradual shift within psychoanalysis away from Freud's original twin preoccupations with the *function* of dreaming as wish fulfilment and the pre-eminence of the latent content, towards a widened emphasis on the *meaning* of dreams, the continuity of manifest and latent content, and the dream as part of a total analytic relationship. These changes are consistent with modern neurophysiological ideas about dreaming. The discovery by Aserinsky and Kleitman (1953) of Rapid Eye Movements (REM) associated with dreaming stimulated a burst of sleep research. An important finding was that REM (or whatever neurochemical events underlie it) appear to be essential for mental health – subjects deprived of REM (by repeated waking while asleep) deteriorate into a confused state much more quickly than those deprived of non-REM sleep. This led Rycroft to claim that Freud's original discovery about dreaming was now reversed in that we do not so much dream in order to sleep, as sleep in order to dream (Rycroft 1979b). However, not all REM is associated with dreaming, and not all dreaming is associated with REM. Dreaming appears to be a response to arousal during sleep, of which REM is the most common, but not the only, source (dreams occur in response to external stimulus like an alarm clock, and during nocturnal seizures), and therefore Freud's idea that a dream is an attempt to maintain sleep in the face of arousal remains plausible (Solms 1995).

The dominant neurophysiological paradigm in dream-research is Hobson's (1988) *activation-synthesis hypothesis*. Freud assumed, teleologically, that the ultimate purpose of mental activity was the discharge of accumulated psychophysiological 'energy' and so a return to a presumed state of quiescence. As we have described, he saw dreaming as a sort of discharge by stealth. It now seems more likely that the main 'purpose' of dreaming is informational rather than energetic – the ordering and storage of accumulated information, so that it can be available in the waking state to enable better adaptation to external reality.

Hobson (1988) has argued that, with external stimulation blocked, the brain stem starts spontaneously to activate neural activity in the cerebral cortex. Recently activated pathways (the 'day's residue') are particularly affected. Presented with an array of disparate activated memories and experiences, the brain, as a compulsive meaning-maker, tries to assemble them into some kind of meaningful pattern – into a coherent story. The bizarreness and vividness of dreams results from the random nature of the activation process, the lack of an external context, and absence of modulatory neural activity.

In Freud's model, meaning is *subtracted* from the latent dream thoughts in order to evade the censor; activation-synthesis sees meaning as *added* to a potentially incoherent array of images. The dreaming brain is not struggling to disguise coherent but unacceptable thoughts, but to make sense of an array of chaotic imagery. However, Hobson's somewhat anti-psychoanalytic views are far from fully established. People with abnormalities in their sensory–motor cortex continue to dream normally – hemiplegic patients move in their dreams, aphasics can speak normally when dreaming, those with cortical blindness and deafness can see and hear – which contradicts the view that dreams result from random stimulation of cortical pathways, and suggests a much more complex representational process at work (Solms 1995), deriving from a 'higher' cerebral level than the motor or sensory cortex.

Freud was right that dreams inevitably reflect the wishes and preoccupations of the dreamer because these organise the incoming material in a meaningful way. This view is consistent with Wittgenstein's (in Gustavson 1964) early critique of the psychoanalytic model of dreaming, in which he argued that anyone offered a random collection of objects on a table and asked to link them together in a story would inevitably create a narrative which reflected his underlying personal themes and wishes. It is also similar to Dennett's (1993) philosophical psychoanalytic party game in which a 'dupe' can be induced to construct a 'dream' out of random answers to his questions, thereby indicating the mind's overwhelming need to create narrative, often based on unconscious preconceptions, out of incoming information, however meaningless.

The relevance of activation-synthesis to contemporary psychoanalysis is that it suggests that the interpretation of a dream is likely to reflect not just the wishes and preoccupations of the dreamer, but those of the analyst as well: the dream itself becomes a sort of Rorschach – or blank screen – upon which each school of psychoanalysis projects its own version of the psychoanalytic story. Freud was right in his insistence on the importance of breaking the dream into its component fragments, and being guided by the patient's free associations: 'dream interpretation . . . without reference to a dreamer's associations, would . . . remain a piece of unscientific virtuosity of very doubtful value' (Freud 1925b). This is not because of the need to unscramble the *dream's* latent thoughts, but because this procedure will guard against the intrusion of the analyst's meaning-making, and leads, via the day's residue, to current conflicts, and so to the *dreamer's* 'latent thoughts' – the assumptions, preoccupations and phantasies that guide his attempts to synthesise experience into a coherent and meaningful whole. If we view the analytic relationship as a 'bipersonal field' (Langs 1976) then we can picture an interpenetration of the patient's and analyst's unconscious phantasy lives, so that the dreams of one will be influenced by those of the other (cf. p. 116).

DREAMS AND THE LANGUAGE OF THE UNCONSCIOUS

The movement from mechanism to meaning suggests that there is a dream *language* which the analyst needs to learn to understand. Ella Sharpe (1937), in her classic *Dream Analysis*, systematically compares the language of dreams with poetic diction, as does her analysand Charles Rycroft (1985) who notes Darwin's quotation of Richter: 'the dream is an involuntary kind of poetry'. She relates condensation to metaphor in which similarities are found in the apparently dissimilar (as, for example, in the use of shots of trains entering tunnels or firework displays to represent sex in pre-war

Hollywood films, at a time when the censor insisted that a man's foot remain in contact with the floor at all times during love scenes). Displacement uses both metonymy, in which comparisons are evoked by linguistic proximity ('*breast-stroke*' which evokes thoughts of both swimming and sex), and synecdoche, in which the part stands for the whole (*fish* standing for the zodiac, the zodiac standing for mother). Punning and onomatopoeia are integral to dream language: *knockers* (in the example on p. 120); Segal's (1991) patient who dreamed of soldiers marching *eight abreast* (ate a breast); names such as *Bournemouth, Master Bates, Chester, Prixford*.

Poetry, like dreams, is *polysemic* (i.e. contains many possible meanings, all of which are mutually compatible) and prefers the particular to the general. My love is not just universal love, but one that's like a rose, a 'red, red' one, that's 'newly sprung in June'. As Sharpe (1937) puts it: 'the bridges of thought are crossed and recrossed by *names*, and names have manifold mutations' – evoking the multiple connections and pathways of the nervous system that underlie memory, and the way in which memory storage is spread throughout the brain rather than localised in any one place.

Lacan's (1966; Bowie 1991) famous aphorism 'the unconscious is structured like a language' is based on the fundamental linguistic distinction between the 'signified', i.e. that which is represented – for example, the furry feline domestic quadruped which has just walked into the room – and the 'signifier', i.e. that which represents, in this case the word 'cat'. In Lacan's view, dream representation is always in the form of Freud's 'rebus', i.e. a picturegram in which the realm of the 'real' or signified – primordial unstructured experience – is encoded in the symbolism of the 'signifier'. Dream language reminds us that what we call 'reality' has been worked on, transformed in the mind, just as language transforms and creates meanings out of the multiplicity of words and grammatical rules. Lacan's view is similar to Bion's notion of 'alpha elements' which emerge from the interaction between 'beta elements' and a transforming mind, whether in the reverie of the maternal breast, or its analogue, the dreamer and his dream. For Lacan, what we call (and reify as) 'the unconscious' is not 'an occult quality or a black box but the conjectural sub-text [i.e. a set of linguistic rules such as condensation and displacement] that is required in order to make the text of dreams ... intelligible' (Bowie 1991) (cf. sense '2' of the unconscious, p. 29). This leads to the idea of a 'good dream' in which feelings have been symbolically represented in a satisfying way.

SYMBOLISM AND THE CREATIVE IMAGINATION

We have already mentioned the tension between Freud's wish to understand dreams in order to illuminate the neuroses, while at the same time wanting to provide a general psychological account of the workings of the unconscious. REM sleep and dreaming are universal among humans, and indeed many other species. Freud viewed the dream as a sort of neurosis, and the psychotic is sometimes described as a dreamer awake. Does this mean that we are all mad, or at least partially so?

This issue was taken up by Ernest Jones (1916) who argued that there was a phenomenon of 'true symbolism' by which repressed ideas, feelings, and wishes are presented to the conscious mind: As Freud (1916/17) put it: 'the number of things which are represented symbolically in dreams is not great. The human body as a whole, parents, children, brothers and sisters, birth, death, nakedness – and one thing more.' The one thing more, of course, being sex itself. Jones, and probably Freud, seemed to believe that due to 'primal repression' some aspects of life could *only* be represented indirectly via symbols, thus putting repression and the potentiality for neurosis at the heart of dreaming, creativity and cultural life generally, where symbolism is a central feature.

This view has been vigorously challenged, especially by Rycroft (1968, 1979b, 1985), who invokes Freud's fundamental distinction between the primary and secondary processes (see Chapter 2, p. 32). Rycroft sees dreaming as primary process thinking in its purest form and argues that to equate primary processes with pathology and secondary process with psychic health is misguided, since normal mental life requires a balance between the two:

Visual, symbolic, non-discursive mental activity is just simply the way in which we think while asleep ... there is no reason to suppose that symbolism is essentially a device by which dreamers deceive and obfuscate themselves, even though it may on occasion be used as such.

Like Lacan (although, to our Anglo-Saxon minds, somewhat more comprehensibly), Rycroft views psychoanalysis as primarily a linguistic discipline, but one that is biologically based in that it is concerned with the fundamental biological issues that affect us all. Symbolism is central to the expression of the 'few things' we have strong feelings about, not because of repression but simply because *symbolism is the mode of representation of affective experience.* The clinical implications of this are twofold. First, analysis concentrates mainly on symbolic expressions, whether in dreams, transference (metaphor and transference are etymologically identical), jokes, slips of the tongue, or art – in order to get in touch with the patient's feelings in their most vivid form. Second, dream symbolism frequently, if not always, contains implicit reference to the body. A patient who dreamed of a *wooded valley swarming with soldiers* turned out to be thinking about his hostile sexual relationships with women – the wooded valley represented the vulva, the soldiers his sperm – the dream depicting a phenomenon with much wider implications (sperm that is hostile and attacking, rather than loving and tender) than the merely physical, just as the inherent ambiguity of a poetic image has resonances far beyond its initial impact (Holmes 1992b). Sharpe (1937) suggests that the 'dead metaphors' of a patient's speech may also contain cryptic reference to bodily experience – the patient who keeps wandering off the point may have had difficulties in feeding; the man who is always beating about the bush may be suffering from fears about penetration, and so on.

A similar, but more systematic, analysis has been developed by Matte-Blanco (1975, 1988). He contrasts *'bivalent logic'*, equivalent to secondary process thinking, which follows the rules of mathematical logic, in which, for example, if *a* equals *b*, and *b* does not equal *c*, then *a* cannot equal *c*, with 'the principle of *symmetry'*, which tends to obliterate such distinctions and is equivalent to Freud's primary processes. In symmetrisation – a form of overgeneralisation – all members of a set are taken as identical, creating feeling categories such as 'motherliness' or 'breastness'. The bizarreness of dreams would be a manifestation of this collapse of distinctions and the equation of psychic and external reality. He postulates not just two types of thought but a gradient from bivalent to symmetrical with *'bi-logical'* in the middle, which has features of both. Emotions tend to be particularly subject to symmetrical thinking. When falling in love we enter an 'indivisible mode' in which our love-object is the 'most beautiful person in the world'. In psychological illness the balance between symmetrical and bivalent logic breaks down. For example, if the part is taken for the whole, then an angry father may mean an 'angry penis', and this may underlie a symptom such as impotence in which a man may experience his penis as potentially damaging. This viewpoint can be related to the procedures of cognitive therapy (Beck *et al.* 1979) in which bivalent logic is used to challenge a neurotic individual's tendency to make unwarranted generalisations (e.g. 'if I don't succeed in this task, I am a failure'), to 'catastrophise' problems, fail to make distinctions and so on.

Segal (1958), from a Kleinian perspective, has revived the attempt by Freud and Jones to differentiate healthy from pathological use of symbolism in her concept of the *symbolic equation*. This refers to an aspect of psychotic thinking in which the sufferer equates ('symmetrises') the symbol with the thing symbolised – the signifier with the signified. Segal contrasts two patients, both violinists, one of whom justified his refusal to perform in public by exclaiming angrily 'do you expect me to masturbate in public?', while the other had dreams suggesting a link between performance and masturbation, but was able in reality to play satisfactorily. For Segal, symbolic equation is associated with the paranoid–schizoid position and the use of projective identification since, she claims, in order to symbolise we need to be able to see ourselves and our objects as separate: 'only what can be adequately mourned can be adequately symbolised' (Segal 1986). This perhaps begs the question of what is meant by 'adequately', but the distinction is clinically useful:

> Every man marries his mother . . . the wife may symbolise and contain some aspects of the mother, or she may feel to *be* the mother, in which case the marriage carries all the prohibitions and conflicts of the relation to the mother.
>
> (Segal 1991: 57)

Segal arrives – curiously given their very different psychoanalytic backgrounds – at very similar conclusions to Rycroft; namely, that symbolisation is a 'core primary activity' of the psyche, rather than, as Freud and Jones seemed to feel, simply one mode of evading the censor. Symbolisation enables transformation to occur: in Bion's terms symbols are 'unsaturated' (the analogy is with chemicals that are free to form bonds with other elements) and so available for 'realisations'. The inability to use symbols can take either the form of Segal's symbolic equation in which reality is so 'saturated' with phantasy that the two cannot be differentiated, or the opposite, in which the capacity to phantasise is so impaired that affects cannot be put into words – a state known as 'alexithymia' (Nemiah 1977). Both conditions present particular technical problems in analysis: the symbolic equator is unable to maintain the necessary state of 'virtuality' in relation to his analyst, becoming, for example, over-dependent or psychotically angry; the alexithymic may find he is being asked to perform the impossible by talking about his feelings.

Conversely, the recovery of creativity is often a critical moment within an analysis, increasing the patient's sense of self-worth and generativity, and, with the discovery of an impersonal creative force within, marking a movement away from narcissism and the use of projective identification, to more mature object relations.

Example: breaching the self-sufficient circle of narcissism
A man in his late twenties entered analysis complaining of depression after a failed marriage. He felt dull and useless, was envious and competitive with women, and was failing to progress in his career. His father had died when he was eight and he saw his sisters as having been close to his mother, who, in the absence of his father, had both revered and controlled him. In the first year of analysis his dreams were all in monochrome, as they had been for as long as he could remember. Then he dreamed of *a snake curled round on itself with a tampon in its mouth. The tampon was removed and the snake began to bleed.* He then realised that the dream was in colour, as were his dreams subsequently. Following the dream he felt a surge of creative energy and began to paint furiously. The dream seemed to symbolise an escape from the circle of femininity within which he had grown up, and a chance to mourn his dead father.

PLAY

Psychoanalytic ideas about play are particularly associated with the work of Donald Winnicott (1965, 1971). Winnicott was analysed by Joan Riviere who was in turn greatly influenced by Melanie Klein. Klein introduced play therapy for children, in which the child's use of play materials is seen, like a dream, as an expression of unconscious communication, and can be interpreted just as a dream might be analysed in therapy with adults. Kleinian analysis with adults, especially in its purest form, similarly approaches everything that the patient brings to the session as unconscious material, to be woven into an interpretation in the same way that the elements of a dream are treated.

Example: 'give sorrow words'
A girl of five was referred for therapy because of delay in speaking. With pipe-cleaner figures and a doll's house she silently

demonstrated how her parents slept apart and how her father came into her bed and abused her. At each stage the therapist described in words what was happening – 'now the daddy comes down stairs...', 'now he is getting into bed ...'. Haltingly the girl repeated the therapist's words. The play reflected her inner world, but could only be expressed verbally in the context of a responsive and attuned therapist.

Just as ego psychologists were troubled by the notion of the dream as simply an expression of disguised desire rather than as also the manifestation of a synthesising and self-actualising self (Erikson 1955), Winnicott doubted that play could be seen as a direct manifestation of unconscious thought. He wanted to emphasise the creative, synthetic aspect of play and to put it into an interpersonal object-relations context, while at the same time retaining the idea that it emerged from the depths of the psyche. His notion of *transitional space* tries to reconcile this potential conflict between wish and adaptation to reality. He states that in the 'play area the child gathers objects or phenomena from external reality and uses these in the service of . . . inner or personal reality' (Winnicott 1971). Similarly, in the Jungian and ego psychologist's vision the creative dreamer synthesises the 'day's residue' with deep wishes into a coherent whole.

Winnicott sees the origins of play in the earliest mother–infant relationship where, by her 'primary maternal preoccupation' and intense involvement with the baby, the mother creates an illusion of omnipotence. By anticipating his (or her) wishes he feels he has *created* the reality of the feeding breast, the playful smile, the nurturing arms. Later there will be a gradual process of dis-illusionment, based on healthy protest tolerated by the mother, but an intermediate zone between phantasy and reality has been opened out, a zone which includes play, transitional phenomena such as the famous teddy bears and security blankets, and, later still, cultural phenomena such as the arts, science and sport. The 'soft space' of the transitional zone is precarious and liable to be threatened from within by instinctual needs (hunger must be satisfied before play can occur), or from without by 'impingements' (another favourite Winni-cottian term) such as parental seductiveness leading to false self and failure of real creativity.

Winnicott (1971) described psychotherapy as 'learning to play', a statement similar to Bion's (1970) more abstract notion of the transformation of beta into alpha elements by the analyst's 'thinking breast'. As treatment progresses the analytic session becomes more and more a 'play space', in which, via the analyst's attunement, there develops greater 'give' or 'play' in the analytic relationship, thus enabling the patient to recover his lost creativity and self-hood. Meares (Meares and Coombs 1994) specifically links the problematics of self found in Borderline Personality Disorder (see Chapter 10) with a deficit in playfulness in childhood, arising from neglectful or abusive parenting, and describes the gradual acquisition of playful self-absorbed inner dialogue as successful analysis progresses.

Casement (1985) also uses Winnicottian ideas in his model of analytic treatment of trauma. The original traumatic situation (he describes a case in which a woman's hand was deformed due to being badly burned when she was two years old) has to be reproduced transferentially in the analytic situation so that it can come into the 'area of omnipotence' (Winnicott 1965) of the subject. Only then can it be transcended: when the sufferer feels that he has some control over what happened, and survives. Casement argues against reassurance – in his case, the patient's request that she hold the analyst's hand – in that it short-circuits this process of re-experiencing the trauma in a controlled fashion, akin to a controlled explosion of an otherwise lethal bomb.

If there are important parallels between play and dreaming then analysis could equally be described as 'learning to dream'. Khan, who was much influenced by Winnicott (1962; in Flanders 1993) describes the 'good dream' in which conflict is metabolised and worked on without the intervention of the meddlesome conscious mind, and Sharpe (1937) discusses the dreams of successful analysands in which, she claims, there is evidence of reduced feelings of shame, and greater integration of past and present, body and mind.

CONCLUSION: THE IMPORTANCE OF DREAMS

Although dream analysis may no longer hold the same pride of place as it did for the analytic pioneers, dreams remain central to analytic work. A dream is an indispensable reference point, a marker of the state of the patient's psyche. A dream cuts through intellectualising, and, however confusing, has a freshness and unquestionable validity that verbal speculation about feelings or emotional tendencies may lack. Via the day's residue, it brings into the analysis the important issues of the patient's day. Awareness of dreams puts the patient in touch with the impersonality of his creative psyche, potentially decreasing narcissism and increasing self-esteem and self-mastery. It often brings the transference into clear focus. A recurrent dream can encapsulate the central drama of a patient's life in a vivid form, and subtle alterations in the emphasis of the dream may mark progress in treatment.

Example: claustro-agoraphobia in a recurrent dream

A middle-aged teacher who had grown up on a working-class estate in Scotland, and who veered unhappily between homosexual and heterosexual relationships, repeatedly dreamed of *being by the door of his mother's house and trying to leave but being held by the testicles*. His father had been a violent drunkard and his mother had turned to him for comfort and protection. Early in treatment he saw the dream as representing the way in which his mother 'had him by the balls'; later he began to experience her holding as protective and nurturing.

The technique of dream interpretation remains essentially the same since Freud's first recommendations: break the dream into its component parts; pay particular attention to the patient's free associations; ask the patient to repeat the dream as a way of capturing more of the dream thoughts; do not let the analyst's assumptions and theories impose themselves on the creativity of the dream; do not ever expect fully to understand the dream which retains its impenetrable 'navel'. Post-Freudian approaches see the dream in the total context of the session and the analytic relationship; pay attention to the form and manner of the dream's telling as well as its matter; see the working through of traumatic experience as a central issue in dreaming; and give equal status to the manifest as the latent content.

The dream continues to offer itself both as a mystery and a treasurehouse of meaning. 'What do you think about while you are asleep?', we ask our patients, or say, with Jung (1974), 'now let's get back to your dream. What does the *dream* say?'.

Part II

Practice

Chapter 7

The assessment interview

He that has eyes to see and ears to hear may convince himself that
no mortal may keep a secret. If his lips are silent, he chatters with
his fingertips . . .

(Freud 1905b: 77)

The psychoanalytic assessment interview is important not just
because it represents a critical moment of choice for both patient and
analyst, but because within the harmonies and discords, the false
starts and emerging themes of the initial encounter, are to be found
in microcosm much of what is to come in the course of treatment.

The word 'assessment' is derived from the Latin *assidere*, to sit
beside, but also contains overtones of legal assizes, and the assessment of taxes, in which an individual's assets are reckoned and
weighed in the balance. There are thus two strands in the assessment
interview: an empathic attempt by the analyst to grasp the nature of
the patient's predicament, and a more distanced effort to sum up his
strengths and weaknesses. The analyst will ask himself how 'analysable' is this patient, while he will try to decide what benefit may
flow from his investment in this treatment.

The term 'analysable' can mean 'understandable' or 'treatable',
which are far from the same thing (Tyson and Sandler 1971). For many
patients an assessment interview may help to clarify and illuminate
their difficulties, even if the final decision is against psychoanalysis
as a method of treatment. The purpose of the interview is to provide
sufficient relevant information, and experience of working therapeutically to enable both patient and analyst to decide how to
proceed. The patient will get a snapshot of what analysis might be
like. The analyst, who may or may not take the patient on himself,
has to be engaged enough for an affectively meaningful encounter

with the patient to happen, while at the same time remaining sufficiently objective for his findings to be generalised to other analysts or therapists.

These dual functions – objective and subjective, a view for the analyst of the patient, and for the patient of the analyst – are reflected in the psychoanalytic literature on assessment. Some writers firmly couch themselves in the language of medicine, listing the 'indications' and 'contra-indications' for therapy (Malan 1979), the characteristics of 'analysability' (Coltart 1986), diagnostic and prognostic features (Kernberg 1982), and the developmental level of his personality organisation. Others stress the interpersonal aspects of the first meeting between patient and analyst (Etchegoyen 1991), the process of mutual accommodation, the importance of 'trial interpretations' and the patient's response to them (Hinshelwood 1991). The latter are summarised in the *formulation*, which brings together the central themes of the patient's current and past life situation as manifest transferentially in the interview.

The diagnostic literature has moved from considering 'indications' to an emphasis on 'suitability' (Tyson and Sandler 1971), and, if necessary, to the modifications of psychoanalytic technique required to change a relative contra-indication to one of suitability (Kernberg 1984). Thus a diagnosis of 'hysteria' might suggest a classical indication for treatment, but Zetzel (1968) pointed out that many hysterics are not in practice accessible to analysis. Conversely, psychosis is usually considered a contra-indication, but some psychotic patients with a suitable analyst may well be able to work psychoanalytically (Rosenfeld 1952, see Chapter 10). In this chapter we shall cover both diagnostic and interpersonal aspects, starting with the conduct of the interview and the formulation, and going on to consider issues of diagnosis, treatability and prognosis.

CONDUCTING THE ASSESSMENT INTERVIEW

In the light of what has been said, the analyst approaches the interview with two potentially mutually incompatible aims – to garner relevant factual information, and at the same time to create an atmosphere in which unconscious material can emerge. If direct questioning is eschewed altogether then important data will be lost; if it dominates then all the analyst may get is unelaborated answers to his questions. Many analytic institutes and psychotherapy departments try to overcome this problem by sending the patient a detailed questionnaire to be returned before the interview takes place. This can form a useful basis for discussion, although it can be intimidating for a patient to be asked to reveal intimate details in an impersonal form, and it also has the disadvantage of depriving the interviewer of hearing *how* the patient tells their story – where emphasis is put, the tone of voice used to describe events and relationships, significant omissions, when the narrative style appears avoidant, when enmeshed (Holmes 1995) – all vital sources of psychodynamic information.

Freud frequently compared analytic treatment with a game of chess in which there are an almost infinite number of possible moves, but where phases can usefully be divided into opening strategies, middle game, and end game. The same analogy can be applied to assessment for psychoanalysis. In opening the interview the analyst will probably proceed in a fairly standard way with each patient; the middle game will include attempts at interpretation and observation of their affective impact; and the end game will involve gathering up the threads and coming to a decision about treatment.

Introduction and preliminaries

From the point of view of the unconscious the interview starts from the moment, or indeed well before, analyst and patient meet (Thoma and Kachele 1987):

Example: the imposter
The analyst noticed a momentary look of surprise and hesitation on his patient's face when he went to the waiting room to collect him for the first time. In the interview the young man turned out to be extremely paranoid, and to have apparently suffered greatly at the hands of a harsh step-father. He spoke of how he thought constantly and in an idealised way about his own father, whom he had not seen for many years. When the analyst mentioned his manner in the waiting room, the patient said that he had been expecting someone fat and short and bald, with a beard and a foreign accent, and had imagined for a moment that the person who had come for him was an imposter. They were able usefully to link this transferential percept with his suspicious feelings about his rejecting step-father, and his longing for a 'real' father of his own.

Each interviewer will have his own particular style and set of opening gambits which have to be adjusted to what is required in order to help each individual patient enter into the spirit of the analytic interview. In our view it is important to behave with ordinary professional 'off the couch' courtesy in greeting a new patient, introducing oneself politely, giving one's name clearly and even responding conventionally to apparently trivial (but often significant) remarks which the patient, driven by anxiety, may make between waiting area and the consulting room, while at the same time noting and, if considered appropriate, returning to them in the course of the interview (Coltart 1993). Others argue, however, that the assessor should always be as neutral and as silent as possible in order to arouse the patient's maximum anxiety, and so gain access to areas of possible disturbance which would otherwise be missed in the more conventional atmosphere of a friendly 'bedside manner'.

Example: difficulty in parking
Say, for example, the patient mentions as he sits down that he had difficulty in finding a parking space. The interviewer might (a) agree that parking *has* become a problem in the area, (b) interpret this along the lines of anxiety about whether there is going to be enough therapeutic space for him to 'park' his difficulties, (c) speculate about sibling rivalry and the patient's competitiveness, (d) say nothing, in order to avoid being drawn into a collusive complaint about the crowded state of the roads, rather than focusing on the patient's internal world!

Opening moves

Menninger (1958) argues that since the patient has implicitly asked a question in coming for help, and is likely to be in a state of considerable anxiety, it is up to the analyst to respond by getting the first session rolling. He will then usually hand the initiative to the patient once analysis proper has begun. In general, the analyst will need to be much more active and encouraging in an assessment interview than in subsequent treatment, although a balance still has to be struck between sufficient warmth to enable the patient to unburden, but not so much that the necessary reticence that enhances transference is lost.

A useful opening question can be to enquire what the patient was thinking about as he was coming to the session or waiting to be collected. This signals, from the start, that the analyst is interested in the patient's inner world, and allows the patient to express anxiety in an accepting atmosphere. From then on there are no firm guide-lines and the analyst needs an 'elastic interview technique' (Balint and Balint 1971) which covers all the important areas without prejudice of the order in which they are tackled.

The presenting problem and its antecedents

A clear definition of why, how and for what reason the patient has come for help at this particular moment is essential (Malan 1979), and this part of the interview should never be skimped, however keen the patient may be to move away from the present to talk about childhood trauma, for example. As we shall see below, dynamic understanding of the presenting problem is one of the three legs upon which the tripod of the psychodynamic formulation rests. A state-ment along the lines of 'I've heard a bit about you from your doctor, but it would be best if you could start by telling me in your own words what has brought you for help' will start the session in motion. If the problem has been present for many years, as it often has, then it is essential to clarify the question: '*Why now?*' For example, a not uncommon scenario is the violent husband whose wife has issued an ultimatum that she will leave unless he gets help, and this will need to emerge if the patient's motivation for change is adequately to be gauged.

The interview plan

The analyst will, by the end of the interview, want to have covered the main features of the patient's current circumstances, family background, detailed developmental history including a psycho-sexual history, early memories, history of major losses and traumata (including specific enquiries about sexual abuse), dream life, main areas of interest and aptitude, and sources of both stress and support. Psychiatric aspects, including history of hospital admissions, psycho-tropic drugs, suicide attempts, substance abuse and 'mental state' features such as depressive, obsessional and psychotic phenomena, will also need to have been covered either in the interview in the case of medical psychotherapists, or by the referrer if the analyst is not medically or psychiatrically qualified. It may not be possible to go over such an exhaustive list in the course of a freely flowing first interview; Winnicott (1965) described psychoanalysis as an 'ex-tended form of history-taking', and much detail will emerge once treatment proper has begun. If the interviewer is unsure of his suitability, based on doubts about how psychiatrically ill the patient may be, a second assessment interview may be needed. As we shall see, thorough assessment pays dividends and may forestall later difficulties.

The interview as a psychodynamic 'probe'

A central purpose of the assessment interview is to act as a stimulus to the patient's unconscious. The therapeutic setting and the person and style of the analyst will in themselves arouse anxiety and hence, if handled with the right balance between support and distance, evoke unconscious reactions. The interviewer may want to tap into phantasy life by asking directly about the patient's earliest memories, what he thinks about as he is falling asleep, what his daydreams and secret ambitions are ('what would you *really* like to happen?'), and, of course, dreams proper ('what do you think about while you are asleep?'). The aim is to create an atmosphere in which innermost fears and phantasies can be explored, and to judge the patient's reactions to the analyst's efforts to foster 'associative freedom' (Spence *et al.* 1994).

Therapeutic interventions: the 'trial interpretation'

Although attentive listening is the key to any psychotherapeutic encounter, the analyst will be far from silent or passive. His interventions will start by questioning, mostly in the form of *open questions* ('Tell me a bit about your family') and move on to *clarifications* ('You mentioned almost in passing that your parents split up when you were 11 years old, can you tell me about your emotional reactions when that happened?').

At some point the analyst will want to probe the patient's analytic potential by *challenge*, *confrontation* and *trial interpretation*. These are a cluster of interventions based on a psychodynamic hypothesis, offered so that the patient is asked to think about himself in a different way. The tone and timing of such interventions is crucial and they should only be attempted once a reasonable therapeutic alliance has been established. If premature they will glance off with little impact; if delivered without finesse they will evoke a defensive reaction and decrease rapport; if too intellectual in content they will fail to elicit an affective response. To be effective they should be fairly brief and simple: 'Do you think perhaps you arrived late for your appointment today because you had mixed feelings about coming?' (confrontation); 'Maybe there is a connection between your depression now and the fact that your daughter is now exactly the same age that you were when your parents split up?', 'I wonder if behind your depression there isn't a lot of anger, similar to what you felt when your mother suddenly had a baby and you were no longer the only object of her affection?' (interpretations); 'Perhaps you see me as rather like your step-father, a rather remote and uncaring figure, out to find fault with you' (transference interpretation). Note that these interventions are best given in a tentative style, allowing the patient to disagree, modify, amplify, or use them as a springboard for further elaboration – a process Malan (1979) calls 'leapfrogging'.

Options, decision, contract

On the basis of the middle phase of the interview, and particularly the response to interventions, the analyst will be looking for three key features which are positively correlated with good outcomes in treatment (Orlinsky and Howard 1986):

(a) the ability to form a good rapport or working alliance;
(b) the ability to work with interpretations;
(c) the capacity to respond affectively within the session – to allow feelings of fear, sadness or anger to surface.

At the end of the interview the analyst will summarise the ground that has been covered and, with the patient's help, reflect on their encounter in order to come to some kind of conclusion: 'We're running out of time, and I think we should spend a few minutes deciding where we go from here'; 'Do you think that working in this way might be helpful to you?', 'Is this the sort of thing you were expecting?' When psychoanalysis was, in the past, virtually the only form of psychotherapy available, the decision was fairly simple – to treat or not to treat. Today, psychoanalysis is but one of a range of therapeutic options. According to Coltart (1988), only 5 per cent of those who consulted her ended up in five times per week analysis. Most analysts consider it good practice to acquaint the patient with the scope of therapeutic possibilities, discussing their various pros and cons. The analyst should then state clearly what he considers, at this moment, to be the best investment (of the patient's time, emotional energy, and money), given the patient's personal and financial resources and in the light of what is realistically feasible. If the assessor plans to accept the patient himself there will also need to be, at this point, a discussion about practicalities: fees, how many times a week they will meet, some idea of the possible length of analysis, holiday arrangements, and so on.

In general, a period of reflection following an assessment interview is no bad thing: both parties may decide *not* to decide immediately. The patient may want to think it over, and to discuss the decision with his family; analyst and patient may come to the conclusion that they need to meet again for a more extended period of assessment or 'trial of therapy'; or the assessor, if he is not in a position to treat the patient himself, may need to explore possible vacancies with colleagues.

THE PSYCHODYNAMIC FORMULATION

As the interview progresses or if the analyst already knows something about the patient even before their meeting, the analyst will be developing hypotheses and ideas about the nature of the patient's difficulties. Ever since Strachey's (1934) seminal paper on interpretation, psychodynamic understanding has been seen in terms of a tripartite formulation, bringing together the current difficulty, the transferential situation and the infantile or childhood constellation of conflict or deficit. This is Malan's (1979) 'triangle of person' – analyst, current other and parent(s) (see p. 170). The aim of the assessment interview is to arrive at a formulation that will guide trial interpretations, help with the decision about whether analysis is suitable, and inform the early stages of treatment (Hinshelwood 1991).

Example: the man who could do everything
John, a vigorous man in his middle forties, came for help because, for the first time in his life, and entirely unexpectedly, he felt he could not cope with his work. From his early twenties, he had built up his own business, a successful building and development firm; he was well respected in his community, happily married with successful children, and with a range of sporting interests. Suddenly he felt tired and irritable, both apathetic and worried about every little detail, and unable to sleep properly. He felt like walking away from everything and had transient suicidal ideas. Anti-depressants had helped only a little. The immediate precipitant of this de-

pression had been a minor car accident, in which he had been run into from behind when stationary while his son, who was driving, was waiting to turn right. He had been jolted, but there was no further physical trauma.

When asked about his parents, he said rather dismissively that his mother had died the year before, but that this was of no significance since he disliked her, and in any case she lived in the USA and was a 'naturalised American citizen'. An only child, it turned out that his parents had split up when he was a baby, and he had been brought up by his uncle and aunt who were childless. They had doted on him and he was the apple of everyone's eye at both school and home: 'The only cloud on the horizon was when my mother or father came to visit, they just stirred things up.'

As the interview progressed, the analyst began to have an almost physical sensation of grappling with this powerful man, as though they were wrestling. He felt that it was very important that he should be firm and assertive. For example, John was clearly nonplussed at finding himself as a potential psychoanalytic patient, since this was very much *not* the image he had of himself as a self-sufficient, strong, well-balanced person who would normally not have dreamed of having any truck with (in his word) 'psycho-business'.

Feeling for the 'point of maximum pain' (Hinshelwood 1991) the analyst saw how, as a child, John had defended himself against the unhappiness of his parents' separation, and the helplessness of his position, by an omnipotent sense of his own invulnerability and importance. The accident and his mother's death had exposed him to these potentially dangerous feelings once more. He dealt with them in his characteristic style by trying to fight his way out of trouble, but now he was battling with himself. Guided by his countertransference, the analyst saw John's shame about asking for help, and their struggle, as being rather like a little boy saying to his uncle (whom he perceived as good but weak) 'you're not my real father'. It was a triumphal oedipal self-aggrandisement that was now slipping away from him. The analyst said: 'Throughout your life it has been very important to you to feel powerful and strong, to be your own self-protector. As a little boy you had no father to turn to for strength. Your sadness about your missing mother could not be expressed. It is as though the accident has exposed some weak and vulnerable part of yourself that you have always kept well hidden. It seems somehow shameful to you to have to consult someone like me, whom you would normally rather despise, in the same way you didn't think much of your uncle.' The patient seemed to relax at this point and responded, while shedding tears for the first time in the interview, by speaking of his impotence, and saying how ashamed he felt of himself, and especially of his angry outbursts. This led to an agreement about the need for a trial of analysis.

This comment based on the 'triangle of person' brought together past relationship, current difficulty and the transference. It similarly illustrates the 'triangle of defence' (Malan 1979; see p. 170) comprising anxiety, defence and 'hidden impulse'. John's anxiety was his fear of losing his strength and vitality; his defence was to work, to fight, to impose his will by brute force, strategies tinged with narcissism and omnipotence; his hidden impulse was the wish to be held and protected and nurtured by someone he could trust.

Reaching a dynamic level is not simply a matter of applying some formula such as Malan's which then automatically yields up the appropriate interpretation. The assessor has to struggle not just with the patient's resistance, but also with his own. The following is an attempt to capture something of the analyst's inner experience (Holmes 1995: 26):

> . . . often I encounter an almost physical sensation of unwillingness within myself when faced with the need to move the patient from a fairly comfortable level of history-taking into the realm of the unconscious. Why disturb the doctor–patient equilibrium? Why run the risk of upsetting or even antagonising the patient? And, above all, how best to do it? More often than not, the key lies in the countertransference, often in the form of an affective response. If I feel a pricking behind the eyes, the patient is probably in a state of grief; if I feel irritated, he is sitting on a powder-keg of rage; if I am bored and detached, perhaps he was never really focused on as a child. I must use whatever sensations or phantasies are aroused in me by the patient's presence and his story to shape my interventions, and so whisk him away, however momentarily, from his static defended state into the fluidity of feelings.

DIAGNOSTIC SCHEMATA IN PSYCHOANALYSIS

The polyglot nature of contemporary psychoanalysis makes it difficult to produce a standardised diagnostic schema – a problem analogous perhaps to that of trying to achieve a single continental currency in the face of diverse national economies. The formulation is necessarily idiosyncratic, reflecting as much the style, pre-conceptions and creativity of the analyst as well as the unique problems of the presenting patient. A different assessor might have formulated the above case differently (cf. Perry *et al.* 1987). A Kleinian formulation might have placed much greater emphasis on aggression, with the accident representing John's primitive split-off destructiveness, uncontained by his abandoning mother, and his depression being a manifestation of the retaliation of a harsh superego bent on punishment and revenge. A self-psychologist might have focused on the mirroring aspect of the transference in which the therapist felt stirrings of omnipotence similar to those that John himself resorted to in the absence of a consistent nurturing self-object. At the same time there are clearly similarities between each approach, albeit couched in the different languages of the separate traditions within psychoanalysis. Standandised approaches to formulation have now been developed by a number of research teams (Perry *et al.* 1989; see Chapter 11).

Despite the difficulties of categorisation, most psychoanalysts use some sort of developmental schema (cf. Chapter 3) as a way of understanding patients diagnostically, indicating the severity of their problems, guiding treatment and predicting prognosis. There is, however, no generally accepted framework for differential diag-nosis. Most are indicators of the *severity* rather than the nature of the patient's disturbance. The distinction between oedipal (three-person, neurotic) difficulties and pre-oedipal (two-person, borderline and narcissistic) problems is used by most authors. Karasu (1990), for example, has proposed a diagnostic matrix based on two-person versus three-person object relations, and the predominance of deficit or conflict in the history. But in practice it is not always easy to decide the level at which the patient is operating, nor indeed whether deficit or conflict is the major theme. John's level of adjustment was undoubtedly 'neurotic' (i.e. three-person), rather than borderline – he had a stable marriage, work pattern and general level of maturity – and yet his illness threw up pre-oedipal narcissistic issues which he had successfully buried since early childhood. Abandoned by his parents he suffered from a 'deficit', and yet his transference was conflictual – he was angry *because* of the deficit.

Ego psychology emphasises the maturity of defences as a guide to developmental level. Vaillant's (1977) distinction between primitive (e.g. splitting), immature (e.g. 'acting out'), neurotic (e.g. obsessionality) and mature (e.g. humour) defences provides a useful hierarchical framework (cf. Chapter 4). Zetzel (1968) tries to capture the essence of 'analysability' in terms of levels of trust, capacity to cope with loss, and ability to distinguish between inner and outer reality. She distinguishes between the 'good hysteric' at one end of a developmental spectrum, whose hold on reality is firm but who suffers from oedipal inhibitions of desire, and, at the other, the 'so-called good hysteric', whose relationships are shallow and who, behind her longing for satisfaction with a man, is in constant search of a nurturing breast.

Kernberg (1984) uses a Kleinian object relations diagnostic schema, in which he sees the two fundamental developmental tasks as the taming of aggression and the achievement of emotional object constancy. Those with severe narcissistic disorders can neither tame their aggressive and genital drives nor escape from splitting, and are rarely suitable for psychoanalysis. In moderate narcissism, the individual is promiscuously dominated by 'part-object' relationships, treating whole people as though they were breasts, penises or lavatories. In borderline conditions the object is whole but unstable and not properly integrated, thus alternately idealised and denigrated. Neurotic individuals have stable, integrated relationships but are genitally inhibited. The mature (?successfully analysed!) individual can integrate genitality into a loving relationship, and harness aggression appropriately while still relating to others as whole beings.

Gedo and Goldberg (1973) ingeniously try to relate developmental levels with the succession of theoretical advances in psychoanalysis. Thus the most mature individuals can be understood in terms of the topographical model, and they require interpretation of repressed feelings. At the next layer down, the tripartite (structural) model applies and help is needed to integrate different aspects of the 'psychic apparatus' – modifying a harsh superego, strengthening a weak ego, channelling an unruly id. Finally, at the most fundamental level, the patient will be struggling with the need to establish a secure sense of self out of his inchoate drives and impulses, and here a soothing, pacifying and unifying (Kohutian) approach will be required.

SELECTING PATIENTS FOR PSYCHOANALYSIS

There is no formula that will decide whether someone should be accepted for psychoanalysis, although diagnostic schemata are invaluable in pointing to possible pitfalls, and suggesting the technical approaches that might be helpful. The decision will always be *contextual* in the sense that it will depend on the relationship between analyst and patient, and their mutual circumstances. To take two unrelated examples: if patients can be contained within a psycho-dynamic in-patient or day-patient setting, than more acutely ill patients can be treated psychoanalytically than would be possible in private office practice. Freud (unlike Jung) cautioned against an-alysis for those over forty, whom he felt lacked the necessary flexibility of mind to change – curiously, since it was only when he himself reached his forties that he invented psychoanalysis. It is now clear that older people can be successfully treated (King 1980; Porter 1991) (see p. 202), and indeed an increasing proportion of psycho-analytic cases comes from this age group not least because they are able to afford such an expensive and intensive treatment. 'An-alysability' is not an objective but an interactional and even soci-ological phenomenon.

Thoma and Kachele (1987) contrast two apparently contradictory statements on the subject by Freud (1905b: 263 and 264; our *italics*):

> To be quite safe one should limit one's choice of patients to those who possess a *normal mental condition* since in the psychoanalytic method this is used as a foothold from which to obtain control of the neurotic manifestations.

But:

> Psychoanalysis was created through and for the treatment of patients *permanently unfit for existence.*

They reconcile these two statements in the aphorism 'sick enough to need it, healthy enough to stand it'. The inclusion and exclusion factors listed by different authors guide the assessor to find this fulcrum between illness and need on the one hand, and healthy robustness on the other. The idea of the 'transference neurosis' captures the essence of the requirement: if psychoanalysis is to succeed, the illness must both manifest itself *and* be contained within the therapeutic alliance. Malan's (1979) 'law of increased disturb-ance' also applies here: during the course of treatment the patient is likely to manifest his most disturbed level of functioning. Casement (1985) sees this as necessary, if the patient is to bring the orginal trauma 'within the area of omnipotence'.

Factors favourable or unfavourable to psychoanalysis fall under three headings: evidence from the *history*, from the *content* of the interview and from the *style* and approach the patient takes to talking about himself (Tyson and Sandler 1971; Malan 1979). A history of at least one good relationship (evidence of 'basic trust', Erikson 1965) and of some positive achievement is encouraging; addiction, serious destructive or self-destructive behaviour suggesting poor frustration tolerance, history of prolonged psychotic breakdown in the face of stress, and entrenched somatisation (with concomitant 'secondary gain') are relative contra-indications. People with severe obsessional neuroses, although originally considered treatable psychoanalytically (Freud 1909), are best treated with a combination of medication and cognitive-behavioural therapy, but obsessional personalities are commonly treated psychoanalytically. Given the existence of a fairly wide range of effective symptomatic treatments (either cognitive-behavioural or pharmacological), many of the patients taken on for psychoanalysis are also likely to be suffering from character disorders.

As we have discussed, key features in the content of the interview are the patient's capacity to form a working alliance, and his affective response to trial interpretations. The patient's narrative style will reveal how 'psychologically minded' or 'accessible' he is, terms which summarise a range of psychological functions: the capacity to see oneself from the outside (Sandler *et al.* 1992), to reflect on one's inner world (Coltart 1986), to tolerate psychic pain, to regress in the service of the ego (Kris 1956), 'autobiographical competence' (Holmes 1992), and 'fluidity of thought' (Limentani 1972).

Finally, the elusive dimension of 'motivation' is probably crucial. The patient who has sought out treatment, who wants it badly, is prepared to work at it, and who views the process and his analyst in a positive light, is likely to do well, to overcome setbacks, to make sacrifices and to cope with regressions. Perhaps this is what Freud (1912a) meant by the need for the patient to have a good 'ethical development', and what Symington (1993) refers to as an essential spark of goodness which counterbalances the 'internal saboteur' of the narcissist – a push towards health within the bleak landscape of neurosis that defies classification and yet forms the germ of a successful therapeutic relationship.

Chapter 8

The therapeutic relationship

> The resistance accompanies the treatment step-by-step. Every single association, every act of the person under treatment must reckon with the resistance and represents a compromise between the forces that are striving towards recovery and the opposing ones.
>
> (Freud 1912b: 103)

The idea of a therapeutic relationship is present in the patient's mind long before analysis begins. He knows something is wrong and begins to wonder how it can be put right. Seeking help from others seems a natural course and the future patient begins to talk either to professionals or to friends, and gradually – sometimes via psychotherapy, at other times through a recommendation, and occasionally by bad experience in other treatments – moves towards analysis. In his mind the individual forms a sense of the style of relationship that he feels will be helpful, whether with a man or woman – a relationship waiting to be actualised in the transference. The patient needs an analyst to fit. Any analyst will not do. As we shall see in this chapter, analysts vary according to their personal style, even though they adhere to basic analytic technique. Individual styles complement some individuals better than others and patient–analyst fit may be an important variable in treatment outcome (see p. 248).

PSYCHOANALYTIC RELATIONSHIP

The therapeutic contract

The psychoanalytic relationship starts when patient and analyst meet, form a contract and begin treatment. Whether the potential patient is naive or informed, the analyst has to set up a contract and to specify certain conditions before treatment begins. He must explain roughly what analysis involves, how long it is likely to last, the risks and possible benefits, costs and any particular 'rules', along with their reasons, that he recommends. Both patient and analyst need to ensure that they are clear about their objectives and expectations, and aware of possible difficulties so that future mis-understandings are minimised. There is no point in treating a patient whose employer is posting him or her abroad within six months of the start of analysis. The patient may believe that six months is an adequate length of time for treatment, and unless this has been discussed beforehand the analyst might fall into the trap of inappro-priately interpreting resistance when the inevitable move takes place. The assessment interview (see previous chapter) should have dealt with these ground rules, but this cannot be taken for granted.

The spirit rather than the letter of the therapeutic agreement is what matters. A patient who requests a change of session may be offered an alternative if he has an unavoidable commitment, such as taking an exam, but not if he simply arranges a meeting with his girlfriend at the time of the session! In this case he is betraying the spirit of the agreement – that both patient and analyst try to adhere to their arrangements, as agreed at the outset, and only vary them by joint discussion. This places equal obligation on both patient and analyst not unilaterally to alter the framework of treatment.

Style

Like all professionals, analysts come in all different shapes and sizes and although their technique may be similar their style may differ markedly. The bearded, white haired, cigar smoking male, sitting behind a couch surrounded by relics of antiquity and poised with pad and pencil is legendary but by no means accurate. Freud (1912a, 1913) made particular recommendations about the setting that he found useful, but prudently suggested that they may not suit all analysts or all patients. Nevertheless, many of his proposals, such as the patient lying on a comfortable couch in a warm room, have become indispensable to analytic technique. The patient may know about the couch but express surprise at lying down, believing it to be outdated and anachronistic. Often, reluctance to lie down is a result of terrifying regressive or sexual phantasies. The patient may need to be informed that lying down can free both himself and his analyst to think, unencumbered from the normal visual cues of human discourse; their removal loosens the control on unconscious process.

The use of the couch has been questioned by some analysts; its removal from the consulting room seeming to symbolise a break with psychoanalysis itself, rather than representing a modification of technique. Adler felt the couch compounded the patient's feelings of inferiority, while Fairbairn (1958) considered it a dehumanising remnant of Freud's hypnotic technique, advocating a face-to-face arrangement which, given his rather reserved personality, may have been equally intimidating. Although the use of the couch has become a mainstay of psychoanalytic technique, the position of the analyst to the couch is more a matter of style. Some analysts sit completely behind the patient, others closer to the side. This is a matter of preference and personal style and may have as much to do with the way an analyst's former analyst positioned himself as with any therapeutic rationale. Many hours are wasted over arguments which confuse analytic *technique* with *style*. Each analyst sets his own style – the way he furnishes his consulting room, greets his patients, finishes the sessions, gives his bills and announces breaks. They all become part of his setting and can only be criticised if they result in a major deviation from the rules followed by the analytic community.

The setting

The therapeutic setting can be seen as a set of counterpoised themes: attachment and separation; opening up and closure; holding/containment and frustration. The generally accepted elements of psychoanalysis include the use of the couch (encouraging regression and free association), sessions 4–5 times a week for 50 minutes (encouraging attachment and continuity), a break at weekends (stimulating separation anxiety), the use of free association (facilitating unconscious expression), an open-ended contract, adherence to the agreed arrangements especially by the analyst (holding), protection of the analytic hour from interruption (containing), neutrality and the 'rule of abstinence' (see below – maintaining frustration).

Certain analysts have deviated from these accepted elements and invariably have been severely criticised. Lacan is said to have worked with free or open time in which the session did not end routinely after 50 minutes but as a significant intervention at any time in a session, either to represent the analysand's 'empty word' or to 'close off a dialectic structure'. This compromises the analyst's use of countertransference and places him in a judgemental position, as presumably if things are difficult or uncomfortable for him the tendency will be to shorten the session and gain free time.

In contrast, Winnicott (1977) at times accepted 'analysis on demand', including prolonged two-hour or three-hour sessions, potentially encouraging pathological dependence and regression. Although rules are made to be broken, such heterodoxy is best reserved for mavericks and masters. The preferred course for ordinary mortals is to stick to the '50-minute hour' even if the patient is distressed at the end of a session. To err on a slight extension may give the message that the analyst can be persuaded to go on, whereas to stop marginally early may imply the opposite. Neutrality is the best course and can only be maintained if the setting is controlled in this way.

It is important not to issue too many directives at the outset of treatment and, although the couch is recommended, it should certainly not be compulsory. If the patient chooses to sit up initially, this will allow the patient's anxieties about lying down to emerge and gradually be understood.

Example: an upright young man
A rather formal 23-year-old man told his male analyst that he wasn't going to lie down as 'it seemed silly'. After some months of face-to-face contact the patient had a dream in which a burly man came up from behind, raised a large stick and stuck it into him. Associations to the dream suggested that the patient was terrified that the analyst would attack him if he lay down; later this linked up with homosexual anxieties.

Free association is more easily recommended than performed. It is possibly best formulated through such a statement as: 'I suggest that you talk about anything that comes into your mind, however irrelevant or inappropriate it may seem, including thoughts and feelings you may have about being in treatment or the sessions themselves.' Such a statement acknowledges that the patient may censor some of his thoughts and feelings, especially if they are about the analysis or the analyst himself, and it implies that it is important to put them into words. In this way some acting out (see later) may be avoided. However, such an invitation can be intimidating, and it is worth remembering one patient's response: 'If I could do that I wouldn't need to be here in the first place' (Rycroft 1979a).

'The rule of abstinence', as put forward by Freud (1915) presents some difficulties for both patient and analyst. The rule applies, first, to the fact that the analyst should not satisfy the patient's desires, and, second, that the patient should not look outside the analysis for immediate gratification. The first aspect of the rule must be adhered to completely – especially if the wishes are sexual – and forms part of the ethical contract. However, it equally applies to other desires, such as responding to curiosity about the analyst's life. It is more important to understand the motivation and phantasies behind questions than to answer them. Any direct satisfaction of the patient's demands for information may interfere with the processes of free association, development of the capacity of self-reflection, and ability to symbolise. However, in some instances acknowledgement of reality is not out of place and is necessary, for example, if the analyst becomes seriously ill or falls pregnant. As Winnicott once remarked, it is important to remember that we are human beings first and analysts second. Equally, perhaps, we may need to remind ourselves that our patients are people first and analysands second.

The second element of the rule of abstinence is problematic as it may become overly prescriptive and authoritarian. Certainly it is important that a patient who experiences unsatisfied needs in relation to the analyst – as they almost inevitably will – does not simply seek satisfaction elsewhere. On the other hand, major life changes for a patient, such as marriage or change of job, frequently occur during the course of an analysis, and it is probably best to consider each one as it is brought to analysis and tease out its meaning rather than issue a prohibition at the beginning. In Freud's 3–6 month analyses, 'abstinence' may have been feasible, but today's years-long treatments make it impractical to recommend any avoidance of major life changes.

The analyst similarly subjects himself to a rule of abstinence. He must not look to the patient for gratification of his own needs. He should be aware of, and learn to curb, his therapeutic fervour or wish to cure, imposing of personal values, or secret pleasure in countertransference experiences. Analytic 'neutrality' can, however, become a much trumpeted ideal devoid of clinical sensitivity. All analyses contain occasional supportive elements such as reassurance and commiseration, in addition to the implicit support of the secure setting and the analyst's attention and empathy. Minor 'gratification'

– for example, allowing a soaking wet patient to dry himself – as long as it remains within an ethical framework – may at times be needed if the analysis is to progress or even survive (cf. p. 162). The important point is not so much to avoid gratification at all times, as to explore its transference and countertransference implications whenever it occurs.

THE TREATMENT PROCESS

The purpose of rules is to establish order. The analytic setting is ordered so that it can become or contain a *process*. Alteration of the setting is an active technique which interrupts the underlying process and should be avoided if possible. However, there is no doubt that inevitable minor changes such as the unexpected absence of the analyst through occasional illness, interruption of the session, lateness on either part, change of consulting room, and alteration of fees may stimulate new material. The setting allows these events to be explored usefully, and their meaning highlighted within the firm boundaries of an orderly contract.

Once the parameters of the relationship have been established the scene is set for treatment to begin, usually with great optimism, if not some trepidation, on the part of both participants. The patient starts by explaining a great deal about himself, fearfully at first but then with increasing confidence as he looks to the analyst for clarification, sympathy and help. Gradually, nagging doubts about treatment intrude into his mind and he hints that the analyst is not behaving or intervening in the expected or desired way. His anxiety increases, his fears are heightened and he thinks that he may have made a mistake in seeking treatment. Early optimism and hopes of a rapid resolution to his problems are replaced by disillusionment. He wishes he had never started on such a course and feels he was either foolhardy or naive.

The analyst's refusal to fulfil the increasing demands of his patient – his adherence to the rule of abstinence – evokes a gradual disillusionment. The resulting frustration increases the likelihood of a reversion to earlier, more archaic patterns of relating and therapeutic regression begins to emerge. Wishes, phantasies, hopes, desires, disappointments, frustrations and longings of the patient's present and past become embodied in the analytic relationship, highlighted by the setting, allowing their origins to be studied. Frustration increases to a level that encourages the emergence of childhood patterns of feeling and behaviour within the transference relationship, without being so overwhelming that the patient abandons treatment or resorts to pathological ways of dealing with the situation.

The analyst's role

The analyst sets himself the task of working 'without memory and desire' (Bion 1967), using 'free-floating' (Sandler 1992) or 'evenly suspended' attention (Freud 1912a) to listen effectively to his patient, to monitor his countertransference feelings and to address central concerns in a helpful way. He allows his mind to wander, reflects on why particular thoughts arise and tolerates feelings rather than avoids them. He tries in his self-monitoring to allow his thought patterns to be dynamic and fluid and to avoid intellectual rigidity. He oscillates between empathic primary identification (see p. 112) with the patient and objectivity, perhaps representing maternal and paternal roles respectively. He tries to strike a balance between silence and speaking and to vary the 'dosage' of interpretation appropriately.

Different authors advocate different approaches here. At one end of the spectrum is Balint (1968) who argues that it is important to intervene as little as possible: when in doubt, keep quiet. At the other extreme lie those, often Klein-influenced analysts, for whom interpretation is the lifeblood of their work (Etchegoyen 1991). In between are authors such as Winnicott (1965), who recommend a non-intrusive attitude, and Green (1975) who believes that excessive speaking *or* too much silence is equally harmful, leading either to intrusions or separation anxiety. Absence and silence are given equal place to presence and interpretation. Inevitably the balance is not solely related to technique but varies according to the analysand's material and the analyst's countertransference. The analyst is also assisted by the development of the therapeutic alliance (i.e. a generally positive attitude towards treatment on the part of the patient (see p. 104)) which enables mistakes and inaccuracies to be tolerated or even found helpful. An inaccurate or inexact interpretation (Glover 1931) can stimulate useful responses which can then be examined, but this is no excuse for sloppy technique and the analyst should make it his prime job to protect the security of the session in the best way he can (Casement 1985).

What, then, is the main task of the analyst in the analytic process?

Is it to reduce conflict and encourage more effective use of mature mechanisms of defence (see p. 92), to establish a continuum between the there-and-then and here-and-now, to understand and give insight, to offer a 'corrective emotional experience', or to facilitate a 'new beginning' through regression? How do the analyst and patient work together to achieve any of these goals? Is it enough to allow the analytic process to take its course relying on the security of the setting and the analytic relationship to bring about change, or is specific and accurate interpretation needed? If the latter is needed what form should it take? Should it be a dynamic interpretation in the present or a genetic reconstruction of the past, a remembering of the there-and-then or an experience in the here-and-now? How far should all interpretations address the transference–countertransference dynamic, or are extratransference interpretations also useful?

The answer surely is that all, and more, are needed. The analyst's craft is to distinguish which is most appropriate for which patient at what time. There is no place for rigid interventions given to a formula, for no two patients are alike and each brings his own unique life to the therapeutic process and forms his own treatment pattern. In an attempt to address some of these questions we shall now turn to some of the central themes of the analytic process: regression, resistance, the spectrum of therapeutic interventions, interpretation, insight, working through and termination.

Regression

Regression, which can be defined as returning from a point in development already reached to an earlier one, is an inevitable part of the analytic process. Freud (1900) distinguished between three kinds of regression: topographical, formal and temporal. *Topographical* regression refers to the move from secondary to primary process, from motor to perceptual systems; thus, in dreaming, as consciousness rests, the unconscious has its freedom. The regressive pull of the analytic setting means that the patient's conscious communications are continuously modified by unconscious phantasies, thoughts and feelings. *Formal* regression, in which there is a 'harking back to older psychical structures' and a use of 'primitive methods of expression' is a common characteristic of the psychoanalytic process. Under stress, a patient utilises more primitive defence mechanisms, behaves in an infantile manner, or moves from a depressive position to paranoid–schizoid functioning. Freud linked *temporal* regression to specific phases of childhood development. As the child moves through different stages, vestiges of the earlier stage are left behind and may be returned to in the face of disappointment, frustration, or emotional difficulty. These points of return are the so-called fixation points (Freud 1916 – cf. p. 50 for a critique of this notion).

Sandler and Sandler (1994a) believe the distinction between the different types of regression is largely superfluous, and Freud (1900) himself claimed that they are 'one at bottom'. They propose that regression is better seen as a release or diminution of an 'anti-regressive function' of the ego. The anti-regressive function is responsible for the maintenance of civilised and independent behaviour when under duress or provocation, controlling unacceptable impulses and needs, and allowing appropriate expression of emotions. As well as the 'anti-regressive function', psychological health requires a capacity to *release* healthy regression and allow latent, often infantile, wishes to be expressed. Failure to allow this may have serious consequences.

Example: the terror of the needy child
A withdrawn man, with schizoid traits, brought up in an orphanage, was referred for analysis. During the assessment he told of how he worked hard, had little social contact, and had never had an intimate relationship. He felt he could never rely on anyone. He related this to an occasion when he had invited a girl out to supper and, although she had agreed, she failed to arrive at their 'date'. He attempted suicide that evening. The analyst took up his fears of dependency and involvement, and how he would rather die than experience abject loneliness, rejection and humiliation. The patient responded by saying he would never give anyone the satisfaction of thinking that he needed them. Sadly, but unsurprisingly, he rejected analytic treatment.

Rigid maintenance of the anti-regressive function of the ego is a potent source of resistance in analysis, but fortunately such a detached attitude and tenacious contol of emotions is rare. As a patient talks and the analyst refrains from excessive interruption, judgemental comments, comforting remarks and critical statements, the patient's less conscious wishes, half-remembered experiences, and earlier expectations come to the fore as if they had been eternally waiting for an opportunity of expression. This benign regressive trend occurs in waves and cycles during analytic treatment, at one moment being apparent, the next retreating to be replaced by more adult functioning; it allows the patient to explore his childhood 'retreats' (*q.v.* p. 226), attitudes, memories and behaviour in the safety of the analytic setting. Kris (1956) characterised this 'regression in the service of the ego' as part of a continuing intrapsychic oscillation between present and past so that the adaptive abilities of the ego in the present are informed by experience from the past.

Balint (1968) pointed to the interpersonal aspects of regression. Analysts vary in their propensity to encourage or discourage regression, a personal quality dependent on a tender acceptance and lack of anxiety in the face of primitive emotions. 'Active techniques' are neither desirable nor necessary. Lying on the couch and the silent presence of the analyst are enough to release a regressive pull. During normal regression a patient rarely loses sight of his curiosity, his ability to experience feelings, and his capacity to observe, and he rapidly regains equilibrium with the help of the analyst's interventions if necessary. The therapeutic alliance should always be maintained. The patient may demand love, crave affection, and require appreciation from the analyst, but he seldom reaches a point where he cannot function without them. The transference relationship allows him to experience wishes, phantasies and feelings from the past in the present; the neutrality of the analyst encourages him to express himself without excessive reasonableness and to talk unencumbered by social politeness, fairness and consideration.

However, if frustrations are too great and demands become excessive, the regression becomes counter-therapeutic and may even lead to a breakdown in treatment or a hospital admission. Now the analytic relationship becomes imbued with grandiose phantasies or dependency needs that cannot be met, alternately idealising and denigrating, indicating that the line between therapeutic and malignant regression has been transgressed. Dangerous acting out and a loss of sense of reality are not far off and the analyst may be pulled into an escalating spiral of pathological transference–countertransference reactions, in which he either 'gives in' or tries to pull away, while the patient scents possible gratification of his infantile desires (see examples, pp. 230–4).

Balint (1949) links regression to the possibility of a *'new beginning'* in which a past trauma is corrected through its appropriate handling within the transference relationship. He considers that in every serious mental or psychosomatic illness there is a *basic fault* which has arisen in the context of the earliest mother–child relationship and that help for such conditions lies in correcting this deficit by addressing the preverbal, empathic and wordless aspects of regression through experiencing rather than interpreting. The patient needs to regress

> either to the setting, that is, to the particular form of object relationship which caused the original deficiency state, or even some stage before it.

(Balint 1968: 166)

Metaphorically at least, the analyst allows the patient to experience the there-and-then within a more favourable relationship and so to heal over the traumatic scar from the past. Winnicott (1971) also stresses how the analytic encounter can become a 'holding environment' or transitional space in which early experiences may be regressively reworked leading to greater creativity and increased awareness (cf. p. 132). This is not far from the idea of the 'corrective emotional experience' (Alexander and French 1946) which fell into disrepute in analytic circles because of its exploitation by ethically dubious practitioners. Discussion about the role of regression continues to inform the current debate between the proponents of emotional experience versus interpretation, relationship as opposed to technical skill, the affective rather than the intellectual content of analysis (cf. pp. 229–33).

The re-experiencing of earlier difficulties is intrinsically painful, even for those patients who are attracted to analysis by its regressive possibilities. The majority of patients resist the regressive pull even if it offers constructive development and progression in the end. The individual who comes for analysis has already found the best possible adaptation to his past difficulties. His solution has been achieved by compromise and trial and error over the years and is not easily going to be given up: change, heralding fear and uncertainty, is defended against. He may use intellectualisation and rationalisation or other defensive styles in the hope of avoiding any path that seems to lead to greater pain. Although he yearns to live more happily and to improve, some of the thoughts, events, ideas, desires and needs that he stumbles across lead to embarrassment and shame. He covers up and may even feel that he is better with his symptoms than without them. His anti-regressive function hardens and becomes a potent source of resistance (Sandler and Sandler 1994a). Thus a state of conflict develops in which he feels pushed and pulled between expressing himself and resisting change.

Resistance

Resistance is a clinical concept that refers to the myriad of methods a patient uses to obstruct the very process that he is relying on to help him. He may feel so resistant that he is compelled to terminate treatment, and the efforts of the analyst to retrieve the situation fall on stony ground. More often, however, the resistances to the analytic process are less severe, with constant fluctuations between recollection, remembering and understanding and the forces opposing them. Clinically, resistance takes many forms, ranging from conscious concealment of facts to unconsciously driven acting out (see p. 194), from intellectualisation and cognitive understanding to 'emoting', from missing sessions to obsessionally turning up on time, from only talking about the analytic relationship to avoiding it, from erotising the relationship to deadening it, and from developing new symptoms to rapidly losing the old and taking a flight into health. In 'Inhibitions, symptoms and anxiety', Freud (1926) introduced a useful classification of resistance into repression resistance, secondary gain resistance, transference resistance, repetition–compulsion resistance and superego resistance. Since that time other aspects of resistance have been named, including 'character resistance' (Reich 1933), the protection of self-esteem in borderline and narcissistic patients (Rosenfeld 1971; Kohut 1984; Kernberg 1988), the preservation of a fragile identity (Erikson 1968), the maintenance of internal safety (Sandler 1968), and avoiding of the integration of experience (Thoma and Kachele 1987).

Repression resistance arises from the individual's need not to know. The emergence of memories, past feelings and phantasies threatens to destabilise the patient's internal equilibrium. The closer the analyst's interventions bring the repressed contents of the unconscious to the surface, the greater the danger to the patient and the greater the resistance. The analyst must pitch his interventions so that they allow repressed content and affects to surface in a way that is tolerable to the patient. Sometimes these buried feelings may themselves become a resistance, and, in *'secondary gain'*, the resulting symptoms become a way of life in themelves.

Example: a cruel sickness

A depressed patient developed nausea and a feeling of fullness in her stomach soon after starting analysis. She complained of feeling bloated and blamed the analyst for her symptoms. She attacked the analysis as detrimental to her health, deriding it about not being able to help her physical condition. She visited her general practitioner but his drugs gave no relief. After further sessions, the analyst felt the treatment was stuck and that the patient seemed to be enjoying her constant attack. He interpreted her wish for him to 'look after' her physically, her disappointment that he did not, and that she felt he had 'force fed' her with his interpretations. While this comment was no doubt partially correct, it missed the sadistic aspect of her symptoms through which she punished not just herself but also those purporting to help her. This linked with her childhood, in which her mother had been a chronic invalid, demanding that the patient wait on her and respond to her every beck and call.

Transference resistance firmly places the concept of resistance within the therapeutic relationship and may take the form of a hostility or indifference to the analyst–patient relationship, or to any mention of it. Even if some awareness dawns, the patient appears blind to the connections with past conflicts, or fails to see any links between his relationship with the outside world and the therapeutic situation. The fate of a patient's internal resistance involves the dyadic relationship and not just the patient's psychopathology. How the analyst interprets, his manner, the atmosphere he creates, will affect the course of the treatment, and his response to the patient's hostile attitudes may lead to counter-resistance in him (Stone 1973). Every analysis requires a degree of mutual accommodation between patient and analyst. Even if this is successful, a patient may continue to find himself developing powerful, uncontrollable aggressive or erotic feelings towards his analyst which eventually leads to a failure of treatment (see Chapter 9). At a loss to explain the failure of some analyses, Freud (1920) attributed such malignant resistances to '*repetition–compulsion*', which he saw as a psychobiological phenomenon insisting on stasis at any cost.

Superego resistance refers to the process by which some patients masochistically accept their lot in a long-suffering way, with little apparent wish to change. In Freud's (1918) case of the Wolf Man, he remarks on the surprising observation that every time progress was made the symptoms seemed to return. At first he thought of this as an act of defiance but he gradually recognised it to be a paradoxical reaction to the accuracy of his interpretations. This became known as a *negative therapeutic reaction* (Freud 1923) and was related to an unconscious masochistic tendency which is determined by aggressive and destructive instincts. It is now more likely to be related to attempts to be independent of an analyst to whom one is attached. ('I'll find out in my own good time and not when you want me to understand'); or it may be related to a wish to remain dependent ('if I show how well I am I'll have to leave'); or to envy (Rosenfeld 1975; Kernberg 1975) ('I can't bear to accept that you could understand so much about me').

Although these different aspects of resistance are useful for clarity, the important thing to remember is that resistance can take an almost infinite number of forms. In all cases, analysis of resistance should be the focus of interpretation. Sometimes a patient seems to be stuck, and that is the point at which he most needs to change. Resistance is often a signpost to change.

Example: a stickler for time
A 30-year-old woman who had suffered from near-fatal asthma as a child, and who had been raped in her teens, looked at her watch at regular intervals throughout her sessions and always insisted on finishing one minute early. Confronting her need to control, and relating this both to the terror she had experienced during the rape and her inability to relax in the presence of her excessively anxious mother, led to greater trust in the relationship. She now deliberately took her watch off for the duration of the session. Once she was more in touch with her emotional needs she was able to leave it on and allow the analyst to bring the session to a close. She did, however, unilaterally decide on termination, although she was by this time much improved, and was able to discuss her fears and her sense that she had had her 'fair share'.

Whenever a treatment feels stuck the analyst needs to recognise the resistance, understand its opposition to change, and address its aggressive and self-defeating nature, especially if it takes one of its more malignant forms such as acting out (see p. 194).

The spectrum of therapeutic interventions

Psychoanalysis has, from the start, swung between seeing insight and interpretation on the one hand, and the emotional relationship with the analyst on the other, as the main vehicles of cure. This polarity, creative at times, has also divided analysts, creating different schools and provoking schisms. In the 1950s Alexander's use of the 'corrective emotional experience' was discredited, and interpretation gained the high ground until Balint and Winnicott reaffirmed the importance of new experience, especially in dealing with pre-oedipal problems. This controversy continues in the debate between contemporary Freudian and Kleinian psychoanalysts on the one hand, who emphasise interpretation, and Self-psychology and Independent approaches on the other, in which non-verbal empathy and attunement are believed to be therapeutic in themselves. Kohut (1984) provocatively argued that nearly all interpretations are 'wild analysis' until proved otherwise, and contrasted the content of an interpretation with the way it is given. He even considered that if the content was well off the mark, the interpretation could be effective if given in the right tone of voice (cf. Chapter 1, p. 18).

In clinical practice, the dichotomy seems artificial: both aspects are essential (cf. Wallerstein 1992, and pp. 168–75 below). The security of the setting and the silent, attentive listening of the analyst form part of the background of treatment; they provide the patient with (a) an experience that allows him to consolidate embryonic feelings of trust in others and (b) a chance of identifying with a helpful, considerate object, which in turn enables him to become more thoughtful about himself and to listen to interpretations. The analyst's capacity to act as a container (see p. 113) (Bion 1959, 1962, 1963) facilitates this process. The analyst collects and integrates projected aspects of the patient's self. His capacity to understand and give meaning to the projected fragments provides the containment which allows them to be transformed into a more tolerable form and reintrojected. Winnicott (1971) and Wolff (1971) contrast the analyst's 'being with' and 'doing to' attitudes, considering them as equally containing. 'Being with the object' depends on the more receptive female element, and 'doing something to the object' with the more active male element, both elements being potentially present in men and women.

In any psychotherapeutic work it is helpful to think of 'being with' the patient as essential to promote growth by providing space and time which frees and facilitates the patient's own potential. In contrast, doing something to the patient, like giving an injunction, commenting on his behaviour, or making interpretations, may artificially force the pace. If 'doing to' is overdone it may deprive the patient of a chance to discover his own answers and solutions and thus interfere with the developmental process. In contrast, too much 'being with' may fail to provide the necessary challenge and intellectual rigour needed to promote growth.

The art and craft of psychoanalysis consists of finding the right balance between 'being with' and 'doing to'. In practice, 'doing to' functions often require a well-established 'being with' relationship before they become effective. 'Non-specific' factors (a term used in psychotherapy research, see p. 247) and 'specific' interventions unique to psychoanalysis are complementary and not alternatives. Nevertheless, the overvaluation of interpretation in the transference as *the* main curative factor in psychoanalysis has led to the neglect of other factors such as affirmation, validation and even praise and support. Whatever the analyst's theoretical allegiance, most work in a flexible way as the balance between interpretive work at one extreme, and supportive interventions at the other, shifts back and forth throughout treatment (see Figure 8.1).

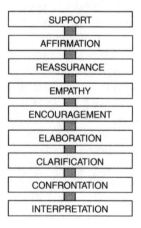

Figure 8.1 The spectrum of therapeutic interventions

In general, the closer the intervention is to the interpretive pole of the continuum, the more 'psychoanalytic' the treatment. *Support, affirmation* and *reassurance* are not mainstays of psychoanalytic technique, but regular 'uhmmm's and 'aah's, which encourage elaboration or stimulate further exploration, are to be found in all analyses. It is important that the analyst is perceived as neither inhuman nor superhuman: most will offer an appropriately sympathetic response in the face of some personal setback or bereavement. Such interventions, as well as mild interjections or grunts, demonstrate that the analyst is still present, alive, listening, following, and trying to understand (Rycroft 1985).

Empathy (see also p. 111), by contrast, is a demonstration of the analyst's attunement to his patient and, although often wordless, may take the form of statements such as 'You seemed to feel really hurt when you were treated in that way'. It is doubtful if one group of analysts will be more empathic than another (Kohut 1984), but in self-psychology empathy is seen as pivotal rather than merely a precursor to interpretation. This emphasis on empathy may have arisen to counterbalance the rather rigid interpretive technique of some ego psychologists, but it also represents a shift from conflict to deficit as a central theoretical theme (see p. 223).

As we move towards those interventions at the centre of the spectrum in Figure 8.1 they become more common in psychoanalytic treatment; when *encouragement* or *elaboration* is used, it is usually as a prelude to clarification or even confrontation. Elaborative techniques usually take the form of open questions such as 'What does that make you think of?', or 'Does that remind you of anything?', rather than a bald 'Why?', which can be impossible to answer and often only serves to stimulate rationalisation. *Clarification* is a reformulation of something the patient has been saying, reflected back after processing by the analyst; it is a trial of a more coherent view, but does not challenge in the way confrontation does. *Confrontation* is not necessarily aggressive and it is likely to be most effective if done in a questioning but firm manner. Finally, *interpretation* usually contains elements of confrontation and challenge by pointing out some distortion, inconsistency or misperception. Whether to be subtle or confrontational depends on the state of the relationship with the patient as well as the degree of the underlying problems. The patient who is in danger of self-destructive acts should be left in no doubt about the analyst's view.

Example: a firm interpretation

A 40-year-old woman, whose mother had recently died, came to the session and talked of her worries about the rainforests, their destruction by humans and the devastation of the environment. Knowing that she was someone who often cut herself and had tried suicide on a number of occasions, the analyst acknowledged her environmental concerns but stated that he believed her pre-occupation with them in the session was an avoidance of her sense of personal devastation following the loss of her mother, which made her feel like cutting herself down and killing herself.

This confronts the patient by addressing the defence head-on, and forms the first part of an interpretation.

Interpretation

The purpose of interpretation is to enable the patient to see what he could not see before, to widen his 'endopsychic perceptual field' (Rycroft 1968), to make sense of the incomprehensible, to find meaning where there seemed to be none, to feel things that he could not feel before, and to turn regression into progression.

Interpretation in its simplest form, by its use of words, makes something conscious that was previously unconscious – 'where id was, there ego shall be' (Freud 1923) – or, more correctly, *pre-*conscious because the analyst should interpret only when a patient nearly knows something but cannot quite grasp it. The theoretical aims of interpretation are clear, but in practice the form, timing and kind of interpretation are more difficult to define.

The Malan/Menninger triangles

Particularly useful in the detailed understanding of when and how to interpret is the 'two triangles' approach, first described by Menninger (1958) and developed by Malan (1979). The *triangle of conflict* consists of defence, anxiety and hidden feeling. The *triangle of insight or person* comprises other (current or recent past), transference (here and now in session) and parent (distant past).

The triangles are linked: the hidden feeling in the triangle of conflict may be related to any aspect of the triangle of person. Interpretation usually involves a mixture of the two triangles and the analyst must decide which aspects need taking up at any given moment. A complete interpretation involving all aspects of both triangles is rare and patient and analyst move around them according to the tension within the session. At the beginning of analysis the focus may be on the current or recent past, because present circumstances are readily accessible and are likely to have brought the patient to analysis.

Example: too near, too distant
An advertising executive came into analysis complaining that his relationships with women swung from being close and romantic to constantly acrimonious, in which he was accused of being uncaring and cold. His present partner was now complaining that he was becoming more distant. He felt that the distancing of relationships was his fault and he already realised that it occurred at a point when marriage and lifelong commitment were looming.

The patient had also changed jobs on many occasions. Each time he appeared to have made a success of his employment in advertising but left suddenly before capitalising fully on his skills. The analyst wondered if the patient had anxieties about too much involvement and closeness and linked his job changes to his changes of women. This simple – but to the patient hitherto unnoticed – link between the presenting problem with other aspects of his life resulted in a deepening of rapport between patient and analyst.

Gradually, or even in an assessment, the current or recent past is linked to the distant past and explored, highlighting those areas of the past that seem to influence feelings and behaviour in the present.

Example: too near, too distant (continued)
The patient began talking about his school friends and whether or not he had experienced feelings of closeness to them as well as exploring his parents' relationship. He felt his parents had rarely shown tenderness to each other, but, on the other hand, his mother had been particularly affectionate to him. However, she left home and travelled around the world for two years when he was seven years old, leaving him with his father. On her return he remembered her wanting everything to return to normal 'as if nothing had happened'. He felt different and spent a lot of time in his room alone. When she tried to play with him or show affection he pushed her away. The analyst suggested that he now had to push his wives and girlfriends away to prevent a repetition of the feelings he had experienced towards his mother when she left home – a link between present and past. The patient described how he felt unmoved by her return, almost as if he did not care if she was there or not. On the other hand, he remembered how close they had been prior to her sudden departure, and his bewilderment when she was not there. He had no knowledge of why she had left so suddenly and the family had never discussed it.

As the relationship with the analyst intensifies the transference–countertransference interaction comes to the fore, quietly at first but with increasing intensity later. All aspects of the triangle of person are then available for interpretation.

Example: too near, too distant (continued)
Soon after this link between distant past and present had been made, the analyst told the patient his holiday dates. As the first

break in treatment approached, the patient said that everyone else seemed to be going away as his girlfriend was going abroad to work for two months. Unwittingly the patient had now linked the analyst in the here-and-now with the present of his outside life. The analyst could now connect the patient's present life with the transference relationship as well as with his past relationship with his mother. Despite the interpretation of the patient's experience that the analyst had gained his trust, fostered warm feelings of dependency just like his mother, and then left him, the patient returned after the break feeling detached, cold and wanting to finish treatment. The analyst linked this with his retreat to his room when his mother had returned from her travels abroad.

While the triangle of person is being explored a watchful eye must be kept on the triangle of conflict. Interpretation should start from defence, with the proviso that it is rare to take up the defence alone, because simply pointing out a defence leads to nervousness in the patient and a feeling that he is doing something wrong. Defence and anxiety should be interpreted together, preferably with a hint about the hidden feeling.

Example: too near, too distant (continued)
At the same time as linking the patient's response to the break in analysis with his reaction to the return of his mother, the analyst interpreted specifically the defensive nature of the patient's aloofness. He suggested that the patient had to be aloof, the defence, in order to control his painful feelings of abandonment. The patient responded by saying that he didn't care what the analyst had been doing during the break. However, when the analyst took this up in terms of his not wanting to know what his mother had been doing when she went away, the patient became more curious about the analyst's activities, hinting at a hidden meaning. Further analysis revealed that his mother had not really travelled abroad during her absence but following an extra-marital affair, had become pregnant, and had gone to live with her parents. The patient had a half-brother about whom he knew nothing. This startling fact only emerged after the transference relationship had intensified to the extent that the patient began to speculate about who the analyst had been with during his holiday. The analytic work around this led the patient to discuss the past openly with his parents.

Diminution of the defences following interpretation may initially lead to an increase in anxiety, which itself will be defended against and need further interpretation, but gradually unconscious feelings come towards the surface through the process of free association. These should not be guessed at: premature interpretation of hidden meanings only leads to incomprehension on the part of the patient, or a decrease in rapport, leaving the patient feeling misunderstood. Interpretation within the triangle of conflict is sometimes called *resistance or defence interpretation* which, of course, does not aim to remove defences altogether but only to soften them and help them become more flexible.

The overall aim within this schematic approach to interpretation is, little by little, to join the hidden feelings of the triangle of conflict with their origins in the parent relationship or distant past. The route by which this is effected is via the transference and its link with the past. Transference interpretation can now be directed towards the here-and now relationship as a repetition of the past – 'you fear that I will reject you if you disagree, just like your father did' – implying a causal connection between present behaviour and past experience. However, especially in very disturbed patients, under the sway of the primary process, past and present may merge into one another. Thus the patient's *present* feelings evoked by the analyst may *appear* as though from the past. This may account for the phenomenon of 'false memory syndrome' (see p. 34), and is consistent with the claim by Spence (1982, 1986) and Schafer (1983) that psychoanalysis is concerned as much with developing a coherent and consistent narrative as it is with 'historical truth' (see also p. 20)

The 'mutative interpretation'

Strachey (1934, 1937) considered interpretation within the transference relationship to be *the* tool for effecting change (cf. p. 103). The analyst acts like a new object for the patient, which, together with the *transference interpretation*, creates a new symbolic structure of meaning with which the patient can approach the world. He gains both new experience *and* insight. Change occurs through identification with the analyst who, rather than behaving like archaic objects adhering to the talion law ('an eye for an eye'), is friendly and available. At first sight this seems to contradict Freud's (1919) demand that the 'patient should be educated to liberate and fulfil his own nature, not to resemble ourselves' and it raises the question of what the patient identifies with. Is it the analyst as Strachey suggests, the psychoanalyst's functions (Hoffer 1950), the analytic relationship (Klauber 1972), the analyst as a self-object (Kohut 1977) or some other component of the therapeutic process? Presumably there is a movement, in Piagetian terms, from accommodation to assimilation (see p. 83), so that the analyst is at first an 'external' internal object, but later his functions become integrated into the patient's personality. Whatever the answer to these questions, all agree that interpretation, however accurate its content, is only effective if given in the context of a trusting, secure and empathic relationship.

Analyst-centred and patient-centred interpretations

The form of transference interpretation is also important. Steiner (1993) divides interpretations into either *analyst-centred* or *patient-centred*, linking them with the projective–introjective systems involved in countertransference reactions. Patient-centred interpretations are concerned with what the analyst imagines is going on in the patient's mind, corresponding with the triangle of conflict: 'You seemed to dismiss that thought (defence) because you became fearful (anxiety) that it may cause you some pain (hint at the hidden feeling).' Here the patient gains a feeling of being understood and that someone is aware of his mental pain.

Analyst-centred interpretations are phrased in such a way as to take into account not just what may be in the patient's mind but also to recognise what the patient thinks is going on in the analyst's mind: 'You are afraid that I might become angry with you.' Here the patient learns about the possibility of another mind in communication with his own (Fonagy 1991; cf. p. 61). Many interpretations contain elements of both, linking together what the patient does, thinks or wishes with the state of mind of the analyst. Excessive use of either form of interpretation leads to problems. Patient-centred statements downplay the importance of the analytic relationship and unconsciously may be experienced by the patient as an attempt to blame and prematurely return projections, while analyst-centred comments may lead the patient to feel that the analyst is only preoccupied with himself and not interested in his real difficulties in the external world.

Extra-transferential interpretation

Strachey's concept of the mutative transference interpretation had a powerful effect on psychoanalytic technique. Some analysts concentrate almost exclusively on the relationship with the analyst, and on the phantasies that are operating in the present and the anxieties that their interpretation awakens (Joseph 1989). Perhaps to redress the balance there has been a resurgence of interest in extra-transference interpretations – that is interpretation outside the analytic relationship itself – especially when a serious impasse (*q.v.* p. 188) has developed in the analysis (Stewart 1989).

Symington (1983) and Coltart (1986) describe the 'analyst's act of freedom', which is a spontaneous and direct communication – often of anger or exasperation, bringing the patient's attention to the fact that the analyst is a real person rather than an all-encompassing, all-knowing 'breast'. This can have a dramatic effect on the progress of an analysis in the doldrums. The element of surprise extricates patient and analyst from mutual imprisonment, and can produce new insight and further development of the therapeutic process. O'Shaughnessy (1992) suggests that the analytic relationship can become an 'over-close enclave' which acts as a substitute for relationships outside. Extra-transference interpretation may break this claustrophobic atmosphere, but equally it can become a self-indulgent excursion out of the analysis and a move into directive therapy and advice. A judicious balance is likely to be the best course.

Irrespective of type, accuracy of content and form, *timing* of interpretation is all-important, as it is in all human interactions, where musical analogies seem particularly apposite. An interpretation should be given at the point of mounting tension, at the moment when affectively charged ideas and associations are firmly attached to the analyst or the analysis, when the atmosphere is ripe, and when the patient almost sees it for himself (Freud 1940a). Such moments – which arise intuitively, presumably on the basis of the analyst's sensitivity, his own analysis and experience – often come at the end of a long process of clarification, elaboration, occasional questioning, testing of the transference–countertransference relationship, and confrontation. A good interpretation restores balance, promotes integration, and leads to insight.

Insight

Although the concept of insight is important in psychoanalysis, there is no agreement as to its exact meaning or to its necessity for therapeutic success. The dramatic portrayal of earth-moving insight in Hollywood films is a far cry from everyday therapeutic reality. The cathartic recovery of buried memories happens rarely in comparison with the daily bread and butter of analytic practice. The gradual acquisition of insight is an intrinsic part of the therapeutic process from the beginning of analysis. The intrapsychic model of insight suggests a recognition by an individual of his own unconscious reality and its effect on his behaviour, his unconscious childhood conflicts and their influence on his present relationships, and an increasing understanding of his inner nature.

It is important to distinguish between cognitive insight and emotional realisation (Zilboorg 1952). Intellectual knowledge on its own is not enough and may act as a resistance to change. Thoma and Kachele (1987), in summarising various views on insight, remark that nearly all authors 'express the opinion that "true" insight or "seeing in" lies between the poles constituted by emotions and intellect'. 'Seeing in' refers to a component of insight related to accessibility of thoughts and feelings, which leads to gradual change. A second element is also important, arising perhaps once or twice per analytic year, when there is a sudden 'ah-ha' experience, or moment of affective 'dynamic insight' (Reid and Finesinger 1952), when the repression barrier is lifted and unconscious knowledge becomes conscious. The dichotomy between gradual preparation and sudden change is familiar to developmental theory and can also be described mathematically by chaos theory (cf. Holmes 1992b).

Etchegoyen (1991) classifies insight as descriptive (i.e. verbal) or 'ostensive' (i.e. 'shown'). Descriptive insight is a verbal account or story about oneself, often built from associations. In contrast, ostensive insight is a more direct form of knowing – for example, when an individual feels he is in emotional contact with a specific psychological situation that he has known before. Proust's epiphany with the 'petite madelaine' would be a prototypical example (Holmes 1992b). Both types of knowledge are necessary if the therapeutic process is to move forward.

Kris (1956) describes insight in the context of the 'good hour' and contrasts it with the 'deceptively good hour'. In the good hour the patient starts the session with hostility and pessimism, but at a particular moment something the analyst says lifts the whole atmosphere and pieces of a jigsaw come together to form a complete picture. In contrast the deceptively good hour starts with an atmosphere of hope and satisfaction. The associations come easily and insight emerges rapidly without obvious arduous work. In these circumstances insight merely gratifies either the patient or the analyst's narcissism. The deceptively good hour often alights on one particular event from childhood and uses it tendentiously to account for all subsequent events. The analyst should be alert to this difficult distinction between the defensive use of insight and its positive role in promoting differentiation and autonomy.

In summary, insight integrates unconscious process with conscious knowledge, links past and present, brings about greater harmony between conflictual wishes and enables the individual to modify and tolerate previous ways of functioning. Insight is not 'given' by the analyst but rather is assimilated by the patient, bit by bit, from the interpretive and non-interpretive elements of the therapeutic process. As the patient reflects on his new understanding from different perspectives and from varied aspects of his past and present life, he gathers together an array of emotions congruent with his insight – a process known as working through.

Working through

In 'Remembering, repeating and working through', Freud (1914c) makes the interesting observation that patients need time to work through their resistances if they are to feel convinced of the power of their underlying impulses. Thus working through can help increase self-esteem – the patient becomes aware of the magnitude of the struggle that confronts him, and the effort he is putting in. Working through takes place in the interval between the time the patient becomes aware of something that the analyst has told him and the moment he accepts it with conviction. It is the process that links intellectual (verbal) insight with emotional (ostensive) insight and is bound up with transference interpretation which aims to turn intellectual verbalisation into immediate experience. Insight leads to working through, and working through consolidates insight.

Given that one of the defining characteristics of psychoanalysis is its duration, it is perhaps curious that working through is relatively underdiscussed in the literature. Apart from the 1914 article, Freud made no systematic study of it (Laplanche and Pontalis 1980). Most analysts would agree that *time* – a minimum of three years, say – is needed for fundamental psychological change to occur in treatment, but this clinical fact remains to be adequately theorised, as does the observation that symptoms may return temporarily shortly before termination. Freud's views were formulated firmly within the drive-resistance-insight era. However, within the context of a developmental model of change, time becomes less problematic. The patient has first to become aware of and so unlearn dysfunctional relational patterns of a lifetime, second to experiment, imitate and accommodate to new ways of relating, and thirdly to assimilate these into a more mature personality structure. Changes begun on the couch have to be tried out in 'real life', and, conversely, everyday life events – of love, loss, success, and disappointment – need to be scrutinised and learned from in therapy. All this, inevitably, takes time, and needs 'working through'. Through this process the ramifications of unconscious forces are traced, as far as possible, in all aspects of a patient's life, both within the analysis and outside, and finally lead to the point at which he feels the time may have come to leave his analyst.

Termination

At first both patient and analyst may dismiss thoughts of finishing analysis, fearing that they may be part of a resistance, but gradually the idea gains credence and is spoken about openly. As a general rule the topic of finishing should come from the patient rather than the analyst, although there may be exceptional circumstances when the analyst needs to broach the subject himself because of personal reasons, because he feels the patient will not get further with the treatment, or even because he cannot tolerate the emotional burden he experiences in relation to a particular patient. He may then advise the patient on a different form of treatment or suggest another analyst more able to deal with the patient's difficulties.

Theoretical objectives of treatment should not be confused with more common-sense indicators of success. In clinical practice observable changes occur in the patient's life and in his relationship to the analyst. Most obviously, symptoms decline, relationships within the family improve, effective working increases, social relationships are better, sexual life is less conflictual, and anxiety and guilt lessen. A psychic quietening seems to take place which is not synonymous with an acceptance of society's norms. An individual may be helped to divorce or not to have to divorce, to change employment or not find himself forced out of a job but gain promotion, to submit a little in his relationships or stand up more often for his own needs, to lose some friendships or gain others. But external changes are not enough. Evidence from within the analysis is also needed.

External changes are corroborated by the analytic process – a patient who talks about how much better his relationship is with his wife may also report a dream that confirms this. He shows more freedom and playfulness of thought, his dreams are more coherent, he is able to negotiate separations such as weekends and breaks more easily without acting out or recourse to excessive use of defensive manoeuvres; his fears of the analyst lessen, allowing him to challenge, consider, show concern, and recognise and accept his failings. There is a move from paranoid to depressive anxieties, oedipal to genital relationships. The balance and oscillation between the two tells the analyst that treatment is nearing an end. In the depressive position a patient becomes aware of his own impulses and phantasies, distinguishes reality from phantasy, recognises his contribution to difficulties and feels concern for others. Projective mechanisms lessen, become more flexible, and greater trust develops. Parts of the self that have been lost through pathological projective identification are regained (Steiner 1989, 1993). Rickman (1950) suggests that a point of irreversibility is reached in a successful analysis when all these factors join together and the patient is able to maintain his changes and continue a self-analysis when necessary.

The process of termination has been likened to a new beginning (Balint 1949), weaning (Meltzer 1967), mourning (Klein 1950a), detachment (Etchegoyen 1991) and maturation (Payne 1950). Whichever framework is used, there is general agreement that termination is difficult for both patient and analyst. The patient struggles for the autonomy that he has wished for and at the same time experiences a continuous regressive pull to former comforting patterns of dependency. He has to surrender his need for the analyst to act as a container. At first the analyst's 'containing functions' are internalised but not integrated into the self so no true separation takes place. The patient's lessening of anxiety continues to require the presence of the analyst. Steiner (1993) considers this the first stage of achieving separateness. The second stage involves relinquishing the object that has been the receptacle of projections, facing its loss, and working through a process of mourning. The patient has to acknowledge the help he has been given as well as accept the loss of its on-going comfort, just as he gave up the breast and was weaned. He needs to accept the limitations of treatment and relinquish a desired but unattainable ideal. For his part the analyst has to follow the fluctuations between regression and integration, accept his own sadness about the ending of an important relationship, mourn the fact that he may never again hear about somone with whom he has become so familiar, and reconcile himself to areas of failure. His patient may pick up, either consciously or unconsciously, these feelings of failure and attempt to convince him of the success of the analysis. Patient and analyst have to work together to accept the analysis as 'good enough' and not resort to mutual admiration or the apportionment of blame.

Pedder (1988) dislikes the word termination, which has connotations of abortion and finality, contrary to the spirit of ending an analysis. He prefers to think in terms of weaning and gradual disillusionment. A relationship that has developed a high degree of intimacy and importance cannot be discarded easily. Many months or even a period of over a year may need to elapse between a suggestion of termination and an actual ending. But once fixed, the date should be irreversible. If changed, the process of termination will have to begin all over again with no more surety than it did the first time. The date must only be finalised after enough work has been done on the final phase of the analysis. Freud (1937) pointed out in his classic discussion of how envy and inability to accept reality may lead to interminable analyses, that a 'lion only springs once'.

Should the analyst alter his technique during this phase? Should there be a gradual reduction in the frequency of sessions rather than a clean break? There are no clear answers to these questions. Some patients seem to like symmetry, and if their sessions gradually increased to five times a week they reduce them in a similar pattern; others prefer to work to a date and stop, often at the time of a normal break, say a summer or Christmas holiday. Patient and analyst have to decide these things together and understand their reasons for any particular course. The analyst may 'lighten' the transference towards the final few months, answer questions more, and be marginally more open, but his basic analytic approach should not change. Just as the reactions of the patient to beginning analysis and during the analysis have their individual quality, so do those associated with finishing. Crucial aspects of the patient's psychic functioning may be revealed and will be lost if the analytic task is abandoned before the end.

With the exception of those training as analysts or therapists, the post-analytic phase has received little attention, perhaps because of the assumption by both patient and analyst that a clean break is best. The clean break is desirable for several reasons. First, meeting outside the analytic hour is difficult enough for both participants during the analysis, let alone soon after finishing when unresolved transferences and countertransferences are likely to be mobilised without any structure within which to work them through. Second, offers of further sessions, if necessary, may undermine the patient's belief in himself. Third, both patient and analyst may have fears about maintaining appropriate boundaries of any future relationship. On the other hand, a clean break with an injunction on no further contact is unrealistic, potentially hurtful and shows little understanding for the vagaries of life. Just as young adults need to return home from time to time even after they have officially 'left', so a patient in trouble may only need to see his former analyst for a few sessions to resolve matters, whereas to see someone else may require going over old ground before the new problem can be tackled. Furthermore, it should not be beyond the bounds of patient and analyst to negotiate any future meetings sensitively, without excessive distancing or over-familiarity on either part. Certainly this has to be done within training organisations where an analysand may see his former analyst on a regular basis, listen to him argue with colleagues, behave badly on committees, and function in other distinctly human ways.

Chapter 9

Clinical dilemmas

Every beginner in psycho-analysis probably feels alarmed at first at the difficulties in store for him when he comes to interpret the patient's associations and to deal with the reproduction of the repressed.

(Freud 1915: 159)

In every analytic session the analyst is faced with technical dilemmas – when to speak, when to remain silent; when to interpret, when to support; when to direct the patient and when to help him clarify his thoughts. In this chapter we shall be concerned with specific issues presenting to the analyst which may cause particular difficulty. We can offer no simple answer to these problems. Psychoanalysis cannot be 'manualised', and indeed the attempt to do so even with short-term therapies is fraught with difficulty (Fretter *et al.* 1994). There is not a unique, correct, solution. Each patient has to be treated according to his particular circumstances. Every analyst deals with complex clinical situations from experience based on his own analysis, knowledge gleaned in case discussions, and from reading and supervision. As a result, the clinical views expressed in this chapter are inevitably personal and we recognise that many clinicians may practise differently. Nevertheless, we hope that our comments will help newcomers to orient themselves around some of the problems. It is especially important to remember that each difficulty has a particular meaning to patient and analyst within the context of the analytic process.

The clinical problems we are concerned with here may be divided into four types (see Table 9.1).

First, there are problems which interfere with the overall *continuity* of the sessions but do not immediately threaten the actual treatment

Table 9.1 Classification of clinical problems

Continuity	Enactment		Special groups
	Acting in	*Acting out*	
Absence	Physical contact	Suicide	Adolescents
Lateness	Persistent questions	Self-mutilation	Elderly
Breaks	Presents	Drug abuse Alcohol abuse	Medication
Impasse	Money		
Family	Silence		Eating disorder Training patients Ethnicity Previous analysis

itself – for example, non-attendance, lateness, breaks and the so-called 'therapeutic impasse'. Second, there are *enactments*, which may be *within* a session, known as 'acting in', such as excessive or inappropriate demands, regular present giving, problems around fees and silence on the part of the patient. Enactments outside the session present the most serious challenge to the analyst and may threaten the treatment itself. These usually take the form of serious acting out, such as suicide attempts, self-mutilation and drug abuse. Finally, there are *groups of patients* that present particular difficulties – for example, adolescents, borderline patients, patients on psychotropic medication, patients suffering from eating disorders, elderly patients, candidates in psychotherapeutic or analytic training, those from ethnic minority groups and those who have had a previous analysis. It is not our intention to cover all these examples but rather to illustrate how to approach some of the clinical issues that they raise. Inevitably problems are often linked. The patient who acts out is also likely to act in, the one who arrives late may also fail to pay bills on time, the patient who makes excessive demands may also threaten suicide and so on.

PROBLEMS CONCERNING THE ANALYTIC PROCESS

Difficulties that interfere with the process of analysis are grist to the mill in all analyses. In general, they are examples of resistance (see p. 164) and will always need to be addressed if an analysis is to progress. All have unconscious ramifications depending on the patient's particular dynamic constellation and the state of the analytic relationship at that moment. The analyst and patient gradually understand that an event, such as lateness or 'forgetting' to pay a bill, a demand, or a feeling, has specific meaning at a particular time, related to their relationship and its representation of the past. However, the same experience may be understood differently later, as their relationship changes and deepens. Any event or symptom is 'overdetermined', each having its own coherence at a particular level of interpretation (Breuer and Freud 1895).

Lateness

Lateness for a session is often associated with resistances within a session such as repetitive material, avoidance of painful topics, reporting of trivial daily events, and silence. Sometimes, the patient is consciously aware that the reason for his lateness is that he doesn't wish to talk about something. More often, he finds himself arriving late for a variety of apparently unavoidable reasons. Apologies are given and the session continues normally. The analyst needs to make a mental note of the lateness and listen carefully to the material. There is usually no point in trying to address the lateness straight away. There will not be enough supporting evidence for interpretation. Questions are likely to divert the session away from spontaneous material and attempts to take up the unconscious motivation behind the lateness too soon will lead to rebuttal and repetition of the manifest rationale for the late arrival. It is best to wait.

Example: the stalling architect
An architect, arriving 15 minutes late for his session, explained that his car wouldn't start and then kept stalling. He apologised. The analyst accepted his explanation without comment but noted that it was unusual for his patient to be so late. The patient continued to apologise saying that he had wanted to be on time as he felt the session the day before was important. He couldn't remember what the session had been about but he had felt upset by it. The session then became punctuated by hesitancy and silence – it did not seem to start properly and 'kept on stalling'. As a result of the hesitancy in the session, the silence and the patient's inability to remember the previous session, which had been about his increasing feelings of dependency, the analyst suggested that

the patient was in fact reluctant to come because of anxiety about his reliance on the analysis. The patient then talked about how he had rather hoped that the car would stop altogether and that he would be forced to miss the session. Further work suggested that the patient was thinking about stopping his analysis, which he felt was demeaning, fearing that he would become addicted to it.

Some patients are persistently late, often by the same number of minutes each day, and others are rigidly early or on time, showing little flexibility in the regime they set themselves. The reasons behind their rigidity may only become clear after years in analysis! In these cases, it is the rigidity rather than the lateness itself that suggests the pattern is defensive in nature and aimed at avoiding painful feelings.

Example: controlling time
A 19-year-old student was 10 minutes late for every session from the start of analysis. He never mentioned it and seemed unperturbed. His father was a dominating man who was rather rigid and obsessional. There had been no period of adolescent rebellion and the patient was successfully completing a university course. Whenever the analyst mentioned the patient's lateness he shrugged and said nothing further. The analyst decided to leave the persistent lateness in the background for a number of months. During one session the analyst had himself been delayed. The patient, arriving at his usual time of 10 minutes late, had seen the analyst hurrying back to the consulting room. The analyst apologised but the patient became increasingly angry and talked about how the analyst had ruined the treatment. He said he expected the analyst to be sitting in the consulting room waiting for him to arrive at the start of the session: it wasn't up to the analyst to dictate when the session was going to start; it was his prerogative. Further work showed the patient's phantasy was of being omnipotently in control of both the session and the analyst. This phantasy had been punctured by the analyst's late arrival. The patient was behaving towards the analyst very much as his father had treated him. If the family were going out, his father would insist that he and his brother were ready and waiting, lined up by the front door at a prearranged time. His father would then slowly gather his things together before inspecting them.

These clinical vignettes show the importance of waiting before trying to understand the meaning of interferences with the analytic process. This is in accordance with Freud's recommendation of interpreting when an unconscious idea is just below the surface – neither so deep that the patient will not understand, nor so near consciousness that the patient can work it out for himself. Resistance occurs at a point of psychological conflict and therefore represents a potential focus of change. A resistance, such as persistent lateness or abject punctuality, needs to become uncomfortable to the patient before its analysis can be effectively accomplished. The architect felt perturbed about his lateness and apologised. As a result it was possible to interpret his lateness in the immediacy of the session. In contrast the student was apparently unperturbed by his unpunctuality and it only became available for analysis when threatened by the analyst's lateness.

Breaks

Breaks in treatment at weekends, for holidays, or unavoidable commitments on the part of both the analyst and patient, are an inherent interference with the analytic process. But, once again, they offer an opportunity for change as a result of the feelings they stir up. Some patients react to a weekend or holiday with relief and celebration. To these patients the analysis is in some way a chore, a requirement, and they struggle under a feeling of oppression by the analyst. In their mind the analyst is a critical superego figure, always ready to comment adversely on their behaviour and fantasies. Weekends and breaks become a freedom that is relished. Friday sessions may be marked by a sense of relief and excitement while Monday sessions are full of foreboding, despondency and guilt about the uninhibited activities of the weekend. Others experience the weekend or holidays as an abandonment. One patient secretly tape-recorded Friday sessions, playing them back to herself throughout the weekend; another would reluctantly leave the Friday session and go to bed for the whole weekend, only able to come alive again on Monday morning. For some the break symbolises primitive feelings of abandonment; in others it will stimulate feelings associated with an early oedipal situation, representing imagined exclusion from the parental relationship.

Example: a needy intrusion
One Friday a patient protested that he would feel better if he knew what the analyst was doing over the weekend. At the weekend he

found himself passing the analyst's consulting room and looking at his house to see who was there. On Sunday evening he phoned to check that his Monday session was at the usual time. On Monday he was sad and depressed as a result of his feeling of exclusion, and guilty and ashamed about his intrusion.

His father had left home when he was 4 years old. From that time he slept in his mother's bed until he was 12. For many years this gave him a feeling of security and safety.

Patterns emerge over weeks and months. Only after they are clear can the analyst begin to address them. Reactions vary according to the transference relationship at the time. Patients in a severely regressed state or in a malignant regression (see p. 162) may refuse to leave the consulting room. Here, a reality based statement such as 'you will have to leave now as I must continue with my working day. When I have finished I shall contact you and we will decide what to do' may help. The analyst has to assess the patient's capacity to manage over a break or weekend and may need the help of another mental health worker or the patient's general practitioner. In general it is best to anticipate such difficulties and to make appropriate arrangements well in advance, always considering the unconscious meaning of such extra-analytic actions (Stewart 1977). The bipersonal field (Langs 1978: p. 116) is never more in stark relief than when the analyst has to take on a management role.

Some analysts send their patients a post-card or write a brief letter during a long break. This may help borderline patients whose fragile hold on reality can be threatened by the prolonged absence of the analyst. The post-card reinforces the patient's recognition that the analyst keeps him in mind even when he is not there. However, it may also provoke envy, resentment and hostility whether from an exotic location or from a local area. The analyst should remember that he has sent the post-card or written the letter when the sessions resume, and to listen out for its effect on the patient.

Example: human contact

A borderline patient, feeling terribly frightened by a forthcoming month-long break, complained of being abandoned and uncared for. She experienced her analyst as sending her away. In her associations she remembered a time when her mother had gone off to hospital to give birth to her younger brother and she had to stay with an aunt for a month. Initially she protested, but after a few weeks of being away she no longer felt the need for her mother.

She expected the same to occur with the analyst's absence. When he sent her a post-card during the vacation to bridge the gap and to help continuity of the analytic relationship, she was amazed that he should understand how bad she felt and the therapeutic alliance was strengthened.

Another technical problem is the timing and dosage of interpretation before breaks. Patients may gradually withdraw just before a long break to protect themselves from uncovering painful experiences with which they will be left to struggle on their own for a number of weeks. The analyst should respect this and weigh up how much distress the patient can bear. The analyst has also to deal with his own countertransference reactions to weekends and breaks. Many take on more work than is sensible. Fridays come as a relief, Mondays as a chore, and holidays a release from exhaustion. Analysis is difficult enough without being subjected to such conditions which may, if unanalysed in supervision, be responsible for a therapeutic impasse.

Impasse

The term 'impasse' is used to denote a state in which the analysis neither progresses nor retreats. The setting itself is not noticeably changed, the patient continues to talk, apparently free-associating, the analyst interprets, but nothing changes and develops. It is tempting *either* to see an impasse as arising out of the patient's resistance *or* to consider it as a technical fault on the part of the analyst. However, an impasse is best seen as a joint problem to which both patient and analyst contribute. Both find themselves bound up in a tangled knot created by the patient's psychopathology and the analyst's countertransference. Rosenfeld (1987) ascribes most blockages in the patient–analyst interaction to the analyst's unconscious infantile anxieties. In order to avoid becoming aware of these areas, the analyst colludes with a complementary part of the patient's personality. In all cases of deadlock, therefore, the analyst has to examine very carefully his own feelings and look for hints of collusion between himself and his patient.

It is important to distinguish an impasse from a negative therapeutic reaction (see p. 165) which follows a period of progress. A true impasse develops slowly, almost imperceptibly, and is only recognised when the analysis remains static or the patient seems fixed in a particular frame of mind. By contrast, hostility, often in the guise of manic defences or manic attacks (Rosenfeld 1975), usually underlies a negative therapeutic reaction and may appropriately be taken up as envy of and triumph over the analyst. In an impasse hostility is conspicuously absent and manic defences are not apparent. Interpreting hostility will be incomprehensible to the patient, as well as unfair, since the analyst's reactions are involved as well (Rosenfeld 1987).

Meltzer (1967) describes a common impasse which develops when a patient is on the verge of moving into the depressive position and finishing treatment. At this time he takes responsibility for his guilt and badness but, rather than experiencing feelings of remorse and facing independence, he remains static. He prefers to use the analyst as a permanent prop. He is symptomatically better and can appreciate the help he has been given but continues to be preoccupied by his own well-being at the expense of his objects. Equally, an impasse based on 'reversible perspective' (Bion 1963) may be so subtle as to be undetected. Reversible perspective consists of manifest agreement between patient and analyst but latent disagreement and hostility. The patient seems to come for one purpose, but in reality has a covert agenda, e.g. to placate a partner, make social contact, or as part of a career plan in psychiatry or psychotherapy.

But what should the analyst do in these situations? Interpretation has already been shown to be ineffective. Sometimes it may be necessary to alter the setting for a short time – for example, by asking the patient to sit up, while the impasse is discussed openly and the patient's criticisms are listened to. At these times it is important not to interpret but to listen carefully and even answer the patient's questions directly. In the case of 'The Wolf Man', Freud (1918) took more drastic action, setting a definite end point to the analysis. Inevitably, such a decision during an impasse is infused with countertransference and such a move is probably best done only after discussion with a colleague. Supervision is essential in this situation.

ENACTMENT: ACTING IN

Clearly, many of the situations discussed above present the analyst with problems within the session, but not so immediately as sudden demands, financial matters, present giving and continuing silence. Once again the primary rule applies. All events must be considered within the patient–analyst relationship, giving special consideration to transference and countertransference.

Physical contact

Requests from patients range from the relatively benign, such as questions and requests to change sessions, to the more problematic such as demands for *physical contact*. Occasionally the analyst may be forced to make physical contact to restrain a patient (Stewart 1992) who sees nothing untoward in his or her expression of need and demand for gratification. A patient with an erotised transference (see p. 109) may be unperturbed by the analyst's refusal of a tenacious demand for sexual gratification. Because of blurring of internal and external reality, the expectation of sexual consummation with the analyst is experienced as reasonable, desirable and, above all, achievable. If the analyst deviates from his rule of abstinence, even in an attempt to create a more 'holding' environment, the outcome is likely to be disastrous (see 'too close, too soon', p. 230). The task of the analyst is to help the patient first to recognise the inappropriateness of the demands and, second, to reflect on their underlying motivation – a move from 'ego-syntonic' demand for gratification, in which there is no obvious anxiety, to 'ego-dystonic' state, in which anxiety and conflict over the desires come to the surface. Although some demands for touching or holding are obviously inappropriate and part of an erotised transference, others, such as looking for reassurance and tenderness from the analyst, appear more reasonable but may represent a subtle denial of aggression.

Careful scrutiny of countertransference and vigilant listening to the patient's material show how acceding to the patient's request may mean that the opportunity for a mutative, albeit painful, experience for both patient and analyst is missed. Every demand for contact needs to be considered in this way. Technically the analyst must ask himself 'What role am I being asked to play for this patient at this particular time, and why?' Winnicott (1958) suggests that a common reason for such a demand is the need of the patient to experience in the present, within the relationship with the analyst, those extreme feelings which belonged to earlier traumatic experiences that were themselves frozen in time because they had been overwhelming for the primitive ego. Casement (1985) argues that analysis enables such traumata to be 'brought within the area of omnipotence'. His refusal to hold a patient's hand – after carefully considering the question and so signalling to her that he took it seriously – brought back for the first time a terrifying memory of her mother fainting just at the moment when she was being anaesthetised following a painful scalding at the age of 2, a wound that had deformed her self-image ever since. Following the re-enactment the patient improved dramatically, in a way that could not have happened had he merely offered her the support she was demanding.

Balint (1968) states that holding the patient's hand can in special circumstances be a helpful first step to a 'new beginning', and overcome a 'basic fault'. Pedder (1986) similarly argues that bonding between a weak individual and an attachment figure can be protective rather than sexual, and therefore that hand-holding is not, as some would argue, inherently seductive.

The patient's family

Patients who create severe difficulties within treatment are also likely to cause problems to other professionals and their families. In the 'basic model' technique of psychoanalysis, relatives are a neglected group often distanced from the treatment in order to protect the therapeutic alliance and the privacy and intimacy of the relationship of patient and analyst. They are viewed as a source of danger, contaminating the aseptic field. Freud (1912a) confessed himself 'utterly at a loss' to know how to treat patients' relatives. However, their lives are inevitably influenced by the patient's analysis and it is natural for them to worry, take an interest, and be affected if the patient changes. It is important to distinguish whether relatives' involvement arises from the patient himself, their own anxieties, the analyst's worries, or a mixture of all three.

Unconscious processes of spouses may have a marked influence on the outcome of treatment.

Example: an involved husband

A married borderline patient relied on her husband to stop her from cutting herself and taking overdoses. She had to report in to him at preassigned times if she was out, he dispensed her medication on a daily basis, and he regularly searched her handbag to remove razor blades. If she failed to phone in at a prearranged time, or if he found razors in her bag, he punished her by withdrawing some of her financial allowance. On many occasions he physically restrained her from lacerating her arms. During the patient's analysis it became clear that she and her husband were engaged in a subtle sado-masochistic interaction disguised as caring support. As the analyst and patient began to address this issue, the husband insisted that he would no longer pay for treatment. By this time the therapeutic relationship was strong enough to allow the patient to challenge her husband's threat. Marital conflict was inevitable. The patient's husband requested a meeting with the analyst and, after asking the patient, he agreed. In discussion it was decided that the patient should continue in analysis while they jointly saw a marital therapist. Athough this was an unusual course, it saved the treatment.

There is an increasing tendency for psychoanalysts to treat border-line and narcissistic personalities. A large number of these will become suicidal or self-destructive and others may have drug and alcohol problems. Serious acting out may occur. In these circum-stances relatives can be allies rather than enemies. It is often helpful to see a spouse or partner at the initial interview in order to discuss the treatment. If a contract is set up, as may be the case for borderline patients (see p. 232), it is important that both patient and relative agree with and understand how it operates. If difficulties are not foreseen, the analyst may be forced to contact relatives in an emergency, overruling the normal practice of not doing so without the patient's permission. However, the analyst needs to think carefully about what he tells the relatives, in order to protect his relationship with his patient. It is best to discuss this with the patient beforehand. Alternatively, the patient should be present at all meetings involving the relatives. This minimises the risk of informa-tion becoming distorted or used inappropriately within the family, but it increases the danger of the analyst basing his treatment on what he perceives as an objective reality rather than on discoveries within the transference.

A request to see the analyst may come directly from the patient's partner rather than from the analyst or patient, especially if the partner feels shut out of the treatment.

Example: too much protection
A 36-year-old man had become seriously depressed and suicidal but not to the extent of requiring hospital admission. One morning he left the house without saying anything and did not return as normal for lunch. His wife and brother were worried, and so phoned the analyst to see if he had been to his session that morning. The analyst refused to answer, saying that she would need the patient's permission. Inevitably the patient's wife and brother were infuriated and drove round to the analyst's house to confront her.

On reflection the analyst felt she was shutting out the relatives in the same way as the patient had shut out his family by walking out without saying anything. She then arranged a meeting between them all and took up the patient's withdrawal and the reasons for creating such anxiety about suicide in his wife and relatives.

Occasionally a patient may bring a relative unannounced to a session.

Example: a heated meeting
A patient who had been in analysis for two years suddenly arrived at a session together with his wife. He told the analyst that his wife had asked to come but his wife contradicted this saying that he had asked her to come. They had had a row the night before and the patient wanted the analyst to adjudicate. The analyst said he would agree to see them together briefly and answer any questions they may have, but in future such meetings should be prearranged. In the ensuing discussion, husband and wife started to argue again, with the patient threatening to hit his wife. The analyst stopped the session and pointed out to his patient that he seemed to want to show him how angry and out of control he could become. The patient's wife responded immediately by saying that she had always felt the analyst didn't know the severity of the patient's difficulties and what she had to put up with.

This vignette illustrates the ambivalence inherent in such situations. For the patient, it was an attempt to avoid working through his aggression and hatred of the analyst. His conflicts were being acted out with his wife rather than contained within the analysis. For his wife, it was to allay her anxieties that the analyst was encouraging the patient's threatening behaviour, and a healthy wish, perhaps unconsciously driven by her husband, to bring his uncontrollable behaviour into the transference and out of the marriage.

Involvement of relatives has always been openly accepted in the analysis of children and adolescents. It is commonplace for parents to be seen at intervals by the analyst, although confidentiality of session material is maintained, or to be offered help in their own right. Nevertheless, in adult analysis, too great an involvement may become defensive on the part of the analyst and detract from enduring and working through conflicts which are central to the patient and to analytic progress. This is particularly likely to happen when patients are suicidal and anxieties are therefore at a maximum.

Example: a secret pact

A borderline patient, working as a dental nurse, had always harboured thoughts of suicide as a solution to her problems. Prior to her marriage she had tried to kill herself by injecting a cocktail of drugs and jumping from a building. She had never told her husband about this and he was unaware of the seriousness of her plight and of her persistent suicidal thoughts. When her suicidal thoughts became compulsive, just before a break in her treatment, the analyst decided that he must talk to her husband. After asking the patient's permission, her husband was invited to a meeting. As a result of the relief that her secret past was now revealed, the patient's suicidal thoughts receded, but returned some months later just before the next holiday. Once again the analyst considered talking to her husband but was now more circumspect, realising that this was not really getting to grips with the problem. He broached the subject with the patient who, this time, refused permission. The analyst became aware that he only wanted to tell her husband of the return of the suicide risk to protect himself from criticism if she killed herself, and because he needed someone else's support in the treatment. The patient's refusal was an implicit statement that patient and analyst needed to deal with the problem within their relationship. However, the analyst requested supervision from a senior colleague to help him tolerate his worries about the patient's possible suicide. This enabled him to address the thoughts and feelings of suicide with the patient, who found them equally intolerable. The previous solution of talking to the husband had, in fact, been an unconscious attempt by the patient, in collusion with the analyst, to undermine or even 'kill off' the analysis itself, which had engendered feelings of dependency and rage in the patient. Further analysis enabled this to be linked to the tendency of the patient's parents to bring in outside help during her childhood when she had a problem. The patient had experienced this as a sign that they did not love her enough to help her themselves, and that when she felt she needed them most they were likely to abandon her.

ENACTMENT: ACTING OUT

Acting out has become an over-inclusive term, often encompassing all behaviours of which the analyst disapproves as well as actions, such as recurrent destructive acts, which form part of an individual's character or personality. In its more restricted sense it refers to those acts or series of acts that are a substitute for remembering and repeating – 'the patient. . . acts it out before us, as it were, instead of reporting it to us' (Freud 1940a). Acts within the session, such as walking round the room, hitting the wall, pushing books off the shelf, or actualisation in the transference, have been known as 'acting in' (Eidelberg 1968). Both acting out and acting in are examples of *enactment*. Acting out implies a regression to a prereflective, pre-verbal level, a belief in the magical effects of action, and a desperate need to get a response from the external world.

The psychoanalytic setting itself therefore encourages acting out by inducing regressive behaviour. Maturity implies integration of action, sublimation, symbolisation and other 'higher' functions. The dis-integration associated with regression is particularly marked in borderline and narcissistic patients (*q.v.* p. 222). For these patients actions speak louder than words, create a more immediate release of tension and frustration, have greater potential for influencing the analyst than continual dialogue and often give a spurious sense of control. However, acting out will occur in every analysis. It is impossible for all aspects of experience, especially certain affects and sensations, to be expressed in words – as all who have been in love can testify. The task of the analyst is to ensure that enactments are a stimulus to the analysis rather than an interference.

Acting out has both positive and negative aspects, the latter often resulting from the consequences of the action rather than from the act itself. On the positive side, the act may be a communication that becomes a useful source of analytic material (Limentani 1966). Balint (1968) describes a patient who enacted a somersault in her session, ushering in a breakthrough in her analysis. On the negative side it is destructive, personally dangerous or even life-threatening and may jeopardise the analysis; the unconscious internal drama or phantasy passes directly to the outside, circumventing thought and psychological defence, and so gains expression. Often close analysis of an episode of acting out will reveal important details of an unconscious conflict.

Example: a problem of expression

A 29-year-old man began psychoanalytic treatment with a male analyst because of sexual anxieties, concerns about his appearance, and difficulty in getting close to people. He had experienced his mother as a dominating, overly organising woman who was so obsessed with cleanliness that she gave him regular enemas as a small boy. As treatment progressed he became more confident and found himself a girlfriend. At the time at which they were planning to buy a flat together, he began to demand that the analyst reassure him about the move. The analyst tried to interpret his fears of intimacy but failed to appreciate the concreteness of his patient's fears. Immediately after a session the patient took an overdose and cut his abdomen, blaming the analyst for not helping. This act was later understood as a communication that he was terrified that his girlfriend would dominate and control him and his 'insides' just as his mother had done, and that his father (analyst) would abandon him to his fate. His body represented the part of him that he felt his mother had abused and he now had to resort to overdose and self-laceration to show the analyst the terrifying nature of his phantasies and demonstrate his need. Following this event, the analyst and patient focused on the patient's serious fears that the analyst would stop seeing him. Such an event did not occur again and the patient gradually settled with his girlfriend.

Destructive acts such as this often have an electrifying effect on the analyst, especially when unexpected, and they may induce complementary countertransferential responses. He may apply rules and regulations, sometimes in panic, which may lead to an escalation rather than a diminution of the self-destructive acts, especially if unaccompanied by understanding. Interpretation is the vehicle through which acting out is best challenged. If the assessment interview suggests that serious acting out is likely to be a feature of analysis, the analyst needs to draw up a contract with the patient at the beginning of treatment (Kernberg *et al.* 1990; Selzer *et al.* 1987) and not wait until something untoward occurs. Appropriate support, set up before treatment, can be activated while the analysis continues. If unexpected, it presents serious challenges to the analyst, not least of which are his feelings of anger, fear and helplessness. Countertransference responses become crucial.

Bilger (1986) has suggested that the pressure placed on the analyst by the behaviour is the primary factor in its designation as acting out, and believes the central quality is one of transgression of an unspoken boundary.

Example: an intrusive greeting
A 48-year-old depressed man became friendly to the point of obsequiousness soon after starting treatment. After entering the

waiting room he would open the consulting room door to say 'hello' to the analyst even if there was another patient there. The analyst felt intruded upon and angry. The patient's act of popping his head round the consulting room door was later understood as a reversal of transference roles in which the patient acted like his mother who continually entered his bedroom when he was a boy to 'see how he was and just to say hello' while the analyst became the angry boy who felt invaded.

Analysts may themselves act out or even enjoy vicariously their patient's misbehaviour, much as a restrained parent may tacitly condone rebellious behaviour in his children. Such countertransferential influence should be considered if acting out escalates despite careful interpretation. Supervision is essential to help the analyst extricate himself from anti-therapeutic involvement.

Suicide

The threat of suicide poses the most immediate challenge to the analyst. He must assess the intensity of the threat and formulate a clear plan within a short space of time. This means gauging accurately the depth of despair, the level of hopelessness, the seriousness of plans, the degree of external support, as well as the contribution of exacerbating factors such as increasing use of alcohol or drugs. If there is no doubt about the seriousness of the threat, the analyst must act decisively, tell the relatives and other carers, and – against the patient's will if necessary – arrange hospital admission by himself or through a third party such as a GP or social worker. The effect this has on the viability of the analytic relationship can be dealt with later. In many cases the decisive action of the analyst may be beneficial to the analytic process which may have laboured for too long, and even been immobilised, under a constant threat of death.

Thoughts and threats of suicide can also become part of a patient's way of life. In these cases the analyst may tell the family that the patient is chronically suicidal and has a definite risk of death, expressing his willingness to enter into treatment but give no guarantee of success. Kernberg *et al.* (1990) suggest that realistic appraisal with relatives early in treatment, or even before treatment starts, helps to prevent the destructive involvement of relatives, and protects the analysis from the patient's attempts to control the therapy by inducing fear of third parties, and guilt about failure.

In order not to overreact to the threat of suicide the analyst needs to hold in mind the affective constellations: hopelessness, rage, and guilt that are commonly found in suicidal patients. These represent the wish to die, the self-directed wish to kill and the wish to be killed respectively. *Hopelessness* may infuse the analysis to such an extent that the analyst himself becomes hopeless. It is at these times that suicide becomes more likely. The analytic relationship should always contain some hope, even if it has to be carried by the analyst alone for a time. *Rage*, and the self-directed wish to kill, may be easier to deal with. The suicidal threats are ways of attacking, coercing, dominating, manipulating and controlling the analyst as well as the outside world. The underlying phantasy may be that of killing oneself to make someone else suffer for ever, and at last recognise one's importance or need. It is particularly important to understand who the analyst unconsciously represents in the patient's mind, and who therefore is the unconscious subject of the attack. Freud (1917) suggested that suicide only becomes possible if an individual becomes fully identified with a lost object. Self and object become fused. In phantasy, the attack is upon the abandoning object rather than the self, and killing oneself is equivalent to murdering the abandoning object who is causing so much pain.

Example: hopelessness, rage and guilt
A borderline patient felt that her life's task was to look after her mother. Her analysis had been dominated by her attempts to control her analyst by demanding session changes, phoning out of hours, and seeking sessions at weekends. When her mother died she became angry and bitter, denigrating herself and saying that she had achieved nothing. Without her mother she had no clear reason to live. She described herself as someone 'who nobody could see' and if she were dead there would only be a 'slight ripple in the world which would be covered over in an instant'. Her analyst suggested that she felt he would not notice that she had gone and would simply replace her with someone else. She then reported that she had begun to plan her suicide because of increasingly horrible thoughts about her dead mother. Her analyst tried to persuade her to go into hospital, but initially she refused. She reported a dream in which she was sitting at a window looking in from the outside. At first she saw her mother through the glass, and then suddenly they were both together on the inside. At that point she and her mother became one person. The patient then

banged her head on the window to try to get out but this only resulted in her smashing up her face, her brains oozing out, and blood gushing everywhere. Someone watched this scene without intervening and then walked up and led her away. She felt relief.

Her analyst interpreted the rage she felt towards her mother who had left her with no role and how she found herself wanting to join her mother, but at the same time escape from her. Escape led to her destruction (the smashing of her head against the window), an inability to think (her brains oozing out), as well as a feeling of guilt. The analyst-figure meanwhile merely sat near and watched. During the session her analyst insisted, and it was agreed, that she should go into hospital. He would not watch her trying to kill herself.

In this vignette, hopelessness is suggested by the patient's sense that her own death would only make a ripple. She tried to dominate the analyst and dictate how he should behave in the same way as she felt her mother did to her. At the point of her mother's death she attacked herself in a way that she wished, unconsciously, to attack her mother. The patient was identified with her mother, as illustrated by the dream. Suicide meant attacking the mother with whom she was identified, but the dream also suggested that it was, in phantasy, a way of differentiating herself from her mother. In the transference the analyst was a passive father who allowed her to remain controlled by her mother.

Analysis of the attack on the analyst by the patient may lead to severe feelings of *guilt* as the patient recognises his own part in his difficulties. This move to the depressive position (Klein 1952) is heralded by a realisation that the analyst has, and always has had, something useful to offer which has previously been denied or treated with contempt. When this is linked to important figures in the patient's past he may become overwhelmed with guilt, believing that he has destroyed those whom he unknowingly loved. The need for punishment becomes so severe as to become a wish to be killed by those whom he has harmed. Suicide becomes the only way of satisfying them. A sense of helplessness may also occur at these times and the patient may feel at the mercy of internal and external events over which he has no control. This further increases the risk of suicide, which becomes an action to relieve the anxiety of helplessness by being in control – to kill before being killed, turning passive into active (Laufer 1987).

It is tempting to translate these three constellations into technical strategies – hopelessness to a counter-response in the analyst of making affirming statements, rage to limit setting and active interventions, and guilt to facilitation of mourning and supportive work. However, things are rarely this simple. What is important about the analyst holding the three leitmotifs in mind is to allow him to empathise with the patient's desire to die, to understand the excitement of suicidal phantasies, to recognise the exhilarating sense of power they release, and not to underestimate their destructiveness.

SPECIAL GROUPS

Analysis in adolescence

Many of the problems discussed above are more common in the treatment of seriously disordered adolescents and young adults (cf. Chapter 3), especially acting out and the need to involve relatives. Adolescence is a time of developing independence. Sexual identity begins to become established. There is intense preoccupation with appearance and change in body image, an exploration of the balance between intimacy and individuation, grappling with fears of merging on the one hand, and isolation on the other. Adolescents are men and women of action as they struggle to understand and renegotiate their relationship with the world in the context of their developing social and sexual powers and frailties. They are wary of adults although desperate for new figures with whom to identify. Their internal world is in a state of confusion. Internal conflicts tend to be externalised, impulses difficult to control, and feelings dangerous to express. Phantasies can only be partially sublimated. Impulsivity, bewildering sexual feelings, and outbursts of anger and emotion result.

Inevitably these developmental processes affect the analytic process and necessitate technical changes on the part of the analyst, particularly at the beginning of treatment. An adolescent who enters treatment of his own accord usually feels that he has failed in his attempt to rework his psychological world, which was hitherto based on childhood relationships and identifications. He feels a sense of self-loathing and despair. At first it is best to listen and not to interpret. Transference interpretations evoke infantile relationships just when the adolescent is trying to move away from his childhood objects. If transference is addressed too early, the adolescent will be unable to distinguish between past and present objects, and will react as he would to the primary objects he is trying to separate from. As a result, he will have no choice but to terminate analysis.

The analyst needs to help the young person to separate past and present, but first must engage him in an analytic process. Some adolescents, especially those who self-refer, make excellent use of treatment and engage easily, but for others the process of engagement is stormy. Any relief from anxiety offered by analytic treatment is attacked because it is experienced as shameful, evoking regressive wishes of being cared for, held and looked after. The conflict between the wish to be cared for and the desire to be independent is externalised (Chused 1990). The analyst becomes a persecutor who is responsible for the pain and needs to be controlled. This is a serious impairment in an adolescent's ability to accept treatment. His experience of painful feelings is turned around and inflicted on the analyst, whom he may deride and taunt, sometimes with threats of suicide or violence. Breaks, weekends and absences on the part of the analyst are all felt as counterattacks and are often dealt with by action, turning passive into active. The adolescent leaves before a break, does not attend on Friday, comes for sessions at whim, and may be silent for long periods if the analyst is himself silent. Of course, not all adolescents who come for treatment are so difficult to engage and some may even idealise the analyst, seeing him as omniscient and the cure for all his problems. However, even this has its difficulties. The initial relief at the offer of help leads to an eagerness to talk, which later may turn to wariness of having revealed too much.

Before beginning analysis with an adolescent, it may be necessary to initiate contact with his parents. This is done for two very practical reasons. First, in contrast to adults, whose parental figures are active primarily in the internal world, adolescents continue to deal directly with parents who exert influence externally as well as internally. Arguments, fights, rejection, collusion, over-involvement and excessive protection are but a few examples of what may occur. Second, analysis of patients in early adolescence can only occur with parental support. Only the parents can back up the stability of the setting, and ensure that treatment is neither interrupted by holidays nor prematurely terminated. Often they will be paying for the treatment. They may also be of help during the frequent demands to stop the analysis. Therapeutic support for the family may also be necessary.

Once analysis has begun, the analyst should not fall into the trap of trying to reassure his patient that he is different from his patient's parents. It is inevitable that an adolescent will imagine that the analyst shares the same beliefs, and will respond to him in the same way, as his parents. The analyst needs to point this out rather than try to show it is not the case. He will come under constant pressure to collude with the denial of problems as the patient tries to repress his feelings of shame and guilt about wanting to be cared for and helped. If his patient has tried to kill himself, the suicidal act will be minimised in importance. It is terrifying for the adolescent to realise that his actions are a result of his inner experiences rather than the fault of others. The task of the analyst is gradually to help the patient (a) to accept internal conflict, (b) to understand that internal and external, past and present, can be differentiated, (c) to tolerate his impulses without acting on them, and (d) to recognise that his struggle for autonomy is hindered as much by internal conflicts as by external objects.

Psychoanalysis with older patients

There is no clear definition of the age at which someone becomes an 'older' patient. Freud (1898, 1904) suggested that patients over 50 years of age were not suitable for analytic treatment. He was concerned about the vast amount of psychological material to be covered and the inflexibility of the mental processes after that age. This view has been increasingly questioned and age is no longer a bar to psychoanalytic treatment (Sandler 1978; Nemiroff and Colarusso 1985). The question is not how old someone is, but whether that person is suitable for analysis. In this way the assessment of an elderly patient is essentially no different from that of other patients (see Chapter 7). The elderly patient who continues to seek new experiences, to form meaningful relationships and to remain active, is likely to show the psychological flexibility needed for analysis. Older patients who are reconciled to their achievements, show a wisdom borne of their experiences and have stable values, are thought to have a good prognosis (Simburg 1985). Some elderly patients have had psychotherapeutic treatment in the past, although it may have been of limited success; others require treatment in old age due to unconscious fears of death (Segal 1958). Another motivating factor behind a request for help is the 'last chance syndrome' (Hildebrand 1995; King 1980).

For the elderly, death is no longer a general concept but a personal matter as they face the crisis of 'integrity versus despair' (Erikson 1968). Death has its own private meaning to each individual, but Jaques (1965) suggests that unconsciously the phantasy is one of immobilisation, helplessness and fragmentation of the self while maintaining the ability to experience the resulting torment and persecution. Along with this, there is a continual requirement for the elderly to face up to changes inflicted as a result of the ageing process. These may involve a decline in physical abilities, loss of relationships, the need to replace sources of self-esteem, and the acceptance of increasing dependency. Facing these issues is painful, not only for the patient but also for the analyst who may be much younger. To face one's own death is hard enough but to do so time after time within the intimacy of an analytic relationship may be too much to bear (Kastenbaum 1964).

Similar problems occur in the analytic treatment of other patients who are faced with death, such as those with AIDS (Grosz 1993). Kastenbaum also suggests that the cultural outlook on the elderly is bleak and is reflected in the tendency to devalue those who work with them, especially within the psychiatric services. Analysts are not immune from such influences which may interfere with appropriate assessment and treatment. It is important to be aware of other countertransference responses in the treatment of the elderly, especially for young analysts. Unresolved rescue phantasies or hostile feelings related to the analyst's parents may be enacted with the patient (Myers 1984, 1986), fears of intense dependency interfere with the therapeutic process (Martindale 1989) and terror of loneliness leads to a denial of need, including extra-analytic help, on the part of both patient and analyst (Cohen 1982; Treliving 1988).

The patient on psychotropic medication

The undesirable polarisation of psychoanalysis and pharmacotherapy may be responsible for the limited discussion in the literature of the use of drugs during psychoanalytic treatment. It is commonly believed that drugs make people inaccessible to psychoanalytic treatment by dampening down the feelings that are the basis of analytic work. This is not the case. There is considerable evidence of the benefit of combined therapy in many illnesses. A combination of anti-depressants and psychotherapeutic treatment results in a better outcome in social functioning and symptom amelioration than either treatment alone (Klerman 1986). Medication may enable a patient to participate in and benefit from treatment. Anna Freud arranged for a colleague to prescribe medication for a severely depressed analytic patient, with highly beneficial results in the analysis (Lipton 1983).

Loeb and Loeb (1987) and Jackson (1993) discuss the necessity for medication and hospital care in the psychoanalytic treatment of manic-depressive disorders. Through psychoanalytic treatment patients were able to recognise some of the unconscious precipitants of their manic episodes, titrate their medication accordingly, and control their impulses better. A similar process has been observed in the treatment of schizophrenia (Robbins 1992). Wylie and Wylie (1987) show how a severely depressed patient was unable to work within the transference until the use of anti-depressants reduced her affective vulnerability and lessened her terror of addressing underlying conflict.

Psychoanalysis and pharmacotherapy are not intrinsically competitive or antagonistic treatments. Each has a different aim and is effective over a different time scale. This has led to the suggestion of a two-stage treatment strategy in which medication alleviates symptoms and sets the stage for later analytic treatment (Karasu 1982). As psychoanalysts take on more seriously ill patients, this is becoming more common. Patients can begin analysis while they are already taking medication, as well as requiring it during treatment. How the analyst deals with this aspect of treatment and how the patient uses the medication may have a profound effect on the course of analysis. Denial of the value of drugs, or overvaluation of their efficacy, may interfere with the analytic process as the following contrasting examples illustrate.

Example: drug denial
A patient, already on medication at the beginning of analysis, cut down her medication with the intention of stopping it, believing that the analyst was 'anti' drugs. Exploration of this fantasy indicated that analysis was idealised as good treatment, medication as bad. The patient even told her psychiatrist that her analyst had advised cutting down medication. In fact the analyst felt any reduction of medication was part of a denial of her psychotic illness and she needed to acknowledge her need of medication. Only regular discussion between the analyst and the psychiatrist about medication prevented an enactment of the patient's polarised views.

Example: a denigrating drug

A borderline patient continually denigrated her analyst quoting newspaper articles critical of psychoanalysis. Despite her rage she attended regularly and rarely missed a session for over a year. At a time of incessant criticism she demanded medication following a series of reports about a new anti-depressant described as a 'wonder-drug'. The analyst felt helpless in the face of her onslaught and was unable to address the issue. He was relieved when she visited a private psychiatrist who prescribed it for her. She brought the tablets to the next session, announcing that she was going to take the first dose of her 'cure'. Taunting him, she swallowed the tablet and left the session. The following day she reported that she felt better than ever before. Recognising that this must be a placebo effect, and taking into account his countertransference reaction, the analyst began to take up her sense of triumph in believing that she had defeated his attempts to help her, leaving him helpless and humiliated. She was now in control. The patient retorted that he should have reached out and stopped her taking the tablet in the session. The analyst took up the cruel elements in her taunts, and her need to remain in control and be out of his emotional reach. She could only get close to her object in this sado-masochistic way. Taking a pill had allowed her to feel that *she* could decide when someone 'got inside her'. Gradually the patient's contempt became available for exploration and she stopped the anti-depressant which had, in reality, made little difference to her symptoms.

It is important to ensure that the meaning of medication is analysed in the transference in the same way as any other action by the analyst such as taking a holiday, increasing fees, giving bills or arriving late. Does the medication have a specific meaning to the patient? Does it evoke any particular feelings, especially about the analyst?

Example: an open verdict

A patient who had been in analysis for two years became severely depressed. She had never seen a psychiatrist in the past; and nor had she needed medication. It was not the medical analyst's policy to prescribe medication and he referred her to a psychiatric colleague. The patient refused to attend the appointment, demanding to know why she had to see someone else and stating that if the analyst thought medication was required he should have prescribed it. It transpired that she felt the analyst was unable to cope with her suicidal and hostile feelings and that he was trying to get someone else to 'do his dirty work'. This related to her experience of her mother, who was herself chronically depressed throughout the patient's childhood, always asking her father to 'take her off her hands'. Eventually she agreed to the appointment and was prescribed an anti-depressant. The drug had marked side-effects and, even though the analyst had not prescribed it himself, she experienced him as having poisoned her, refused further medication and considered terminating analysis.

Would it have been better for the analyst to prescribe in this case? If he had, some of the rage may have been avoided but perhaps his role of poisoner would have been heightened. To have acquiesced to the patient's demand may have fuelled an omnipotent phantasy that she could control the analyst, escalating acting out. On the other hand, if the analyst had prescribed medication, this may have led her to have greater trust in him as a result of his decisiveness. On balance the analyst erred on the safe side and maintained his analytic role.

The analyst also needs to question whether countertransference feelings or personal opinion are complicating the use of medication. This can work both ways. On the one hand, the analyst may not wish to accept the limitations of his treatment or his theory and may therefore fail to suggest medication when he should; on the other hand, he may suggest psychopharmacology out of frustration, anger and hopelessness which should be dealt with analytically. Clearly, whenever medication is used, it becomes relevant to the analytic process. The task of the analyst is not to take sides in the psychoanalytic/pharmacological debate but to ensure that the effect of medication on the therapeutic process is constantly scrutinised, with special regard given to the transference–countertransference relationship.

Gender

Gender is an increasingly important issue in psychoanalysis. Despite Freud's (1931) recognition that the sex of the analyst in relation to the patient may inhibit or influence certain pre-oedipal and oedipal processes, he paid little attention to gender as a topic. Indeed, many of his generalisations and assumptions about sex and gender have been seriously questioned (Grossman and Kaplan 1989). Chasseguet-

Smirgel (1984) argues that analysts bring to their work a balance of masculine and feminine traits, 'paternal legislative power and maternal aptitude' respectively, formed through their own maternal and paternal identifications, and that these form the basis of psychic bisexuality. The influence of actual gender on the analytic relationship is thereby lessened, although Chasseguet-Smirgel distinguishes such identifications from a more deeply rooted masculinity and femininity. Thus a woman has a profound and unbroken identification with her mother as a nurturer and container, prototypically made complete through her own pregnancy. On the other hand, the man has to disidentify with his mother, with separation taking precedence over connection, distinction over similarity, and has to ally himself with father. This cuts the boy off from the emotional attunement, sharing of states of mind, and capacity to perceive the other's needs and feelings, that was part of the primary bond between him and his mother. Emotional closeness can now be experienced as dangerous and enveloping, potentially giving rise to the 'core complex' that is found in adult perversions (Glasser 1979, 1986), if not reintegrated. This has led to the suggestion that, although male and female identifications may be present in both men and women, the female analyst is more likely to draw out nurturing maternal transferences from both male and female patients, which develop into dependent wishes of merging (Lester 1990). The female patient accepts and learns from the experience but the male patient reacts strongly as such wishes threaten his masculine identity (Stoller 1985). Similarly, the male analyst may react countertransferentially to powerful symbiotic wishes from a female patient by distancing himself, or, by misinterpreting them as erotic strivings rather than recognising them as a need for maternal care.

Gender-related oedipal transferences are easier to identify as, at this stage, sexual and aggressive urges are directed primarily towards one or the other parent. Generally speaking, powerful erotic strivings are most commonly described in the male analyst–female patient dyad and are strikingly absent from the literature on female analyst–male patient dyads. Not surprisingly the male analyst–male patient dyad is often described as being dominated by aggressive competition with the oedipal father, while erotic heterosexual wishes are directed towards people outside the analysis. Homosexual wishes are inevitably present and may form a resistance in both patient and analyst. Bernstein (1991) sees an equal level of danger in the female analyst–female patient mix. For the analyst there may be a defence against homosexuality, an over-identification with the patient's strivings for independence, career success and complaints against men, a difficulty in experiencing herself as a penetrating person, and a tendency to regress to the original mother–child relationship. Only if the analyst can extricate herself from regressive and sexual aspects of her relationship with her own mother can a successful analysis take place.

Ethnicity

Psychoanalysis, despite its origins among an oppressed ethnic minority, has never fully addressed the place of ethnic issues within treatment, perhaps because the vast majority of analysts and their patients are caucasian. It has been said that ethnic differences have a negative effect on the process and outcome of psychoanalysis (Bradshaw 1978, 1982), that they distort countertransference feelings (Sager *et al.* 1972), that they serve as a defence from underlying conflicts (Evans 1985) and that they induce analyst-guilt, leaving a white analyst with a black patient unable to maintain an analytic stance (D. Holmes 1992). The internal world may be distanced, with both patient and analyst becoming identified with the down-trodden (Goldberg *et al.* 1974). Underlying problems of aggression, internal conflicts and affective responses may not be adequately tackled but, rather, explained according to social attitude to race.

However, recent research reveals more positive aspects. Studies of outcome of therapy with cross-race and same-race therapist–patient dyads show similar outcomes, although notable differences in process (Jones 1978). Racial difference is a useful avenue for transference reactions and a facilitator of analytic treatment. D. Holmes (1992) shows how racial issues in both same-race dyads and cross-race dyads are powerful landscapes on which to project all that is unacceptable. The danger is that the analyst will accept the prejudice without looking at more psychological causes of conflict. For many patients the use of racial issues may be a potent source of expression and elaboration of defences, object relations and impulses. What is important is that the ethnicity is tackled, and not ignored as if it were a non-issue. Perhaps the clearest clinical instances of the interaction between psychoanalysis and ethnicity are to be found around questions of identity and identification, and where oedipal feelings of rivalry and exclusion are intertwined with themes of race.

Example: identity confusion

A young woman entered analysis following an episode of severe depression in which she had heard voices accusing her of being a 'racist'. She was the offspring of a mother of Indian origin and a French father, and had been adopted soon after birth into a liberal middle-class family who already had two children. Her father, who had come from an impoverished working-class background and had a strong social conscience, had particularly wanted to adopt a 'black baby'. Her adolescence had been stormy, and, unlike her two academically successful older sisters, she had left school early and had lived a somewhat rackety life. Her depression coincided with her splitting up with a working-class black boyfriend who had told her she didn't fit in with 'his sort of people'. She felt neither fish nor fowl, but returned to live with her parents, while feeling convinced that they did not really want her. Initially she was superficially friendly and collaborative in treatment, but she arrived for a session one day in a state of fury and accused the analyst of being in conspiracy with her parents, of patronisingly seeing her as inferior, of having no idea what it was like to be black in a racist society, and of taking her into treatment 'just to salve your grimy little conscience'. The analyst acknowledged that there might be some truth in these accusations, but on further discussion it emerged that she deeply resented the fact that her parents had pushed her into treatment and that the bills were sent to them, even though this had been agreed at the start. As the transferential implications of all this were unravelled, she grasped how her anger towards the analyst paralleled the anger, and later compassion, she felt towards her natural mother for having abandoned her. She then began to see how her risk-taking behaviour had been a challenge to see if her parents really cared about her, expressing her wish for a more loving relationship with her mother, and to see herself as 'special' rather than second-best. A discussion with one of her sisters revealed that she also felt that their parents were much more interested in themselves and each other than in their offspring. Paradoxically, following this, the patient could begin to allow herself to think of her parents as a loving couple, and the split between the angry 'black' and the compliant 'white' side of her became less pronounced.

MONEY

Ever since Freud compared the symbolic meaning of giving and
withholding to defecation and linked faeces with gifts and money in
a symbolic equation, the literature on the meaning of money has been
plentiful. In contrast, comment on the significance of money as a
transaction within analytic treatment, and the influence of the source
of finance on the treatment process, has been muted. Recently,
perhaps as a result of social and economic changes, greater interest
has been taken in the influence of payment on treatment (Thoma and
Kachele 1987; Nobel 1989). In countries with high inflation or where
payment is fixed by insurance companies or government schemes, as
in Germany and Holland, fees are part of an external reality shared
by analyst and patient alike. Where they are part of a private contract,
however, analysts tend to analyse financial matters within the
transference relationship rather than concentrate on reality. Late
payments may be seen as resistance, offers of cash as an attempt to
draw the analyst into a joint criminal act of tax evasion, and sending
the bill to a private insurer as a way of avoiding an intimate
transaction with the analyst. Conventionally bills are given to the
patient at the same time each month, with payment due at the time
agreed.

There seems to be an unspoken and largely unquestioned consensus that there is a hierarchy of which source of payment is
preferable. Direct payment by a patient, unsupported by outside
finance, is 'best'. After that there is a slippery slope of payment by
relatives, insurance or government, to questionable free treatment
even though it is funded indirectly through taxation. Personal
sacrifice is felt to be necessary to sustain motivation, to mobilise self-
determination, to reduce gratification of narcissistic wishes, and to
keep the patient in touch with reality. Even training institutes insist
that a patient makes a contribution to treatment, dependent on
earnings, to bring in a sense of reality. However, direct payment
between a self-sacrificing patient and a better-off analyst must also
result in palpable transference–countertransference problems involving resentment, envy and hostility. Eissler (1974) found few
problems in payment by relatives, but certainly it may sometimes
cause difficulties (see 'an involved husband' on p. 191).

Whatever the source of finance, money has a significant part to
play in all analyses. Each source brings its own advantages and
disadvantages, opens up channels for phantasies, fears, enactments

and defences. In patients who are in free or heavily subsidised treatment, special attention needs to be paid to underlying wishes to be a favoured patient, and fears of expressing hostile feelings. In the case of third party payment, patient and analyst need to be careful not to collude in minimising the importance of payment or ignoring it completely. Direct payment may give rise to transferences involving control, power, envy, dominance, avoidance of dependence and self-sacrificing masochism. Influences on the analyst may be equally significant. He relies on his patients for his living and may hold onto wealthy patients while feeling less concerned about those paying less, resent the patient who is heavily subsidised feeling he has it too easy, keep patient's in treatment for too long, and slant recommendations for treatment according to vacancies. T. Reik (1922), one of the analytic pioneers, provides an interesting discussion of the moral dilemma presented to him by a millionaire who offered to pay him a huge fee – which would have enabled him to pursue his writing and research – on condition that he was his one and only patient.

In general, the attitudes of a patient and his analyst to money may be more important than the source of funding. Many analysts offer some patients treatment for a low fee and younger analysts often continue with their training patients for many years. The fee should not be so low as to lead to resentment or too high as to result in greed or excessive reliance on one patient for income. The ethics of psychonalysis and its role within a National Health Service are important areas of concern (Holmes and Mitcheson 1995). Most analysts would agree with Freud (1919) that 'the poor man should have just as much right to assistance for his mind' as the well-off. How this can be achieved is a topic requiring urgent debate.

Chapter 10

Psychoanalytic contributions to psychiatry

> Psycho-analysis stands to psychiatry more or less as histology does to anatomy; in one, the outer forms of organs are studied, in the other, the construction of these out of the tissues and constituent elements.
>
> (Freud 1916/17)

Our original aim in writing this chapter was to consider the specific psychoanalytic contribution to the understanding and treatment of the variety of different psychiatric diagnoses – obsessional neurosis, the addictions, schizophrenia, manic-depression, the personality disorders and so on. Freud made significant contributions to the classification of psychiatric disorders. His distinction between what he called the 'actual neuroses', which would now probably be classified as panic attacks, and 'anxiety neurosis', a more diffuse sense of worry or dread, has stood the test of time, even if his idea that the 'actual neuroses' are the result of sexual frustration has not. Similarly he attempted to differentiate the mechanisms underlying anxiety neurosis, depression and psychosis: 'Transference [i.e. anxiety] neuroses correspond to a conflict between the ego and the id; narcissistic neuroses [i.e. depression], to a conflict between the ego and the superego; and psychoses, to one between the ego and the external world' (Freud 1924).

But at this point we encounter a number of problems. First, as Freud's formulation reveals, psychoanalytic thinking is highly theory-laden. Each disorder is related to the central psychoanalytic concept of psychological conflict; however, as we shall see later, some idea of non-conflictual *deficit* is also probably needed to comprehend fully the devastating effects of mental illness, a shift characterised by Kohut (1977) as a move from Guilty to Tragic Man.

Freud also tended to pick up on one aspect of an illness – overactive conscience in depression, for example – and build his theory around that, while contemporary descriptive psychiatry tries (with only varying success admittedly) to approach the phenomena of mental illness without theoretical preconceptions. Psychiatry also attempts to make a clear differentiation between the description of the phenomena of illness and causal explanations for their occurrence – a distinction often confused in psychoanalytical thinking.

Second, contemporary psychoanalysis is more concerned with psychological *processes* than specific *disorders* – it is possible to browse through several volumes of the *International Journal of Psycho-Analysis* without finding any reference to psychiatric disorder: psychoanalysis is more interested in the uniqueness of the individual than in broad categories of diagnosis. Third, psychoanalysis as a specific treatment is only relevant to a restricted number of psychiatric patients, whereas psychiatry is concerned with the whole range of therapies – biological, social and psychological – included among the latter are cognitive-behavioural and systemic therapies as well as psychodynamic. Fourth, psychoanalysts and psychiatrists often use the same words to mean different things; for example, 'psychosis', 'borderline' and even 'defence mechanism'. Finally, while psychiatry aims for specificity, psychoanalytic formulations and treatments tend to be elastic and broad-spectrum – for example, the notion of projective identification is relevant to patients with addiction, eating disorder, borderline personality disorder, paranoid psychosis and perversion.

In approaching this topic we have returned, therefore, to Freud's analogy between anatomy (psychiatry) and histology (psychoanalysis). Psychiatry, through its diagnostic schemata – DSM IV or ICD-10 – anatomises and categorises the variety of psychiatric illness. Histology is concerned with general pathological processes – response to injury, tissue repair, degenerative changes, autoimmune diseases – which apply to a wide range of different illnesses. Similarly, psychoanalysis can provide insight into the underlying mechanisms and meaning of a variety of different mental disorders. While strictly psychoanalytic treatments may be applicable mainly to a relatively restricted group of people suffering from mild to moderate personality disorders, a psychoanalytic perspective can illuminate the general and psychotherapeutic management of many illnesses, including somatisation disorders, and, for example, can be especially helpful in understanding countertransference reactions among staff looking after difficult patients (see pp. 233–4 below).

Kernberg (1984) writes of 'borderline personality *organisation*', a constellation of defences and psychological dispositions that applies, among others, in Borderline Personality Disorder, Narcissistic Personality Disorder, and Antisocial Personality Disorder. Similarly, Klein's depressive and paranoid–schizoid *positions*, or Steiner's (1993) pathological organisation are not specific diagnoses, but modes of thought and behaviour, constellations or nodal points in the spectrum of mental activities that help one to think about the inner experience of psychological illness. Following this tradition, we divide our discussion into three broad categories of abnormal mental processes: psychotic processes, borderline processes and neurotic processes.

PSYCHOTIC PROCESSES

The psychoanalytic project began, and remains, as an attempt to make *meaning* out of the apparently incomprehensible phenomena of mental life – dreams, slips of the tongue, hysterical symptoms. By placing 'madness' – the non-rational primary processes – at the heart of psychic life, Freud opened up the possibility of understanding psychosis. It is certainly true, as we shall see, that personal meaning is to be found in psychosis, but *understanding* should not be confused with *explanation*. Until the discovery of a chromosomal abnormality in 1956, Down's syndrome was thought to be caused by physical or emotional trauma in pregnancy, since, when closely questioned, mothers of affected babies were much more likely to recall traumatic incidents than those with normal babies. Thus the personal meaning of the experience of Down's syndrome has no connection with its actual cause – an abnormality of cell division in the formation of the ovum. Psychoanalytic accounts of psychosis often strain to explain what they more accurately describe.

The psychopathology of schizophrenia

Freud's first shot at understanding paranoid schizophrenia came in his analysis of Judge Schreber's autobiographical account of the psychotic episodes which punctuated his life (Freud 1911b). Freud understood Schreber's delusion of the end-of-the-world catastrophe as a manifestation of the internal catastrophe of his illness. He saw his illness as a *regression* to a primitive state of *narcissism* in which 'the person's only sexual object is his own ego' (Freud 1911b: 463). Having withdrawn from the world, the paranoiac, in Freud's view, then proceeds, by *projection* of his inner world onto the outer, to build it up again in a delusional way: 'The delusion-formation, which we take to be a pathological product, is in reality an attempt at recovery, a process of reconstruction' (Freud 1911b: 457); a 'delusion is found applied like a patch over the place where originally a rent had appeared in the ego's relation to the external world' (Freud 1924: 215).

The three themes of regression, narcissism and projection form the basis of most subsequent psychoanalytic accounts of psychosis. Freud considered patients with schizophrenia unanalysable because their self-absorption made them incapable of forming a transference relationship with an analyst. Post-Freudian authors have disagreed about this: Searles (1965), for example, describes intense and exquisitely sensitive transferential relationships, but the treatment of patients with schizophrenia requires much modification of technique, and few, if any, would now see psychoanalysis as a first-line treatment for schizophrenia. Freud also remained neutral about the aetiology of psychosis; some post-Freudian psychoanalysts have tried to relate the regression to faulty parental attunement in the first few months of life (Fromm-Reichmann 1959; Stolorow *et al.* 1987): Schreber's father was cruel and abusive to his sensitive son (Schatzman 1973). But as the evidence for a biological basis to schizophrenia accumulates, the notion of schizophrenogenic parents has, rightly, been increasingly discredited.

A more plausible account of the role of dynamic factors in psychosis assumes some sort of biologically-based abnormality which leads to the breakdown of the normal perceptual and experiential boundaries between the self and the external world. Whether this is a true 'regression' to normal but primitive modes of thinking is open to question: it seems unlikely that all babies' experiences of the world are 'schizophrenic' (Gabbard 1990), although they do probably at times feel powerless, confused and experience the world in an animistic way in which objects are imbued with projected feelings (Bradley 1989). Faced with this confusing breakdown, the ego then tries to contain and make sense of the primary process material (see p. 32), normally kept repressed, with which it is flooded. Grotstein (1977a and b) sees a primary failure of 'stimulus barriers' – both to external and internal stimuli, which leads to excessive projective identification as an attempt to keep the ego from being overwhelmed. For Roberts (1992) delusions represent the attempt to maintain meaning in the face of threatened chaos, and are likely to be suffused with personal themes, just as dreams combine the day's residue with the dreamer's deeper preoccupations. The 'strength' of the ego *does* reflect previous favourable or adverse experiences. Thus childhood trauma, and later parental negativity or over-involvement, may influence the way a biological propensity to schizophrenia is expressed.

This model combines the idea of a biological deficit with the psychodynamic notion of conflict, in that the ego is struggling to maintain coherence and make sense of essentially 'non-sensical' experiences. Analogies with infantile experience can help us empathise with this process, but they remain analogies rather than aetiological explanations.

Kleinian views

The most concerted psychoanalytic attempt to understand the phenomenology of psychosis has come from the Kleinian school, especially through the work of Bion, Rosenfeld, Segal, Rey and Sohn (Spillius 1988; Hinshelwood 1989; Rey 1994). They identify abnormalities in feeling, thinking and relating with consequent defensive responses. The following is an attempt to summarise their views.

Affect

Schizophrenia is characterised by an excess of destructive impulses, in which reality, both internal and external, is regarded with violent hatred. The origins of this hatred is not really explained, sometimes attributed to 'constitutional factors', or the 'death instinct' (Segal 1993). Hatred is linked to envy: the sufferer is enormously envious, for example, of the 'good' qualities of the maternal breast, and transferentially of any therapeutic help he may be offered. The patient also turns his hatred inwards towards such potentially positive feelings as guilt or even the recognition of psychic pain itself. The projection of hatred (see below) is therefore a fundamental defensive manoeuvre in these patients. When this fails, self-murderous feelings emerge, accounting for the high suicide rate in schizophrenia.

Some authors have been critical of this conflict-based model; for them, to say that the psychotic has a hatred of reality is rather like saying that a one-legged man has a hatred of walking! Emphasising deficit rather than conflict, Winnicott (1965), Laing (1960), and Searles (1965) describe the basic affective state in schizophrenia as a dread of annihilation due to the lack of a stable integrating autonomous ego, and relate this to presumed maternal intrusiveness in infancy.

Cognition

For Bion (1957, 1961), schizophrenia is dominated by what he calls 'minus K', the desire *not to know*, due to failure to transform 'preconceptions' (alpha elements) into 'conceptions' (beta elements) via the transmuting introjected maternal breast (cf. p. 53). Creative thought depends on bringing ideas and words together so that transformational 'intercourse' can occur between them. What is found in schizophrenia, he claims, is an 'attack on linking', a precursor of the oedipal child's envy of parental sexual relationship. Segal (1981) emphasises the presumed 'concrete thinking' of psychosis, in which symbol and reality become confused, leading to what she calls the 'symbolic equation' (see p. 131). Thus, using Winnicott's idea of 'hate in the countertransference', the non-psychotic might say that the end of an analytic session or a break made him feel 'as though you can't stand me, want to get rid of me'; whereas the psychotic might *actually* experience the break as a murder, rather than, as with the neurotic, merely murder*ous*.

Both these viewpoints emphasise phenomena that are far from universal in schizophrenia; some patients are highly creative (not excluding one of the analytic pioneers, Wilhelm Reich) – for Segal, creativity requires transcendence of the symbolic equation. In many, symbolism and concrete thinking seem to coexist side-by-side, when, for instance, a patient attends for an appointment while simultaneously claiming the doctor is a murderer. This fits in with Bion's idea of the psychotic and non-psychotic parts of the personality, the analyst's task being to establish contact with the latter in order to reach the former. As Searles (Mullen 1973) put it, 'the analyst must use the mad part of himself to make contact with the sane part of the patient'.

Example: post-psychotic depression
Mary had suffered from schizophrenia for 20 years. Now in her forties, her symptoms controlled by drugs, she entered analysis in

order to try to cope with what she called her 'whirling attacks'.
During these episodes she would lie on the bed and moan for hours
while her distraught mother with whom she lived would watch
helplessly. In analysis it soon became clear that during these
moments she was in fact feeling terrible panic as she contemplated
the devastation in her life that her illness had wrought. She saw
how all her youthful ambitions had come to nothing, and that it
was unlikely she would marry, have children, or find a job
commensurate with her talents and intelligence (which had been
considerable). As she began to moan in her sessions, complaining
that the analyst was doing 'nothing' to help, the regressive aspect
became apparent: she was like a miserable 3-year-old simultaneously intruding, attacking and craving love. Gradually she
began to own the feelings during these episodes, rather than seeing
them concretely as 'attacks', and as she mourned the many losses
the illness had brought, she was able tentatively to form a
relationshp with a man, who, although 'unsuitable' and unacceptable to her mother, was someone she could care for and
cherish in a way she had longed to be looked after herself.

Relationships

Object relationships, while not, as Freud thought, non-existent in
schizophrenia, are certainly problematic. Bion described transference
in schizophrenia as 'thin', 'premature' and 'tenacious'. Rey (1994)
sees the schizoid dilemma as claustro-agoraphobia – a desperate
loneliness and at the same time a terror of intimacy. Rosenfeld (1987)
emphasises the 'parasitic' aspect of schizophrenic relationships, a
defence, as he sees it, against separation anxiety, in which the patient
attaches himself to carers or institutions in a passive dependent
embryo-like way, feeding off them without any real reciprocity.
There is certainly a static or even repetitive feel to much interaction
in schizophrenia – the pace of change, in therapy of any sort, is
painfully slow – but this is as much the result of the inherent deficits
of the schizophrenic state as of defensive manoeuvres.

Defences

A number of characteristic defensive patterns are commonly found
in an attempt to maintain some kind of psychic coherence in the face
of cataclysmic changes. Fragmentation and helplessness may be

compensated by omnipotence and idealisation, as Freud (1911b) noted with Schreber's delusional communication with God. Hatred of reality is dealt with by grandiosity and triumph over the envied object. Hatred and destructiveness are projected. Bion describes the schizophrenic world as inhabited by 'bizarre objects'. These are elements of the fragmented self projected into the outside world, which then take on characteristics of the projected self. For example, a patient who feels that the television is sending frightening messages to him has projected a malevolent part of himself which now confronts him in a frightening way, but perhaps less terrifyingly than if the hatred had remained entirely inside him.

Example: psychotic embarrassment
A man in his twenties was horribly embarrassed by his 'big penis', which he felt everyone would notice and which prevented him from going out in the street. He came from an ambitious family in which his brothers and sisters had all done very well academically. All had spouses or partners. His illness and social and academic failure were a constant source of humiliation to him. He heard voices telling him to harm members of his family. He wanted to live with his parents, but his continuous angry outbursts and search for reassurance had exhausted them, and he had moved into a hostel. His 'big penis' could be seen as a 'bizarre object' which contained his omnipotence, his longing for closeness but also feelings of being 'too much to handle', his desire for triumph, and aggression. The feelings around his 'bizarre penis' embarrassed him but were not entirely overwhelming as they might have been had he not externalised them in this way.

The ego in psychosis

Rosenfeld and Sohn have concentrated on the nature of the ego in psychosis. If the normal ego is seen as a 'precipitate of abandoned object cathexes' (Freud 1923), i.e. as reflecting a synthesis of parental and other influences, what happens in psychosis where the 'narcissistic' ego has withdrawn from other people? The ego is seen as fundamentally split, with a 'pathological identification' in which the object (an unresponsive or abusive care-giver for example) is omnipotently taken in without being fully integrated or assimilated into a coherent self, forming an 'incorporated object'. Any good objects will be squeezed out while the threatening object is held within in an idealised way rather than actually related to, with all the dangers that implies for the oversensitive schizophrenic. Sohn calls this pathological introject 'the identificate', a sort of unintegrated foreign body that can dominate and take over the personality, or form, in Rosenfeld's striking metaphor, a Mafia-like gang that dominates and obscures the fragile non-psychotic self.

All this leads, in a Manichean way, to a swing away from life to anti-life, from love to hatred, from relationships to omnipotent self-sufficiency, from eros to thanatos.

Example: murder and salvation
A divorced woman in her thirties became convinced that there was a plot against her and that her life and that of her 9-year-old daughter were in danger. She had been regularly sexually abused by an uncle at the age of 9. When a taxi driver asked if she lived on the left or right side of the street, she 'knew' that the left side was the devil's side and that she and her daughter were in mortal danger. Later that evening, when her daughter was asleep on the sofa, she saw her making what she thought were pelvic thrusting movements. Again, she 'knew' that the devil was having sex with her, and violently attacked both her daughter and herself with a knife in a vain attempt to protect them both.

Her 'identificate' contained the abusing uncle projected into the 'devil', and then reintrojected into herself and her daughter whom she attacked with such ferocity.

Therapeutic strategies

Conflict and deficit models of schizophrenia lead to two differing psychoanalytic therapeutic strategies. Interpersonal psychoanalysts such as Searles, Fromm-Reichmann, Sullivan and Winnicott tried to make good the hypothesised lack of maternal attunement and consequent ego deficit in the early months of life by advocating a flexible hyperempathic stance with prolonged daily or even twice-daily sessions, and an emphasis on non-verbal and intuitive elements in the therapeutic relationship. Rosenfeld and Bion, by contrast, stressed the need to contact the conflicted non-psychotic part of the self by the use of words and accurate, if sometimes extravagant, interpretations.

Example: a wild interpretation
An over-enthusiastic trainee saw a disturbed young paranoid schizophrenic man in the emergency clinic one evening. The

patient had had a row with his girlfriend, who, he then became convinced, was plotting against him and who had informed the media that he was a homosexual. The trainee saw him for three or four follow-up sessions in the course of which he made a number of quite powerful 'conflict'-type interpretations, including one based on Chasseguet-Smirgel's (1985) notion of the 'faecal penis', i.e. an omnipotent quasi-delusional attempt to deny the reality of oedipal or pre-oedipal helplessness and inadequacy. Some five years later he received a letter out of the blue from the patient which stated: 'You may recall how you told me when we met five years ago that "my trouble was that I thought my penis was made of shit"; well, I have come to the conclusion that you were completely right . . .'!

As mentioned earlier, conventional psychoanalysis is rarely if ever indicated in the present-day treatment of acute schizophrenia, although psychoanalytically informed management strategies can produce good results (Alanen *et al.* 1994). Self-psychologists such as Stolorow (Stolorow *et al.* 1987) advocate a supportive therapeutic stance, and criticise the emphasis on aggression and hate and general negativity inherent in some approaches which, they argue, may reinforce the patient's already fragile self-esteem. Where a supportive psychoanalytically informed approach is tried, flexibility, holding, a need to limit regression and to focus on the here-and-now, and 'respect for the illness' (Gabbard 1990) – i.e. *not* seeing it as something for which the patient, albeit unconsciously, should be held responsible – are essential. The emphasis is on strengthening the non-psychotic part of the personality. This can be done by cognitive strategies in which the reality of the psychotic experiences is challenged (Chadwick and Birchwood 1994) and by concentrating on separating the healthy part of the self from the identificate or 'cohabitee', by asking the question 'Who is the mad voice inside?' (Sinason 1993).

Example: the African queen

Rosy was a normally quiet, friendly, submissive, divorced woman in her late twenties who had had several schizo-affective episodes in which she had become floridly deluded – on one occasion living for nearly a week naked at the bottom of her garden, saying that her voices had told her she was 'Eve' and was in paradise. She had two children who, due to her illness, had been taken into care

but were now happily settled with their father's parents. Rosy
came from Uganda and had, with her sister, been 'rescued' by a
missionary at the time of the Amin regime. Her mother, who had
apparently been mentally ill, had died, and Rosy had been brought
up by her father who sexually abused her, and was subsequently
killed in the civil war. Normally quiet and submissive, in one
psychotic episode she became very violent and threatening,
shouting that she was 'Nafekerra', an African queen with healing
powers, and that those who crossed her did so at their peril. When
she had recovered she explained that 'Nafekerra' was in fact her
mother who spoke with a deep voice and whom Rosy actually felt
dwelling within her, controlling her and uttering sounds for her.

The staff's attempt to 'rescue' Rosy from her illness infuriated
and terrified this 'identificate' internal mother who felt that her
child was being taken from her. This helped them to adopt a firm
but compassionate management strategy for Rosy. When, thanks
to neuroleptic medication, the psychotic storm was over, Rosy
could talk about the loss of her own children with great sadness,
and linked this to her childhood terror and mental pain when she
was whisked away from Uganda.

In summary, a psychoanalytic approach to psychosis can provide
useful insights into psychotic processes, can help in the general
understanding and management of psychosis, and occasionally is
indicated as a specific treatment. Flexibility, firmness and patience
are essential, and should always be carried out in collaboration with
psychiatric management, including drug treatment (see p. 203).

BORDERLINE PROCESSES

The inherently ambiguous term 'borderline' evokes an ambivalent
response within the psychoanalytic and psychiatric community.
Many authors complain of its imprecision, and predict its eventual
replacement by some more satisfactory formulation (e.g. Higgitt and
Fonagy 1992). At the same time there is an increasing interest in the
nature of borderline disorders and their treatment by modified
psychoanalytic methods. Indeed it appears that this may well be one
of the major contributions of psychoanalysis to contemporary psychiatry.

The term 'borderline' has emerged from a confluence of psychiatric and psychoanalytic research. Gunderson (1984) and his co-

workers identified a group of patients with a characteristic set of personality features who present frequently to psychiatrists and who pose considerable therapeutic and management difficulties. The DSM 111-R descriptive criteria for a diagnosis of Borderline Personality Disorder (BPD) can be summarised as 'stable instability' comprising: intense but unstable personal relationships; self-destructiveness; constant efforts to avoid real or imagined abandonment; chronic dysphoria such as anger or boredom; transient psychotic episodes or cognitive distortions; impulsivity; poor social adaptation; and identity disturbance.

The psychoanalytic concept of borderline came from a combination of clinical experience and theory. Deutsch (1942) wrote of the 'as if' personality, and Zetzel (1968) of the 'so-called good hysteric' (who turns out in treatment to be highly disturbed and difficult), Winnicott (1965) and Laing (1960) of the 'false self'. All were trying to capture the essence of people who, while not diagnostically psychotic, evince psychotic mechanisms, often regress dangerously within psychoanalytic treatment, and yet prove challenging and sometimes rewarding patients. They exist, as Rey (1994) summarises it, on the borderline between oedipal and pre-oedipal, between psychosis and neurosis, between male and female, between paranoid–schizoid and depressive positions, between fear of the object and need for the object, between inner and outer, between body and mind.

BPD has evoked intense theorising among psychoanalysts, and, perhaps because of its clinical difficulty and variability, represents a battefield upon which many of the controversies and schisms of contemporary psychoanalysis have been played out. The main difference, as with psychosis, is between authors who emphasise conflict and those who stress deficit as the central psychopathological theme, each group advocating apparently very different treatment approaches. The 'conflict' group include both the classical Freudians and neo-classical Lacanians, and the Kleinians and their followers, while the 'deficit' group comprise, in Britain, the Independents, and in the USA, the Interpersonalists and Self-psychologists (see p. 45). In practice this divide is somewhat artificial: as we shall see, the evidence suggests that both conflict *and* deficit are important in the aetiology of BPD, that both intrapsychic and environmental factors play an important part, and that different authors are probably describing and treating different patient populations with different clinical needs.

Conflict models of borderline

It is often diagnostically difficult to distinguish between Borderline Personality Disorder (BPD) and other personality disorders such as Narcissistic Personality Disorder (NPD), Histrionic Personality (HPD) and some types of Antisocial Personality Disorder. Research shows that several different personality disorders can coexist within one individual. Kernberg (1984) has used Kleinian ideas, combining classical instinct theory with object relations (see p. 40), to define an underlying *Borderline Personality Organisation* (BPO) which occurs in many psychopathological situations, including BPD, NPD, HPD, psychotic disorders, some eating disorders and in normal individuals who are exposed to extreme stress (cf. Garland 1991).

Kernberg's BPO has, in attenuated form, many of the features of psychotic thinking described previously. These include:

1. Ego weakness. This leads to poor impulse control, a deficient capacity to cope with anxiety, and therefore difficulty in sublimating instinctual demands into socially acceptable channels.

2. A shift from secondary to primary process thinking (see p. 32). This is particularly manifest in the dream-like quasi-psychotic states common in BPD individuals, in which the capacity for reality-testing disappears. Thus they may feel that those who care for or love them actually detest and hate them, which, indeed, by projective identification, they may be induced to do.

3. The use of 'primitive' defence mechanisms. These include splitting and projective identification, idealisation, denial, omnipotence and devaluation. The world in BPO is split into good and bad, black and white, friend and foe. Such people swing between feeling all-powerful (often all-powerfully destructive) or helplessly inadequate; rushing from one idealised 'answer' to another, only to be bitterly disappointed as each God turns out to have feet of clay. Perceptions of the world are powerfully coloured by projection and a characteristic feature of analytic work with these patients is projective identification in which feelings are communicated not by symbolism or words but by direct transfer into the therapist's inner world.

Example: Gotcha!

A borderline patient, a woman in her early fifties, spent many therapeutic hours trying unsuccessfully to get some token of love from her male therapist, asking him if he liked her, describing how most men found her enormously attractive, pleading with him to say something that would counteract the contempt and despair she felt she had received from her physically and sexually abusive father, and going into great detail of her romantic and sexual phantasies about the therapist. These entreaties regularly reached a crescendo just before breaks, and were steadfastly interpreted as a response to separation and as an identification with her importuning father, but to little avail. One day, weakened by a session of relentless demands, the therapist explained how if he were to respond to her advances it would completely jeopardise the therapy. He sensed at the time that this was an error, but it did in fact result in a lessening of her demands, and therapy appeared to progress. About a year later the patient remarked in passing on how much she admired the therapist for his strength in restraining his sexual impulses for her sake! When he heard her say this he felt intruded upon, assaulted and almost physically sick, bitterly realising that his misguided attempt at explanation and reassurance had come home to roost. On clarifying her comment, it was clear that the important point was that she felt that she had at last got him to admit that he really *did* desire her – as the therapist put it to her: 'You felt: Gotcha!' Then, turning to his countertransference, and using 'internal supervision' (Casement 1985), he grasped, not without some difficulty, the projective identification: only by getting him to feel this way could she communicate her own feelings of disgust and self-loathing deriving from her father's sexual assaults.

4. Pathological internal object relations. The inner world in BPO mirrors these external manifestations of splitting and projection. Instead of stable and smoothly integrated internal representations of people and their relationships, the self and others are experienced in chiaroscuro, or as part-objects – breasts, penises and objects for evacuation or exploitation. At different times the subject is in the grip, in Fairbairn's (1952) terms, of a split off libidinal or anti-libidinal self, choosing perversity or self-destruction as a defence against inner emptiness or complete fragmentation.

Kernberg relates BPO to Mahler's 'rapprochement subphase' (see p. 61) in which the child begins to separate and to explore the world for himself, but needs to rush back to his mother for comfort and reassurance and 'narcissistic supplies'. If the mother is physically or psychologically unavailable, the child may not be able to integrate good and bad maternal imagos. The child then reacts to abandonment with an excess of aggression which is projected outwards onto his objects and reintrojected into a split self in a way that often resists therapeutic efforts:

Example: 'I hate myself'
Anna, a 29-year-old married woman had felt there was something 'wrong' with her since she was at least 14, when she entered a sexually abusive relationship with an older man. She disliked her body which she saw as both fat and flat-chested, and had only really liked herself for the six months when she was breast-feeding her daughter, when she had a visible bosom. She had shown many aspects of psychological disturbance including heavy drinking, anorexia, considerable cannabis use, and increasingly determined episodes of self-harm in which she took tablets, cut or burned her face, legs, arms and genitals. She 'knew' that she was 'rotten' and 'hateful', and kept a secret diary of poems in which she recorded her self-hatred. When Anna was 10 her mother, on whom she was very dependent, began an affair of which Anna was aware, often seeing the lovers kiss and hearing them make love. Anna felt utterly abandoned and desperate, furious with her mother but unable to say anything for fear of betraying her to her father. It was at this point that she began to experience self-hatred, which seemed to be based on an identification with her feelings towards her mother – the 'absent' breast symbolising her feelings of abandonment. Despite numerous therapeutic efforts this core belief in herself as 'bad' persisted throughout Anna's very stormy course of treatment, and she seemed almost to take pleasure in her ability to thwart those trying to help her, including the analyst. She would regularly harm herself whenever she felt there was some possibility of progress in therapy. The only escape from it seemed to be when she felt numb – as she put it: 'Not bad, but nothing'.

This position of an identified internal 'bad parent' object, who is clung to, who punishes and persecutes in the way that the original 'bad object' did in reality, combined with elements of revenge and triumph over the object, is a common constellation in BPD. One patient described this split-off identificate as 'Him', an evil male who took over her personality and made her do destructive things.

Steiner (1993) describes the inner world of the borderline in spatial terms. Between the splitting of the paranoid–schizoid position and the pain of the depressive position lies the 'borderline position'. The sufferer seeks out 'psychic retreats', safe havens, free from pain, but also sequestered from real emotional contact with people and the flux of life. Steiner suggests that silent, aloof, overtalkative or pseudo-cooperative patients may be operating from such retreats, which are often symbolised in dreams as caves, fortresses, houses or parts of the body. Fanatical affiliation to political or religious groups may have a similar defensive function as a way of containing disturbance, but also potentially impeding psychic growth.

Narcissistic Personality Disorder

Kernberg views NPD as a more mature but no less therapeutically problematic variant of BPO, in which there is a fusion between the ideal self and the actual self. Real intersubjectivity is obliterated in an attempt to avoid feelings of rage, disappointment, envy, contempt and despair. Two types of narcissism may be distinguished. Rosenfeld (1987) writes of the 'thick skinned' oblivious insensitive type of narcissist, obsessed with himself and his achievements, whose relationships reflect the need to be admired and lack depth or substance. By contrast, the hypervigilant 'thin skinned' oversensitive often hypochondriacal type of narcissist, whose emotional life is the subject of intense and constant scrutiny, is perhaps best seen as vulnerable to Winnicottian 'impingement', due to a deficit of maternal attunement.

Deficit models

Deficit models identify similar features of BPO, but tend to put a different emphasis on the clinical phenomena:

1 *Aggression*. For Kernberg, excess aggression is the primary abnormality in BPO. For Kohut and Fairbairn the aggression is secondary to environmental failure, a protest against an unresponsive mother, or a way of holding onto an object through hatred in the absence of the capacity to love. The fragmentation and inner loneliness of the borderline patient are not seen as defences, but as 'breakdown products' of an individual deprived of vital supplies of love (Adler 1985).

2 *The ego*. Conflict theorists see the ego as 'weak', and unable to contain aggressive impulses. Deficit theorists emphasise the failure of self-soothing function often found in BPO. Unable to calm themselves psychologically, patients with BPD turn to

dependent relationships with others, to drugs, compulsive sex, binge-eating or self-harm. Many 'cutters' describe escalating agitation which, at the moment of self-injury, turns into an almost post-orgasmic sense of calm.

3 *The role of the environment.* Kohut and Winnicott have a rather idealised view of the early mother–infant relationship, in which the mother's responsiveness and attunement, her capacity to foster transitional space, and to supply 'self-object' needs, leads to a secure, stable sense of self. Where the basic 'good enough' maternal functions were missing, the child is vulnerable to BPD in later life.

4 *The necessity of narcissism.* For Kernberg, the narcissist is in a state of conflict between his need for an object and the rage he feels towards his objects – hence he obliterates the gap and self-absorbedly 'becomes' his ideal self. For Kohut and Winnicott the narcissist is faced by an insensitive, absent or abusive primary object, and so retreats into himself, trying vainly to 'be' the missing mother to himself he so desperately needed, in order to preserve some sense of inner coherence.

Empirical studies of BPD

This polarisation of models can be confusing for the clinician. For some theorists the problem lies within the individual who is burdened with an excess of aggression; others picture a mother who discourages the development of an autonomous self by reinforcing clinging, dependent behaviour (Masterson 1976); for others the holding, soothing mother is absent or neglectful. Does the research evidence help to resolve these differences, and what are the implications for treatment?

There is increasing evidence for the existence of severe environmental disruption in the childhoods of patients with BPD. Gunderson and Sabo (1993) suggest that at least one-third of BPD patients fulfil the criteria for post-traumatic stress disorder, having been subjected to physical and sexual abuse in childhood or being the survivors of traumatic loss. Van de Kolk (1987) found histories of sexual abuse in 60–70 per cent of hospitalised patients with BPD. Fonagy (1991) has built his theory of BPD around these facts, suggesting that borderlines lack what he calls 'mentalising capacity', the ability to see oneself and others as having minds, which for him is a necessary defence against the realisation that the parents upon whom the child depends have the ability to attack and harm. Fonagy

(1991) and Westen (1990) both make the point that the increasing evidence of child abuse in the histories of BPD throws doubt on the psychoanalytic focus on 'pre-oedipal' years in these patients since abuse occurs most frequently in latency and early adolescence.

Long-term outcome studies in BPD have revealed a number of facts relevant to psychoanalytic treatments (Stone 1993; Aronson 1989). Disturbance lasts for several years – at least five or six – but then has a tendency to settle down, but may return in the forties or fifties, especially in women whose children have left home. Suicide rates are high in the early years, especially in patients who abuse alcohol. More research is needed into the efficacy of psychoanalytic treatment of BPD. Stevenson and Meares (1992) found that 60 per cent of patients with a personality disorder improved after one year's treatment with psychoanalytic psychotherapy, but Aronson (1989) claims that only about 50 per cent stay in treatment for more than six months, and of these only about 50 per cent improve. Aronson (1989) is highly critical of the psychoanalytic outcome literature in BPD which he sees as based on overgeneralisation from small samples; uncontrolled, often anecdotal evidence; and with a failing to tackle the problems of dropouts and treatment failures:

> The limited empirical evidence suggests that the intensive psycho-therapies of the borderline are for the elite patient by the elite therapist ... the proponderance of theoretical as opposed to practical writings in this field may be seen as an intellectual denial of the limitations of therapy.
>
> (Aronson 1989: 524)

Stone, however, takes a more optimistic view, suggesting that about one-third of patients with BPD are suitable for analytic/expressive psychotherapy, and those that remain in treatment tend to do well. Gunderson and Sabo (1993) believe that the single most effective strategy for maintaining BPD patients out of hospital is a secure psychotherapeutic relationship.

Treatment strategies

The theoretical polarisation is reflected in differing treatment strat-egies. Kernberg and the Kleinian school tend to emphasise the importance of verbal interventions and need for early interpretation of negative transference, while the deficit group see the creation of a holding environment through empathic responsiveness and valida-

tion as the prime necessity. Conflict theorists accuse the deficit group
of creating a collusive relationship in which real aggression is
denied, mirroring the maternal deprivation in childhood which led
to the development of false self and inhibition of autonomy and
exploration. Deficit theorists believe that too much emphasis on
negative transference reinforces the already fragile self-esteem of the
borderline, and even creates the very aggression it attempts to
interpret (Ryle 1994).

Each approach in pure culture can lead the analyst into serious
difficulties. A 'Kohutian' (or 'Winnicottian') strategy can lead to
regressive dependency, escalating demands, erotic transference, with
the therapist shifting abruptly from over-involvement to rejection:

Example: too close, too soon
A nurse in her early twenties was seen for assessment. She had a
history of self-harm, mood swings, unstable relationships and
alcohol abuse. She had felt utterly neglected by her mother when
a much favoured younger brother was born, and was sexually
abused by her father between the ages of 11 and 14. She rang up
the day after the assessment demanding to be taken on immediately, and treatment was hurriedly organised with an inexperienced male therapist. After a few sessions she stated that
words were not enough, and requested to sit near the therapist so
that she could 'feel the closeness I longed for but never never had
with my mother'. Her request was granted, but she then insisted
that he stroke her hair, which again he naively agreed to do. Like
the fisherman's wife in the fairy story, she next stated that 50
minutes was not nearly long enough; when the therapist explained
that he could not extend the sessions, but that she could remain
behind for a few minutes to compose herself if she wanted, she
barred his way out of the consulting room. The end of each
session came to consist of a wrestling match as he tried to
extricate himself from the room. The therapist attempted to
interpret these events as a repetition, via projective identification,
of her intense jealousy of her 'sibling' patients, and the feelings
of claustrophobia she felt during the sexual abuse, but to no avail.
The therapy came to a dramatic and catastrophic close, and the
patient, who was seen again by the original assessor, was banned
from the unit.

The problems created by more confrontational tactics may be less
dramatic and, as Kernberg (1984) states, 'It is easier to move from

expressive to supportive therapy than in the other direction', but if used insensitively causes many dropouts in therapies which might otherwise have progressed, since many patients with BPD find silence and negative interpretations confusing and unbearable. In a study of therapy dropouts in BPD, Gunderson and Sabo (1993) found that half had left feeling unbearably angry following a confrontation with the analyst.

Again, these differences may be more important as ideological rallying cries than as clinical guidelines. All would agree that establishing a sound therapeutic alliance is both essential and extremely difficult. The interpretation of negative transference *and* a high degree of acceptance and holding may, in varying circumstances, be appropriate. Containment and acceptance are needed. The patient, lacking the capacity for self-soothing, needs gentleness; equally needed is some confrontation with a constantly projected inner world, held in the grip of bad objects. Fosshage (1994) relates treatment in BPD to Gedo and Goldberg's (1973) developmental sequence of empathy, moving from physiological regulation in the newborn, through attunement in infancy, to 'consensual [i.e. verbal] validation' in the toddler. He argues that in order to mobilise analysable transference in BPD some non-interpretive work is required: because such patients are operating at a developmentally preverbal level, this in BPD is still 'analysis', whereas with neurotics it would not be.

Kohutians are often treating very fragile out-patients who may need to feel utterly secure with their therapist, to be reassured that they can make contact in emergencies, and to be offered special arrangements during breaks, such as a 'backup' therapist and being sent postcards from their therapist. Many of Kernberg's patients are treated in hospital settings where the holding environment is already in place. Interventions which help them to face up to their destructiveness, although shocking, may also be an enormous relief, representing a small first step towards the realisation that they can master their misery from within, rather than constantly blaming circumstances or other people.

In summary, the following is a list of the essential conditions for successful analytic work with patients with BPD (cf. Waldinger 1987; Gabbard 1990):

1 A stable treatment framework which safeguards the integrity of the patient, the therapist and the analysis. The therapist needs to

recognise that some patients will not be able to tolerate strict analytic boundaries and will have to make themselves more available than is conventionally recommended.

2 Limit-setting. The counterpart of condition 1 above is the need for clear boundaries and to ensure that the patient understands them. For example, one patient was allowed to contact her analyst between sessions once per week, but if she contacted the analyst more often than that, then a session was forfeited the following week.

3 Interpretive focus on the here-and-now rather than reconstruction. Minute-by-minute microfailures of empathy will inevitably occur, and will be responded to by the patient with withdrawal and/or paranoid feelings of being abandoned, toyed with or even tortured. These need to be focused upon within the session as they arise. Similarly, the patient's inevitable feelings of hatred and rejection towards the therapist need to be taken up, so that good and bad imagos can be gradually reconciled – the 'good' attentive analyst listens to how horrible and 'bad' the patient feels he is.

4 Constant monitoring of countertransference. As the examples above suggest, extensive use of projective identification means that countertransference is a key therapeutic tool in BPD. The therapist will be cast in the role of both rescuer and attacker and must be able to 'treat those two imposters just the same', and when the inevitable therapeutic mistakes and muddles occur, to disentangle his own contributions from those of the patient. His overall stance – whether a follower of Kernberg, Winnicott or Kohut – is likely to be, at least in part, a product of his own unconscious needs and experiences, producing, respectively, a punitive or an indulgent attitude towards vulnerability. This will need to be examined through personal analysis or vigilant self-scrutiny.

5 Avoidance of a passive therapeutic stance. 'Classical' silence and complete non-directiveness may produce unbearable anxiety for the BPD patient. Most analysts will admit to 'breaking the rules' (Steiner 1993), and often include more supportive elements such as reassurance, analytic transparency and guidance than they would with less disturbed patients.

6 Containment and confrontation of anger and self-destructiveness. Angry outbursts or self-destructive behaviour will almost in-evitably arise in the course of an analytic treatment of a BPD

patient. These need to be handled firmly but non-punitively. The therapist should not react in the heat of the moment but 'strike when the iron is cold'. Analysts may be confronted by patients who arrive at sessions drunk, having cut their wrists or taken an overdose. They may be subjected to unrestrained wailing or screaming in sessions, or intrusions into their private lives. Clear guidelines or even a contract may be needed to keep this behaviour within manageable bounds. Such patients may need to have it firmly stated that while everything possible will be done to try to prevent them harming or even killing themselves, the ultimate responsibility lies with them, not with the therapist. Contracts around self-destructiveness are best handled in co-operation with the patient's general practitioner, general psychiatrist with access to in-patient beds, social worker and/or spouse. The patient may be greatly reassured by the example of a collaborative 'parental couple' (Bateman 1995), and this may help to reduce splitting.

7 Therapeutic focus on the connection between feelings and actions. In addition to the limit-setting implicit in condition 6, the therapist must, through minute reconstruction of the events in the inner world leading up to episodes of aggression or despair, help the patient to identify the thoughts and feelings associated with destructive actions.

8 In summary, progress in treatment will be shown within sessions by all or some of the following (Wallerstein 1994): (a) the capacity to expand on the analyst's comments; (b) tolerance of phantasy – including hatred and eroticism – as opposed to acting out; (c) tolerance of interpretations directed at grandiosity and projective identification; and (d) the capacity to experience guilt.

The difficult patient; hospital treatment in BPD

Sooner or later the analyst will be faced with the need to admit a BPD patient into hospital (Gabbard 1986, 1989). Such admissions may be brief or prolonged. If possible, prolonged admissions to general psychiatric units should be avoided, but brief crisis admissions can be very useful to help patients over difficult moments in their lives or treatment. Here the hospital acts as a temporary haven, auxiliary ego, container, or 'self-object', freeing the analyst to continue with interpretive work.

Example: rationing hospital admissions

A very disturbed woman in her early twenties regularly acted out during each weekend break – climbing dangerous scaffolding, getting drunk and entering into dangerous sexual situations with men she hardly knew. She often presented or was brought to the hospital casualty department by the police in the small hours. Her diagnosis was Multiple Personality Disorder (in which BPO is very evident) and by Monday morning she would have 'forgotten' these episodes or attributed them to 'Him', one of her subpersonalities. Once it was established that it was she who felt abandoned and helpless and desperate on the days when she could not see her analyst, a contract was drawn up in which she had automatic rights of access to a hospital bed for the weekend up to two weekends per month. She only rarely used this facility, and eventually found a sympathetic general practitioner who supported her when the analyst was not available.

Gabbard (1990) defines four often overlapping types of BPD patient who need, or achieve, prolonged admissions to hospital: (a) the relentlessly self-destructive; (b) 'special' patients – often members of the caring professions – who manage to split and divide their carers so powerfully that out-patient treatment breaks down; (c) 'hateful' or 'heartsink' patients who are expelled from community settings into hospitals; and (d) the passively oppositional often determinedly silent patient.

All need to be treated in specialist units since their capacity for splitting and projective identification means that they will inevitably cause disruption and therapeutic failure in general units, which are usually unable to enforce tight limit-setting and to maintain the vigilant staff countertransference monitoring, as well as lacking dedicated analytic facilities that these patients need. Splitting is an ever-present danger (Main 1957): fragments of the patient's inner world are projected into likely staff members, often resulting in violent clashes between those who see the patient as a pitiful victim in need of unconditional love, and those who perceive him as 'bad', malevolent, manipulative and argue for confrontation or discharge. These different aspects of the patient need to be contained and examined in regular staff groups dedicated to monitoring group countertransference. Close communication between the patient's analyst and the 'management' team is essential, if escalating spirals of anger or despair – within the team as well as the patient – are to be avoided.

NEUROTIC PROCESSES

In Chapter 1 we suggested that affect has replaced instinct, impulse and libido as the central theme in psychoanalytic thinking. Anxiety and depression are undoubtedly the most common of all the painful affects that lead patients to seek psychoanalytic help. Aspects of anxiety and depression have been touched on throughout this book. As with psychotic and borderline processes, psychoanalytic under-standing of neurosis cannot easily be mapped directly onto specific psychiatric diagnoses. In the concluding section of this chapter we shall look briefly at the relationship between anxiety and depression, as conceived psychoanalytically, and their manifestations in psychi-atric disorders.

Anxiety

Freud's (1926) volume *Inhibitions, Symptoms and Anxiety*, pub-lished in his seventieth year, marked an important shift in his thinking. His earlier idea about anxiety was that it represented 'unbound' psychic energy or libido that had escaped the forces of repression. This may still be a useful way of looking at the overwhelming waves of anxiety which survivors of disasters and other traumata often feel (Garland 1991). But once the structural model (see Chapter 2) was in place he began to conceive of anxiety as an adaptive response of the ego, and a stimulus to psychological or behavioural action. 'Signal anxiety' arises when there is a conflict between different parts of the 'psychic apparatus'. This leads to a hierarchy of different types of anxiety, depending on where the conflict predominantly lies (cf. Gabbard 1990), moving from the most 'mature' to the most 'primitive'.

Superego anxiety

Here the conflict lies between the ego ideal, with its guardian conscience, and the actual performance of the ego. Thus those with perfectionistic obsessional characters worry constantly about their inability to achieve the high standards they set themselves. Behind this may lie a sense of a demanding internal parent who cannot be satisfied. Since anxiety and aggression are often inversely related, superego anxiety may contain a fear of a retaliatory punishment for these overwhelming demands, itself a projection and reintrojection of the patient's own demanding neediness.

Castration anxiety

The analysis of male impotence was the counterpart of Freud's early focus on female hysteria (Mitchell 1989). Freud understood 'castration anxiety' in terms of the oedipal fear of the little boy that his punishment for loving his mother, and so challenging his father, would be castration, and consequent relegation to what he presumes to be the position of women. While 'oedipus' is no longer thought of so literally in bodily terms, castration anxiety as a sense of powerlessness within a phallocentric society is an important theme in feminist-influenced neo-Freudian thought (Chodorow 1978; Benjamin 1990). 'Fear of success', difficulty with assertion, and sexual inhibition can also be understood within the rubric of castration anxiety. In Kleinan terminology, 'castration anxiety' can be related to depressive-position feelings of having damaged the object and so harbouring a wound within oneself.

Separation anxiety

Bowlby (1988; Holmes 1993) expanded on Freud's idea that a fundamental conflict in neurotic disorders was that between the need for an object and fear of losing the object. Constantly seeking approval, over-dependency, agoraphobia, or conversely excessive detachment, can all be understood in terms of separation anxiety and defences against it. Bowlby saw separation anxiety as a response to real parental inconsistency or absence in childhood, leading to clinging and fearful behaviour in the victim whose fears of being abandoned are realistic. Here, too, conflict over aggression often plays an important part in the dynamic:

Example: a fugitive from injustice
Peter was a 40-year-old headmaster of a secondary school who suffered from escalating anxiety. One day he left work as usual, but instead of going home, booked himself into a hotel in a neighbouring town, staying in his room for two days without informing anyone where he was. Eventually he phoned the local psychiatric hospital, and following a brief admission was referred for psychoanalysis. The precipitant of his 'fugue' was what he saw as the increasing bureaucratic demands that government-imposed changes in the teaching profession placed upon him. Until this time he had been a model and successful teacher, but had felt

increasingly anxious, frustrated, angry and guilty, all of which he had kept to himself.

He was the younger, by ten years, of two sons. When his older brother was killed in a climbing accident at the age of 19, Peter's mother became intensely anxious and found it harder and harder to allow Peter to do the normal adventurous things a 9-year-old wanted to do. Peter became adept at placating her, but was left with a feeling of always being second-best, and having to look after his own emotional needs. At times he was similarly polite but subtly controlling and distant in therapy, inducing mild feelings of guilt in the therapist that he was never quite giving enough.

His anxiety-driven fugue could be understood in part as a replaying of the brother's disappearance, a way of testing whether his wife (who had become very engrossed in a business she had only recently started) really wanted and cared about him; in part, a revenge on the educational system that had ensnared him and taken him for granted and, therefore, indirectly an attack on the mother on whom he depended (and who depended on him) but with whom he also felt furiously angry for the inhibitions she had imposed on him.

Persecutory anxiety and disintegration anxiety

Psychotic mechanisms of anxiety have already been discussed in which the sufferer projects his own feelings of hatred and envy, and then is persecuted by these feelings which he attributes to others. Disintegration anxiety is also part of the more psychotic picture discussed above and reflects the 'primitive' fears of fragmentation and annihilation experienced in some psychotic states.

Treatment

As the above types of anxiety imply, there is no single psycho-dynamic formulation or interpretive method that applies to all anxiety disorders. The consistency of the analytic setting is often enough to counteract the crippling effects of separation anxiety. The techniques described in the preceding two chapters – working from anxiety to defence to underlying feeling or impulse – forms the basic strategy needed in approaching anxiety clinically. The anxious patient will test the analyst's ability to orient the treatment along the expressive–supportive spectrum (Wallerstein 1986). There will inevitably be overt or unconscious pressure for reassurance and support. The research evidence available seems to suggest that more disturbed patients benefit from a supportive slant, whereas psychologically sophisticated patients using mature defences do better with a more strictly expressive mode of treatment (Horowitz *et al.* 1984).

Depressive processes

Psychoanalytic theories about depression centre around the themes of (a) ambivalence around aggression, (b) loss and (c) self-esteem. Freud initially saw depression in terms of a conflict model, picturing a regression to the 'oral stage' of development in which the sufferer experiences ambivalent guilt at having destroyed the very object he loves. This would explain the anxious dependence that is often a feature of depression.

Stimulated by discussions with Abraham, Freud (1917) in 'Mourning and melancholia' suggested that loss was a central precipitant and precursor (vulnerability factor) in depression. The triggering current loss reawakens earlier childhood losses – either actual or symbolic – and through 'identification with the lost object', the sufferer attacks himself with reproaches that rightly belong to the loved one who has left him or let him down. Freud saw depression as a 'narcissistic disorder' because of this withdrawal from the object into oneself.

Klein (1986) used these ideas in her model of normal psychological development in which external loss – loss of the breast, of the exclusive preoccupation of one's mother, or the admiration of the father – is compensated by the establishment of an internal world into which the lost external object is 'reinstated'. She saw the successful achievement of the depressive position in childhood as immunising the individual against loss in later life and, conversely, that in depression he is thrown back to the earlier failure to integrate good and bad into whole objects in the inner world. The depressive believes himself omnipotently to be responsible for loss, due to his inherent destructiveness, which has not been integrated with loving feelings. The sado-masochistic element in depression arises from projection and reintrojection of these feelings of envy and hatred. For Winnicott, if the depressive position – or stage of concern – has been achieved, the reaction to loss is grief; if not, the reaction is depression.

Pedder (1982) relates these Kleinian ideas to Brown and Harris's (1978) research findings in depression, which confirms the role of childhood loss, especially of mother, as a vulnerability factor. Brown and Harris see loss of self-esteem as central to the psychology of depression. For Pedder, self-esteem implies an internal object relationship in which one part of the self is 'held' lovingly by another. If this structure has not been achieved – i.e. if, in Kleinian terms, the depressive position has not been reached – the individual will depend excessively on external sources of positive regard, and if these are lost he will be vulnerable to depression.

Treatment

Psychoanalytic treatment in acute depression is unusual, although Interpersonal Therapy (IPT) is a form of brief psychoanalytically informed psychotherapy that has been shown to be effective in depressive disorder (Klerman and Weissman 1984; Elkin *et al.* 1989). Some patients with chronic depression can be treated psychoanalytically, although, as with all treatments for this intractable condition, the results are very variable. The basic therapeutic strategies are: mobilising aggression; working through unmourned losses; externalising and understanding internal sado-masochistic patterns in the transference; neutralising excessive superego demands; and providing a secure base that is neither clung to nor shunned.

The analyst will inevitably experience times of despair, rage and hopelessness in working with these patients. Winnicott's insight that the limits on therapy – 50-minute hours, breaks and holidays – express the analyst's countertransferential 'hate', similar to that shown by the good-enough-mother when she puts her child to bed and attends to her own needs, is particularly relevant to working with chronic depression. This links with Strachey's basic model of mutative factors in psychoanalysis (see p. 173), since the patient will project his own hopelessness and hatred into the analyst, who, through continuing concern combined with warm limit-setting, disconfirms the vicious circle of depression. This enables the patient to feel safer about expressing aggression, and to integrate these feelings with positive ones and so gradually to build up a more benign set of internal objects.

Example: a death as a new beginning
Nancy had suffered with depression since her teens, and, while at

university, she had made a major suicide attempt and been admitted to a psychiatric hospital for 18 months. The younger of two sisters, her mother had had a severe puerperal depression following a stillbirth and had herself been in hospital for nine months when Nancy was about 3 years of age. Nancy had been looked after by her father, whom she grew to detest, and, in the course of analysis, began to believe that his care at that time was severely defective or even abusive. Her parents were publicans; she experienced her mother as intrusively offering the 'affectionless control' that is often a feature of depression.

Throughout her twenties and thirties she lived the life of a semiinvalid, restricting her social life, plagued with overwhelming feelings of rage and despair, spending large parts of the day in bed, and working only very intermittently in her job as a librarian. Her first marriage had foundered, but in her second she had married an older man who was immensely tolerant, appearing to be immune to her violent verbal attacks and enormous dependency. She entered analysis after the birth of her son, fearful that without help she might not be able to manage motherhood.

The first four years of analysis seemed to produce little benefit other than, perhaps, stabilising her life and providing a container for her aggression and dependency. She would at times launch into a vicious attack on the analyst, whom she saw as a superior, heartless treatment machine on whom she had become inextricably dependent, and whose sole purpose was to humiliate her. The sessions were often silent, repetitive and static, leaving the analyst feeling trapped and impotent, although in her less furious moments she confessed that she did value the treatment since, apart from her husband, the analyst was the only person in the world to whom she could express her hatred. On two or three occasions she required brief hospitalisation when her depression became overwhelming, but this too only served to remind her of her hopelessness and inability to cope.

Then, suddenly, her husband became ill and, after a period of illness in which she nursed him magnificently, died. The two years following his death saw a remarkable transformation. She grieved greatly but at the same time her confidence increased; she began to think of herself as normal rather than an alien creature; she started to enjoy her son and her friends; she began to travel, venturing into territory that she would have avoided in her previously restricted life. She made a partial reconciliation with her parents, from whom she had completely cut herself off. Eventually she met another man with whom she developed a much more equal relationship, and with whom she could, when necessary, argue in a productive and mature way, compared with her previous dependent destructiveness.

Pari passu with these external changes, the analysis became far less static, and a warm relationship began to develop. Breaks, which previously had often led to breakdown, were tolerated without mishap. Interpretations, almost for the first time, seemed to be meaningful to her. The analyst began to feel more like a real person in the sessions rather than a vague object which she attacked, or from whom she gained some frail warmth.

Nancy's analysis was one of those in which change was gradual, with no virtuoso breakthrough interpretations or overwhelming mutative moments. Perhaps the most important contribution was that the analyst continued to 'be there', and survived her vicious attacks without retaliation. He was both challenging and tolerant of Nancy's need for physical as well as psychic retreat, however much she tried to provoke him into telling her she had had enough, should get a job, had no right to sleep every afternoon, was not fit to be a mother, etc.

Presumably on the basis of an introjective identification with this analytic function, Nancy seemed to take on more and more of the positive qualities with her dead husband. She said that she felt that he was inside her, and that she was drawing strength from his guidance. When faced with difficulty, she would ask herself what he would have done, and it was usually right! He became the good object who, although physically dead, had at a psychological level, survived her attacks. He had, in Klein's word, been 'reinstated' within her. Her inner world was, for the first time in her life, secure. She was amazed to discover, after eight years of analysis, that she was finally free of dependence.

CONCLUSION

Although the above case has been presented as an example of neurotic processes, it illustrates how psychotic, borderline and neurotic aspects are layered within the personality and often all need to be addressed in the course of analysis. At times she developed a psychotic transference in which she projectively saw the analyst as a mocking persecutor, cruelly toying with her like a cat with a baby bird. There were many 'borderline' features, including her feelings of emptiness and boredom, and explosive rage, all of which seemed to revolve around a defect of self-soothing. Her low self-esteem and avoidance of competition with other women were examples of more neurotic aspects. The identification and timing of interventions addressing these different layers is one of the most important aspects of the craft of psychoanalysis – whose exposition has been one of the aims of this book.

Chapter 11

Research in psychoanalysis

> In psychoanalysis there has existed from the very first an inseparable bond between cure and research.
>
> (Freud 1926b: 256)

Subjected to professorial inquisition about his research output in a job interview at a famous postgraduate teaching hospital, a prominent analyst explained, 'but each time I take on a new patient, that constitutes a fresh research project'. As the quotation from Freud implies, his riposte was consistent with analytic tradition (and he got the job) – but contained in that exchange was a clash of cultures highlighting the troubled relationship between psychoanalysis and contemporary science. Freud had a nineteenth-century conception of research: the intensive and disinterested study of phenomena. Consistent with that notion, leading psychoanalytic thinkers have continued to make conceptual and practical advances building on Freud's pioneering ideas. But developments in the philosophy and technology of science have meant that contemporary understanding of the term 'research' has acquired a specialised meaning, with an emphasis on measurement, the rigorous use of controls, statistical manipulation of data, and replicability. If, as we suggested in Chapter 1, psychoanalysis is perhaps best seen as a craft rather than as a science, then its findings, while clinically valuable, do not by these standards constitute a body of scientific knowledge.

Contemporary scientific research comprises three sets of operations: agreed data, which are available to the scientific community; methods for experimentally manipulating such data; and refutable hypotheses about how the phenomena might be understood (Wolpert 1992). Because of its reliance on the case history as a basis for its theorising, psychoanalysis has had great difficulty in fitting this paradigm. As Fonagy (1993: 577) puts it:

> Its almost unique emphasis on anecdotal clinical data, however, left the epistemology of psychoanalysis and psychotherapy dependent on an outmoded epistemic paradigm: enumerative inductivism [i.e. generalising from a number of examples]. Enumerative inductivism, finding examples consistent with a proposition, is at most an educational device and not a method of scientific scrutiny ... The almost universal application of this epistemic tool in psychoanalytic writings [including in this volume! – authors] has created a situation where, currently, psychoanalysis has no method of discarding ideas once they have been proposed and made to sound plausible.

Moreover, there are also great problems in agreeing what the raw data of psychoanalysis actually *are* (Colby and Stoller, 1988; Fonagy 1989). A 'case history' is a sophisticated creation, in which the events of a clinical encounter are filtered, shaped, tidied up, reflected upon, romanticised, condensed and generally tailored to fit theoretical preconceptions, in ways that makes it highly unreliable (and unreplicable) as a source of information about what actually happens between analyst and patient.

Thus many aspects of psychoanalysis fall far short of the standards usually required for acceptance within the scientific community. Conversely, for practising psychoanalysts the preoccupations of contemporary science seem largely irrelevant to their day-to-day experience. One psychoanalytic response to this seemingly unbridgeable gulf is to concede the territory of science altogether, arguing (as, ironically, does behaviourism) that the inner world with which psychoanalysis is concerned can only be reached by introspection, and so, like the arts, is *inherently* unresearchable (Steiner 1985). A more sophisticated elaboration of this position views psychoanalysis as a 'hermeneutic' discipline (Ricoeur 1970) agreeing that the attempt to find external validation for its truths is doomed to failure, and advocating instead the criteria of internal coherence and narrative plausibility as the basis for settling disputes (Spence 1982, 1987).

But, from the early days of psychoanalysis, there have been those who have tried, more or less successfully, to overcome these practical and philosophical objections, starting with naturalistic 'field studies' of psychoanalysis and moving gradually towards a more firm scientific footing. We believe that it is important for clinicians to be aware of this research for several reasons. First because it links psychoanalysis with the wider scientific community and helps to break down the esoteric and inward-looking world that at worst it can become. Second, because, as has been shown, research can reassure clinicians that their work is an effective and useful treatment for psychological distress. Third, research helps sift fact from myth and so enables psychoanalysis to scrutinise and refine itself in order to discard what is outmoded or unworkable, and to develop what is most valuable. Fourth, because if psychoanalysis is to survive as a publicly funded form of therapy, it will be required to prove itself scientifically. Finally, by grounding psychoanalysis in reality, research acts as an antidote to the besetting dangers of wildness or ossification.

METHODOLOGY

As with all science, research in psychoanalysis depends on the development of suitable techniques and methods. The central task of psychoanalytic research is to navigate a channel between the Scilla of the near-unmeasurability of the issues that really matter to psychoanalysts – meaning, phantasy, the minutiae of patient–analyst interaction – and the Charybdis of the triviality of much behavioural research.

Psychotherapy research is conveniently divided into *outcome* studies, looking at the results of psychoanalytic treatment, and *process* research, which, as its name implies, studies what goes on in the psychoanalytic process itself. Process–outcome research studies the relationship between the two. Sound psychoanalytic research inevitably involves the introduction of a third party into the analytic relationship – an 'oedipal' procedure which in itself has unconscious reverberations. In outcome research the researcher will administer questionnaires or interview patients before and after treatment. The most obvious technique of process research is the use of tape- or video-recorded sessions which, either in their raw state or transcribed, can be studied by a neutral observer. This material can then be subjected to further research procedures. For example, therapist interventions can be classified by agreed criteria as transference interpretations, non-transference interpretations, reassurances, etc., and the effect of these interventions on the process of the session can be studied; independent judges can be asked to make psychodynamic formulations based on their reading of the scripts, and these in turn can be looked at by a second set of independent judges and assessed for their inter-rater reliability and ability to predict outcome in therapy; the narrative structure of the transcript can be studied, looking at its fluency or associative freedom.

PSYCHOTHERAPY RESEARCH AND PSYCHOANALYSIS

Research findings in psychoanalysis itself are relatively sparse and, among these, few are methodologically robust. There many reasons why this should be so, including the prolonged nature of psycho-analytic treatments, the traditional reluctance of most analysts to subject themselves to scientific scrutiny, the problem of accumulating a sufficient number of analytic cases for statistical purposes, and the difficulty in operationalising its theoretical concepts. By contrast, the study of psycho*therapy*, most of which focuses on methodologically manageable brief treatments, has become an expanding field, some of which is relevant to psychoanalytic work. Before looking specifically at psychoanalytic research, therefore, we shall survey some relevant general findings from psychotherapy research.

The effectiveness of psychotherapy

Eysenck (1952) threw down the gauntlet to psychotherapy researchers nearly half a century ago with his manipulation of Fenichel's data, which he claimed showed that patients in psycho-analysis improved no more than untreated controls. By the 1980s this view had been conclusively refuted with several well-controlled studies and meta-analyses showing the effectiveness of psycho-therapy compared with untreated controls (Smith *et al.* 1980; Lambert *et al.* 1986). About 30 per cent of people on waiting lists improve spontaneously, compared with the 70 per cent of treated patients who benefit from psychotherapeutic treatment. Also the *rate* of improvement among 'waiting list controls' is slower than for those in active treatment (McNeilly and Howard 1991). Howard *et al.* (1986) studied the 'dose–effect curve' in psychotherapy, and found that, in general, the more prolonged the treatment the greater the benefit. However, this is a negative logarithmic curve, and the greatest demonstrable gains (which usually measure symptomatic rather than dynamic change) are concentrated in the early stages of therapy, with 75 per cent of total improvement being achieved in the first thirty sessions or so. Another important issue is the stability of improvements in psychotherapy. Several studies have shown that treatment gains in psychotherapy are maintained at long-term follow-up (Luborsky *et al.* 1988), but a recent review (Fonagy 1993) suggests that the gains of brief therapy are not always maintained at long-term follow-up, thus strengthening the case for prolonged treatments such as psychoanalysis.

The placebo problem in psychotherapy research

The fact that a patient benefits from a particular form of therapy says nothing about the particular aspect that is curing his problem. The 'equivalence paradox' (Stiles *et al.* 1986) in psychotherapy research arises from the finding that although there is a vast array of different therapeutic methods, in general none can be shown consistently to be more effective than any other. As Luborsky *et al.* (1975) famously put it, quoting Lewis Caroll's 'dodo-bird verdict': 'Everyone has won and all must have prizes.' Frank (1986) explains the equivalence paradox on the basis of his triad of 'common factors' in therapy: 'remoralisation', or the giving of hope; the offering of a relationship with the therapist; and providing a rationale and a set of activities which suggest a pathway towards health. In psychoanalysis these would include: regular attendance at sessions; focus on dreams and phantasies; the use of free association; and the expression of uncovered feelings.

The use of 'placebo' therapies – such as 'clinical management' by non-psychotherapists or vague self-help groups – is an attempt to tease out the differential contribution of 'common factors' and specific interventions (such as transference interpretations which, in the classical psychoanalytic view, are the 'mutative' ingredient). When active therapy is compared with placebo therapy the 'effect sizes' (i.e. the difference between the group mean for a particular measure in the treatment group compared with controls) are generally less impressive than with waiting list controls (see, for example, Crits-Cristoph 1992, for a meta-analysis of placebo-controlled trials of brief dynamic psychotherapy). 'Common factors' appear to produce effect sizes of about 0.5, as opposed to waiting list controls and active treatments where the figures are around 0.2 and 0.8 respectively. As we shall see, psychoanalytic research findings are consistent with these results, suggesting that the efficacy of psychoanalysis is based on the combination of a 'non-specific' supportive component, and a more specifically *psychoanalytic* contribution based on interpretation, transference neurosis, etc.

Therapist and patient contributions to psychotherapy outcomes

The therapist–patient relationship appears to be a crucial factor in producing good outcomes – a not unexpected finding and one that was anticipated by Freud (1940a) in his notion of the therapeutic 'pact' which he saw as the basis for successful analysis. Patients tend to attribute the success of treatment to the personal qualities of their therapists rather than technical procedures. 'Positive transference' features such as seeing the therapist as warm, sensitive, honest, caring, understanding, supportive, possessing a sense of humour, etc., are associated with good outcomes. Conversely, where patients perceive their therapists as disliking, disrespecting or finding it impossible to empathise with their clients, outcomes are poor (Eaton *et al.* 1993). Therapists, of course, vary in their effectiveness, some consistently producing good outcomes, some being regularly ineffective, and most being somewhere in between. This is not simply a function of personal qualities since there is some evidence that therapists who adhere to a particular model of therapy, of whatever variety, are more successful than those who deviate too much from standard procedures (Horowitz *et al.* 1984). Patient characteristics contribute even more than therapists to outcome in therapy (Bergin and Lambert 1986). In general, and again unsurprisingly, the more disturbed the patient the worse the outcome, although Malan (1976) found that in Brief Dynamic Therapy good motivation could compensate for severity of illness to produce good results.

Given the importance of patient characteristics, attempts have been made to match therapy and patient. There is some slight evidence (Benjamin 1993), again as might be expected, that introspective, 'psychologically-minded' patients do better with nondirective insight-oriented therapies such as psychoanalysis, while 'externalising' patients do better with behavioural approaches. Relevant to the Menninger Psychotherapy Research Project which we discuss below is Horowitz *et al.*'s (1984) finding that, in abnormal grief reactions, patients with poor ego integration did better with supportive approaches, while the more integrated subjects benefited from a more psychodynamic type of therapy.

IMMEDIATE AND LONG-TERM OUTCOME
OF PSYCHOANALYSIS

Analysts have, from the pioneering years, been aware of the need to study outcome in psychoanalysis and this effort has continued sporadically up to the present (Bachrach *et al*. 1985, 1991; Kantrowitz *et al*. 1990a, b and c). By the standards of contemporary psychotherapy research, few if any of these studies would be considered methodologically acceptable, and are perhaps better seen as attempts at audit rather than research proper. As mentioned above, controlled studies of psychoanalysis, because of their prolonged nature, are almost impossible. Most studies rely on analysts' assessments of the outcome of their patients. Independent observers are seldom used, and the records fail to use standard outcome measures, simply asking analysts to classify the results of treatment as 'good', 'poor', 'mixed', etc. – an approach which may tempt practitioners to overestimate the benefit of their treatments. The distinction between symptomatic improvement and dynamic change is also one that has, at least until recently, bedevilled psychoanalytic outcome research since the kinds of improvements that psychoanalysis hopes to produce are difficult to quantify. Many studies asked naturalistic open questions of analysts about such issues as the development of an 'analytic process' without specifying in a reliable way what was meant.

One of the earliest outcome reports came from the Berlin Psychoanalytic Institute which pioneered free treatments for the poor (Bachrach *et al*. 1991): 60 per cent of neurotic and 20 per cent of psychotic patients were judged to have received substantial benefit. Slightly better results were reported from London (Bachrach *et al*. 1991), Chicago (Alexander 1937, who seemed to do particularly well with psychosomatic cases, 77 per cent of whom improved substantially) and from the Menninger Clinic (Knight 1941). On the whole, these early studies anticipate subsequent research showing that 60–70 per cent of patients can regularly be expected to show substantial improvement with all forms of psychotherapy.

A major concern of several post-war studies (e.g. Weber *et al*. 1985a and b; Sashin *et al*. 1975; Kantrowitz *et al*. 1990a, b and c) has been the relationship between outcome, 'analysability' as judged at the initial assessment, and the development of an 'analytic process' (i.e. a transference neurosis which is gradually resolved in the course of treatment). In most studies assessment interviews proved to be poor predictors of who would eventually do well in analysis (Erle and Goldberg 1979), although Malan's (1976) original finding – that establishing a strong therapist–patient bond, the capacity to show affect at assessment, and evidence of achievement either at work or in a relationship all predict good outcome in Brief Dynamic Therapy – has stood the test of time. Perhaps more perturbing has been the poor correlation, especially in long-term follow-up studies, between the development of an 'analytic process' and outcome:

> those patients who were seen by their analysts to have had a successful analysis, as defined in the traditional way [i.e. development and partial resolution of the transference neurosis] were no more or less likely to have achieved long-term stability of psychological changes than their counterparts who, according to their analysts, had *not* developed a transference neurosis.
>
> (Kantrowitz *et al*. 1990a: 493)

In long-term follow-up the capacity for 'self-analytic function' – presumably a measure of the extent to which the patient had internalised the analytic process – seemed to be an important aspect of good outcomes. Pfeffer (1963) offered a period of brief therapy to patients several years after completion of analysis, and then compared the formulations of the new therapists with their analysts' original assessments. He found that neurotic conflicts had not so much been obliterated as mastered by analysis and that they remained in a dormant form in all the patients studied. Bachrach comment:

> These studies, therefore, caution against perfectionistic expectations and suggest that criteria such as 'resolution of conflicts' or 'resolution of transference neurosis' are unrealistic measures of psychoanalytic outcomes; perhaps outcomes are better conceptualised as beneficial shifts in pathological compromise formations or in transference/resistance configurations.
>
> (Bachrach *et al*. 1991: 903)

Another consistent finding from these US studies has been the large numbers of post-analytic patients who return for further treatment. In Kantrowitz's study (1990b), for example, out of 17 patients 5–10 years after completion of analysis, 7 (40 per cent) had either remained stable or had improved, 6 (35 per cent) had deteriorated but had been restored to psychological equilibrium after further treatment, and 4 (25 per cent) had deteriorated whether or not they went back into therapy.

THE MENNINGER PROJECT

The outstanding example of naturalistic studies of psychoanalysis is undoubtedly the Menninger Project (Wallerstein 1986), which began in 1954 as a prospective study and spanned a 25-year period looking at assessment, treatment, and outcome in patients referred to the Menninger Clinic for psychoanalysis, 42 of whom were selected for intensive study. The Clinic provides an in-patient as well as an out-patient service, and the patients were mostly much more ill than those who would normally be seen in out-patient or office practice. Many were referred because of the failure of standard treatments. They would be comparable to the more difficult patients seen in NHS psychotherapy departments, or admitted to a unit such as the Cassel Hospital or the Halliwick Day Hospital (Bateman 1995) for intensive psychoanalytic psychotherapy. A few patients have been in continuous treatment since the start of the Menninger Project, while others have been followed-up 20 years after completion of therapy. Patients, their families and their therapists have been subjected to a battery of tests, and process notes and supervisory records have been kept, charting the progress of therapy.

A major thrust of Wallerstein's analysis of this enormous mass of data has been the attempt to compare classical psychoanalysis with psychoanalytic psychotherapy. He classified 22 of the cases as psychoanalysis, 20 as psychotherapy, but there was a clear spectrum from classical psychoanalysis, modified psychoanalysis, expressive–supportive psychotherapy (probably equivalent to the British category of psychoanalytic psychotherapy), supportive–expressive psychotherapy to supportive psychotherapy. Some of Wallerstein's most important findings, many of which are consistent with results we have outlined from other studies, can be summarised as follows:

1 There was no evidence that psychoanalysis was more effective than supportive therapy with this group of patients: 12/22 (46 per cent) of psychoanalytic cases and 12/20 (54 per cent) of psychotherapy cases did well, with good or moderately good outcomes. The improvements brought about by supportive therapy were

   just as stable, as enduring, as proof against subsequent environmental vicissitudes, and as free (or not free) from the requirement for supplemental post-treatment contact, support, or further therapeutic help as the changes in those patients treated via . . . psychoanalysis.

(Wallerstein 1986: 686)

2 Of the 22 cases initially started with psychoanalysis, only 6 remained within the parameters of classical analysis; 6 had 'modified classical', which included some supportive elements such as sitting up, the analyst wrapping blankets round a rain-drenched anorexic, telephoning suicidal patients at home, and admissions to hospital in crisis; 6 were converted to supportive therapy, one of whom became a 'therapeutic lifer', receiving 25 years of continuous therapy from four different therapists.

3 A 'positive dependent transference' seemed to be the basis of *all* successful therapies, whether analytic or supportive.

4 Overall there was only a weak relationship between 'insight' and change, although psychoanalysis was particularly associated with the presence of insight – whether this was because analysis led to insight or that insightful patients were selected for analysis was unclear. In summary, 25 per cent showed neither insight nor change; in 45 per cent change occurred with little insight (the majority of these were, unsurprisingly, in the psychotherapy group); in 25 per cent insight and change were evenly balanced (these were virtually all in the psychoanalysis group); and in 5 per cent there was insight but little change.

5 An important aim of Wallerstein's study was to elucidate the controversy about the 'widening scope' of psychoanalysis (Stone 1993) – the use of psychoanalytic techniques to treat much more severely disturbed patients than had previously been thought possible. Kernberg's (1975) contribution to the Menninger Project suggested that a modified analytic approach, including the use of 'psychodynamically guided hospitalisation', early interpretation of negative transference and a focus on the here-and-now inter-actions rather than reconstructions, enabled severe borderline and even some psychotic patients to be treated successfully. Wallerstein looked in detail at this group of 'heroic indication' patients. The overall results were not good. He identified 11 such patients with paranoid features, major alcohol or drug addiction, or borderline pathology. Six of these patients were in the psycho-analysis group: 3 died of mental-illness-related causes (2 from alcoholism, 1 by suicide); and 3 dropped out of analysis (2 of whom did badly, and 1 well – the psychotherapeutic 'lifer' already

mentioned). The psychotherapy group contained the other 5 patients, of whom 2 had mental-illness-related deaths; 4 of these 5 patients were total failures and 1 did moderately well.

The conclusions about this group of patients, with whom psycho-dynamically-minded psychiatrists will be all too familiar, were: that the best form of therapy is 'supportive–expressive' for however long it is necessary; that periods of hospitalisation will be required during long-term therapy; and that a network of informal support, often centred around the subculture associated with a psychiatric unit, is also an important ingredient if these patients are even to survive, let alone thrive.

Finally: 'even if they had little chance with psychoanalysis, they might have had no chance at all with other forms of treatment' (Wallerstein 1986).

More optimistic conclusions can be drawn from two comparable but much less comprehensive British studies of in-patient psycho-analytic therapy with highly disturbed patients, both of which included a cost–benefit analysis of the impact of therapy. Rosser *et al.*'s (1987) five-year follow-up study of patients admitted to the Cassel Hospital showed that about 60 per cent of patients benefited overall, although those with borderline pathology did less well than those with affective disorders. Menzies *et al.*'s (1993) three-year follow-up report from the Henderson Hospital similarly showed that, after discharge, patients with psychopathic disorder made signifi-cantly less use of medical and social service facilities than before admission.

CAN MEANING BE QUANTIFIED?

One of the most widely known attempts to put psychoanalytic insights on a reliable, replicable and scientifically reputable basis, is Luborsky and his group's Core Conflictual Relationship Theme (CCRT) method (Luborsky and Crits-Cristoph 1990). The method is laborious, but it yields psychodynamically meaningful data about the inner world. It starts from the idea that every therapy session contains a number of unconscious personal themes which can be identified through studying transcripts of the sessions. Identifying the CCRT is a two-stage process. First, pairs of trained judges extract from the transcript a number of 'relationship episodes' (REs) which have been described or enacted by the patient in the session – a story about work, home or his reactions to the therapist. Most patients generate about four such REs per session. The list of REs is then passed on to a second set of judges who analyse them into three components: (a) the patient's wishes, needs or intentions; (b) the response elicited from others, either positive or negative; and (c) the reactions of the self to the reactions of the others, again positive or negative. Common examples of *wishes* are for closeness, dominance or autonomy, of *responses* are those of being rejected, controlled or dominated, and of *self-responses* are anger, withdrawal and disappointment. These categories are initally made freehand by the judges in order to produce 'tailor-made' categories, which are then translated into a predetermined list of standard categories to allow for more reliable comparisons. From these standard categories there emerges a CCRT, or set of CCRTs, which characterise the patient's core state – a typical example would be: the wish for closeness, feeling rejected, and responding with withdrawal.

By far the most reliable markers of change in psychotherapy are symptom ratings. These, however, are unsatisfying to psychodynamic researchers, who have tried to operationalise dynamic hypotheses. A significant early example was Malan's (1963) studies of brief therapy. An example involves a man with recurrent psychogenic blackouts, in which it was hypothesised that

> He is afraid that he cannot cope with the responsibilities of masculinity. To take responsibility entails being aggressive and his fear is that this will result in (1) triumphing over his father and possibly (2) damaging the woman. . . . he expresses his anxiety by losing consciousness . . .
>
> (Malan 1963: 118)

However, it has proved impossible to achieve good inter-rater reliability by the Malan-type method in which raters attempt an overall formulation based on a case summary (DeWitt *et al.* 1983). CCRT formulations are much closer to experience and do not use sophisticated psychoanalytic concepts or terminology, but as they are highly reliable (Crits-Cristoph *et al.* 1988) they thus have considerable flexibility as a research tool. They can be modified into a set of statements which the patient can then use to think about himself (cf. Ryle 1990) – in the CCRT example above the patient might agree to the statement 'I want to be close but whenever I try to reach out and am rejected I withdraw, thereby perpetuating my isolation'. CCRTs correspond with the 'core beliefs' found to be important in cognitive therapy.

Luborsky has used CCRTs to research a number of important psychoanalytic issues. CCRT 'pervasiveness' decreases in the course of successful therapy, so that by the end of therapy patients are less dominated by their core themes. Wishes change less than responses, therapeutic change being associated particularly with the capacity to cope with negative responses and to elicit more positive ones from others, rather than some idealised 'resolution of underlying conflict' – a finding consistent with Bachrach's conclusion quoted earlier. Another study used CCRTs to look at the relationship between the 'accuracy' of interpretations, as measured by their closeness to CCRTs. In general, the more skilful the therapist, the better the outcome, especially insofar as they were able accurately to identify wishes and other responses. In both this study and a comparable one using the Plan Diagnosis Method (PDM, see below), the accuracy of interpretation was related to good outcome, but the type of interpretation was not – i.e. non-transference interpretations were just as effective as transference ones (Fretter *et al.* 1994). Indeed, in another study, a high frequency of transference interpretations in Brief Dynamic Therapy actually predicted *negative* outcomes (Piper *et al.* 1991), perhaps because therapists focus more and more on transference in an attempt to retrieve a deteriorating therapeutic situation.

Luborsky (Luborsky and Crits-Cristoph 1990; Luborsky *et al.* 1994) believes that the CCRT approach provides the first scientific confirmation and objective measure of the concept of transference. By comparing the features of CCRT with Freud's statements about transference they confirm that (a) individuals have only a few basic transference patterns, (b) these patterns are manifest both in their relationships generally and with the therapist, (c) transference patterns seem to derive from early parental relationship patterns, (d) transference patterns are as evident outside therapy as in it, (e) these patterns are susceptible to gradual change in the course of treatment.

An important feature of any research method is its capacity to be used by all workers in the field, not just by those who devised it. This has not perhaps been the case with CCRT, but it is certainly true of a new instrument, the Adult Attachment Interview (AAI), devised by Mary Main and her colleagues (Main 1991) based on the principles of attachment theory (Bowlby 1988; Holmes 1993), which is being widely used in psychodynamic psychotherapy research. The AAI also starts with interview transcripts, but, unlike most instruments, it is concerned not so much with the content as the *form* and *style* of the patient's narrative. Like therapy itself, the AAI tries to 'listen with the third ear' (Reik 1922), but in a way that can be researched. A psychodynamic-type assessment interview is carried out, concentrating on the subject's past and present attachments and losses. It is assumed that a person's underlying relational dispositions (which may well be unconscious) will be evident in the structure of his narrative, its consistency, coherence, elaboration or restrictedness.

Interviews are assigned to one of three major categories: *autonomous-free*, in which the subject can talk openly and coherently about his childhood and parents, including painful experiences from the past; *dismissive-detached*, in which narratives are not elaborated and subjects have few childhood memories, tending to deny difficulty or devalue relationships in a grandiose way; and *preoccupied-enmeshed*, in which the narrative style is muddled and confusing and the individual appears to be dominated by affect from the past such as anger or overwhelming sadness. In a fourth category, *incoherent*, the AAI also identifies significant 'breaks' or incoherence which may appear in any type of interview and may reflect past trauma, such as sexual abuse, that has been repressed but momentarily surfaces during the interview.

The AAI has been used to track change in psychoanalytic therapy showing how individuals can move from dismissive or enmeshed to secure narrative styles as therapy progresses (Fonagy *et al.* 1995). It has also been used to trace the intergenerational transmission of attachment patterns, showing how the classification of prospective parents on the AAI before their babies are born correlates well with the subsequent child's attachment status at one year. An unexpected but important finding of this study was that infants appear to develop quite independent attachment patterns with each parent, so that they may be secure with father and insecure with mother and vice versa – depending on the parent's AAI. This is consistent with the psychoanalytic view of an inner or representational world containing models or prototypes of relationships which may act independently of one another. Presumably similar internal models of attachment are built up in the course of therapy which then supersede previous insecure relationship patterns.

SINGLE CASE STUDIES: 'MRS C'

Research that is remote from therapeutic reality is likely to be seen as irrelevant by most clinicians (Denman 1995). Since psychoanalysis is concerned primarily with single cases, there is an increasing literature looking at the psychoanalytic process using single-case, or 'N = 1', design. This has been made possible by the use of computer analysis of the vast amount of data generated by a single analytic treatment. One example of this approach is the Ulm Project (Thoma and Kachele 1987) in which the computer analysed frequently occurring key themes, suggesting that therapy is always 'focal', with a gradually shifting focus as therapy progresses. The Mount Zion Psychotherapy Research Project (Weiss and Sampson *et al.* 1986) is another outstanding example of how important and scientifically reputable research can derive from the study of a particular case. Mrs C underwent a six-year analysis, every hour of which was audio-recorded and transcribed. Her main problems were poor sexual adjustment and chronically low self-esteem. The eventual outcome was very good.

Weiss and Sampson tackled the material with the help of their operational formulation of psychoanalytic ideas, the Plan Diagnosis Method (PDM). They assume that patients carry with them a set of pathogenic beliefs about relationships, and, through the 'Plan', with which they unconsciously test their therapists, hope that they will be disconfirmed. For instance, they saw Mrs C as suffering from 'success guilt' which prevented her from enjoying her marriage or allowing herself to have sexual pleasure. They linked this with her relationship to her handicapped younger sister, on whom a huge amount of parental attention had been lavished, and with whom, therefore, Mrs C felt it was unsafe to compete successfully. Her consequent aggression about this neglect was transferred onto her husband.

Weiss and Sampson see the Plan as a cognitive–affective structure to which unconscious feelings and intellectual functions both contribute. Interpretations that are compatible with the Plan are assumed to be beneficial. Treatment went through several phases – initial attachment, resistance in the second and third years, a much freer but eroticised relationship to the therapist in the fourth and fifth years, and eventual termination with ambivalence and gratitude. Using the PDM they tried to communicate with the unconscious impact of interpretations, finding, for example, that there was an increase in the 'experiencing scale' following interpretations which corresponded to the overall Plan as determined by independent raters.

In another 'N = 1' study, Moran and Fonagy (1987) followed the progress of a highly successful analysis in a 13-year-old diabetic girl, using blood sugar readings as a marker of the state of her internal world and relating these to the analyst's detailed session recordings. Using the statistical technique of 'lag correlation', they showed that there was a temporal relationship between the interpretation of oedipal conflicts and the emergence of better diabetic control. They argue that findings such as these help to counter Grunbaum's (1984) claim that psychoanalysis is based on 'suggestion', since the analyst was ignorant of, and made no reference to, the state of the patient's diabetic control.

More recently, Spence *et al.* (1993) have studied the Mrs C transcripts using a linguistic method known as 'co-occurrence'. This measures the frequency with which certain affectively linked words follow one another – for instance, 'man–woman' co-occur more frequently than emotionally unrelated pairs, such as 'man–field'. Such co-occurrences are more frequently found in fiction than in non-fiction, and it is likely that they reflect underlying affective links, following associative pathways. They studied seven blocks of transcript hours from different phases of treatment and found that co-occurrence increased with the progress of treatment, suggesting reduced rigidity, or an increase in 'associative freedom', as therapy advanced. They also found that three types of therapist interventions – interpreting defences, picking up on recurrent themes, and the investigation of dreams and phantasies – were particularly followed by an increase in co-occurrence which lasted for the next three sessions. This finding is consistent with Malan's (1979) notion of the 'leapfrogging' (cf. Chapter 7) which characterises successful therapist–patient interaction, and also provides some justification for the frequency of analytic sessions needed to maintain therapeutic momentum.

CONCLUSION

The relationship between psychoanalytic practitioners and researchers has not always been easy. At worst, research merely demonstrates the irrelevant or the obvious, while clinicians ignore their findings or adopt an actively Luddite attitude towards them. Present-day research methods have become increasingly applicable to psychoanalytic practice as theoretical positions become less rigid, and modern computer technology enables much more subtle probing of clinical reality. Clinicians, especially if publicly funded, increasingly recognise the need for scientific evaluation of the overall efficacy of their therapy, the robustness of their concepts, the impact of their interventions and the nature of analyst–patient interactions. Freud's insistence that psychoanalysis be accepted as a science remains a legitimate contemporary hope and possibility.

References

Useful introductory texts are marked with an asterisk.

Abend, S.M. (1989) 'Countertransference and psychoanalytic technique', *Psychoanal. Quart.*, 58: 374–95.

Abraham, K. (1953) *Selected Papers of Karl Abraham*, New York: Basic Books.

Adler, G. (1985) *Borderline Psychopathology and its Treatment*, New York: Jason Aronson.

Alanen, Y., Lehtinen, V., Rakkolainen, V. *et al.* (1994) (eds) 'Integrated approach to schizophrenia', *Brit. J. Psychiat.*, Suppl. 23.

Alexander, F. (1937) *Five Year Report of the Chicago Institute for Psychoanalysis: 1932–1937*, Chicago: Chicago Institute for Psycho-Analysis.

Alexander, F. and French, T.M. (1946) *Psychoanalytic Psychotherapy*, Lincoln: University of Nebraska Press.

Alvarez, A. (1992) *Live Company*, London: Routledge.

Arlow, J.A. (1991) *Psychoanalysis: Clinical Theory and Practice*, Madison, C.T.: International Universities Press.

—— (1993) 'Discussion of Baranger's paper on "The mind of the analyst: from listening to interpretation"', *Int. J. Psycho-Anal.*, 74: 1147–54.

Aronson, T. (1989) 'A critical review of psychotherapeutic treatments of the borderline personality: historical trends and future directions', *J. Nerv. Ment. Dis.*, 177: 511–28.

Aserinsky, E. and Kleitman, N. (1953) 'Regularly occurring periods of eye motility and concurrent phenomena during sleep', *Science*, 118: 273–4.

Auden, W. (1952) *Selected Poems*, London: Penguin.

Bachrach, H., Weber, J. and Solomon, M. (1985) 'Factors associated with the outcome of psychoanalysis', *Int. Rev. Psycho-Anal.*, 43: 161–74.

Bachrach, H., Galatzer-Levy, R., Skolnikoff, A. and Waldron, S. (1991) 'On the efficacy of psychoanalysis', *J. Amer. Psychoanal. Ass.*, 39: 871–911.

Balint, E. (1993) *Before I was I*, London: Free Association Books.

Balint, M. (1949) 'On the termination of analysis', *Int. J. Psycho-Anal.*, 31: 196–99.

—— (1952) *Primary Love and Psychoanalytic Technique*, London: Hogarth.

—— (1957) *Problems of Human Behaviour and Pleasure*, London: Hogarth.

—— (1968) *The Basic Fault: Therapeutic Aspects of Regression*, London: Tavistock

Balint, M. and Balint, E. (1939) 'On transference and countertransference', in *Primary Love and Psychoanalytic Technique*, London: Tavistock (reprinted London: Karnac Books, 1985).

—— (1971) *Psychotherapeutic Techniques in Medicine*, London: Tavistock.

Balint, M., Ornstein, P. and Balint, E. (1972) *Focal Psychotherapy*. London: Tavistock.

Baranger, M. (1993) 'The mind of the analyst: from listening to interpretation', *Int. J. Psycho-Anal.*, 74: 15–24.

Bateman, A. (1995) 'The treatment of borderline patients in a day hospital setting', *Psychoanal. Psychother.*, 9, No. 1.

Beck, A., Rush, A., Shaw. B. And Emery, G. (1979) *Cognitive Therapy of Depression*, New York: International Universities Press.

*Benjamin, J. (1990) *The Bonds of Love*, London: Virago.

—— (1995) 'An "overinclusive" theory of gender development', in A. Elliott and S. Frosh (eds) *Psychoanalysis in Contexts*, London: Routledge.

Benjamin, L. (1993) 'Every psychopathology is a gift of love', *Psychother. Res.*, 3: 1–24.

Bergin, A. and Lambert, M. (1986) 'The evaluation of therapeutic outcomes', in S. Garfield and A. Bergin (eds) *Handbook of Psychotherapy and Behaviour Change*, Chichester: Wiley.

Bernstein, D. (1991) 'Gender specific dangers in the female/female dyad in treatment', *Psychoanal. Rev.*, 78.

Bettleheim, B. (1985) *Freud and Man's Soul*, London: Fontana.

Bilger, A. (1986) 'Agieren: Problem und Chance', *Forum der Psychoanalyse*, 2: 294–308.

Bion, W. (1952) 'Group dynamics: a review', *Int. J. Psycho-Anal.*, 33: 235–47.

—— (1955) 'Language and the schizophrenic', in M. Klein, P Heimann, and R. Money-Kyrle (eds) *New Directions of Psychoanalysis*, London: Tavistock Publications, 220–39.

—— (1957) 'Differentiation of the psychotic from the non-psychotic personalities', *Int. J. Psycho-Anal.*, 38: 266–75.

—— (1959) 'Attacks on linking', *International Journal of Psychoanalysis*, 40: 308–15 (reprinted in *Second Thoughts*, London: Heinemann, 1967, pp. 93–109).

—— (1961) 'A theory of thinking', *Int. J. Psycho-Anal.*, 43: 306–10.

—— (1962) *Learning from Experience*, London: Heinemann.

—— (1963) *Elements of Psychoanalysis*, London: Heinemann.

—— (1967) Notes on memory and desire, *The Psychoanalytic Forum*, 2: 272–273 and 279–80; also in E. Bott Spillius (ed.), *Melanie Klein Today, Vol. 2: Mainly Practice* London: Routledge, 1988, pp. 17–21.

—— (1970) *Attention and Interpretation*, London: Heinemann.

Bleuler, E. (1924) *Textbook of Psychiatry*, New York: Macmillan.

Blum, H. (1973) 'The concept of erotized transference', *J. Amer. Psychoanal. Ass.*, 21: 61–76.

Bly, R. (1988) *Iron John*, New York: Basic Books.

Bollas, C. (1987) *The Shadow of the Object: Psychoanalysis of the Unthought Known*, London: Free Association Books.

—— (1989) *Forces of Destiny*, London: Free Association Books.

—— (1993) *Being a Character: Psychoanalysis and Self Experience*, London: Routledge.

Bolognini, S. (1994) 'Transference: erotised, erotic loving, affectionate', *Int. J. Psycho-Anal.*, 75: 73–86.

Bond, M. (1992) 'An empirical study of defensive styles: The Defense Style Questionnaire', in G.E. Vaillant (ed.) *Ego Mechanisms of Defence*, Washington, DC: American Psychiatric Press Inc.

Bond, M., Gardner, S.T., Christian, J. *et al.* (1983) 'Empirical study of self-rated defence styles', *Arch. Gen. Psychiat.* 40: 333–38.

Bower, G. (1981) 'Mood and Memory', *American Psychol.*, 36: 129–148.

Bowie, M. (1991) *Lacan*, London: Fontana.

Bowlby, J. (1988) *A Secure Base: Clinical Applications of Attachment Theory*, London: Routledge.

Bradley, B. (1989) *Visions of Infancy*, Cambridge: Polity.

Bradshaw, W. (1978) 'Training psychiatrists for working with blacks in basic residency programmes', *Amer. J. Psychiat*, 135: 1520–24.

—— (1982) 'Supervision in black and white: race as a factor in supervision, in M. Blumenfield (ed.) *Applied Supervision in Psychotherapy*, New York: Grune and Stratton.

Brazelton, T. and Cramer, B. (1991) *The Earliest Relationship*, London: Karnac.

Brenman-Pick, I. (1985) 'Working through in the countertransference', *Int. J. Psycho-Anal.*, 66: 157–66.

Brenner, C. (1979) Working alliance, therapeutic alliance, and transference, *J. Amer. Psychoanal. Ass.*, 27 (supplement): 137–57.

—— (1982) *The Mind in Conflict*, New York: IUP.

Breuer, J. and Freud, S. (1895) Studies in Hysteria, *S.E. 2*, London: Hogarth.

Britton, R., Feldman, M. and O'Shaugnessy, E. (1989) *The Oedipus Complex Today*, London: Karnac.

Brown, G. and Harris, T. (1978) *The Social Origins of Depression*, London: Tavistock.

*Brown, D. and Pedder, J. (1993) *Introduction to Psychotherapy: An Outline of Psychodynamic Principles and Practice*, 2nd edn, London: Routledge.

Bruner, J. (1986) *Actual Minds, Possible Worlds*, Cambridge, Mass.: Harvard University Press.

—— (1990) *Acts of Meaning*, Cambridge, Mass.: Harvard University Press.

Byng-Hall, J. (1991) 'The application of attachment theory to understanding and treatment in family therapy', in C. Murray Parkes *et al.* (eds) *Attachment Across the Life Cycle*, London: Routledge.

*Casement, P. (1985) *On Learning from the Patient*, London: Tavistock.

Cavell, M. (1988) 'Solipsism and community: two concepts of mind in philosophy and psychoanalysis', *Psychoanal. Contemp. Thought*, 11: 587–613.

—— (1994) *The Psychoanalytic Mind*, Cambridge, Mass.: Harvard University Press.

Chadwick, P. and Birchwood, M. (1994) 'The omnipotence of voices: a cognitive approach to auditory hallucinations', *Brit. J. Psychiat.*, 164: 190–201.

Chasseguet-Smirgel, J. (1984) 'The femininity of the analyst in professional practice', *Int. J. Psycho-Anal.*, 65:169–79.
—— (1985) *Creativity and Perversion*, London: Free Association Books.
Chodorow, N. (1978) *The Reproduction of Motherhood*, Berkeley, CA: University of California Press.
Chomsky, N. (1972) *Language and Mind*, New York: Harcourt Brace.
Chused, J. (1990) 'Neutrality in the analysis of action-prone adolescents', *J. Amer. Psychoanal. Ass.*, 38: 679–704.
Clulow, C. (1985) *Marital Therapy, an Inside View*, Aberdeen: University Press.
Cohen, N.A. (1982) 'On loneliness and the aging process', *Int. J. Psycho-Anal.*, 63: 149–55.
Colby, K. and Stoller, R. (1988) *Cognitive Science and Psychoanalysis*, Hillsdale, NJ: Analytic Press.
Coltart, N. (1986) 'Slouching towards Bethlehem – or thinking the unthinkable in psychoanalysis', in G. Kohon (ed.) *The British School of Psychoanalysis*, London: Free Association Books.
—— (1988) Diagnosis and assessment for suitability for psycho-analytic psychotherapy, *Brit. J. Psychother.*, 4: 127–34
*—— (1993) *How to Survive as a Psychotherapist*, London: SCM Press.
Cooper, A.M. (1987) 'Changes on psychoanalytic ideas: transference interpretation', *J. Amer. Psychoanal. Ass.*, 35: 77–98.
Crits-Cristoph, P. (1992) 'The efficacy of brief dynamic psychotherapy: a meta-analysis', *Amer. J. Psychiat.*, 149: 151–8.
Crits-Cristoph, P., Luborsky, L., Dahl, L., Popp, C. *et al.* (1988) 'Clinicians can agree in assessing relationship patterns in psychotherapy', *Arch. Gen. Psychiat.*, 45: 1001–4.
Dahl, H., Kachele, H. and Thoma, H. (eds) (1988) *Psychoanalytic Process Research Strategies*, New York: Springer.
Denman, C. (1995) 'Questions to be answered in the evaluation of long-term therapy', in *Research Foundations of Psychotherapy Practice*, M. Aveline and D. Shapiro (eds), Chichester: Wiley.
Dennett, D. (1993) *Consciousness Explained*, London; Penguin.
Deutsch, H. (1942) 'Some forms of emotional disturbance and their relationship to schizophrenia', *Psychoanal. Quart.*, 11: 301–21.
Dewitt, K., Kaltreider, N., Weiss, D. and Horowitz, M. (1983) 'Judging change in psychotherapy: reliability of clinical formulations', *Arch. Gen. Psychiat.*, 40: 1121–8.
Dicks, H. (1967) *Marital Tensions*, London: Routledge.
Dixon, N. and Henley, S. (1991) 'Unconscious perception: possible implications of data from academic research for clinical practice', *J. Nerv. Ment. Dis.*, 79: 243–51.
Eagle, M. (1984) *Recent Developments in Psychoanalysis; A Critical Evaluation*, New York: McGraw-Hill.
Eaton, T., Abeles, N. and Gutfreund, M. (1993) 'Negative indicators, therapeutic alliance, and therapy outcome', *Psychother. Res.*, 3: 115–23.
Eidelberg, L. (1968) *Encyclopaedia of Psychoanalysis*, New York: The Free Press.
Eissler, K. (1974) 'On some theoretical and technical problems regarding

the payment of fees for psychoanalytic treatment', *Int. Rev. Psycho-Anal.*, 1: 73–101.

Elkin, I., Shea, M., Watkins, J. *et al.* (1989) 'NIMH treatment of depression collaborative research programme; 1: General effectiveness of treatments', *Arch. Gen. Psychiat.*, 56: 971–82.

Elliot, R. and Shapiro, D. (1992) 'Client and therapist as analysts of significant events', in S. Toukmainian and D. Rennie (eds), *Psychotherapy Process Research: Paradigmatic and Narrative Approaches*, Newbury Park, CA: Sage.

Ellenberger, H. (1970) *The Discovery of the Unconscious*, New York: Basic Books.

Emde, R. (1981) 'Changing models of infancy and the nature of early development: remodeling the foundation', *J. Amer. Psychoanal. Ass.*, 29: 179–220.

—— (1988a and 1988b) 'Development terminable and interminable, I and II', *Int. J. Psycho-Anal.*, 69: 23–42 and 283–6.

Engel, G. (1968) 'A life setting conducive to illness', *Ann. Internal Med.*, 69: 293–300.

Erikson, E. (1954) 'The dream specimen of psychoanalysis', *J. Amer. Psychoanal. Ass.*, 2: 5–56.

—— (1965) *Childhood and Society*, London: Penguin.

—— (1968) *Identity, Youth and Crisis*, New York: Norton.

Erle, J. and Goldberg, D. (1979) 'Problems in the assessment of analyzability', *Psychoanal. Quart.*, 48: 48–84.

Etchegoyen, H. (1991) *The Fundamentals of Psychoanalytic Technique*, London: Karnac.

Evans, D. (1985) 'Psychotherapy and black patients: problems of training, trainees, and trainers', *Psychother.: Theory, Res. Prac.*, 22: 457–60.

Eysenck, H. (1952) 'The effects of psychotherapy: an evaluation', *J. Cons. Psychol.*, 16: 319–24.

Fairbairn, W.R.D. (1952) *Psychoanalytic Studies of the Personality*, London: Routledge.

—— (1958) 'On the nature and aims of psychoanalytical treatment', *Int. J. Psycho-Anal.*, 39: 374–85.

Fenichel, O. (1941) 'Problems of psychoanalytic technique', *Psychoanal. Quart. Inc.*, New York: Albany.

—— (1946) *The Psychoanalytic Theory of Neurosis*, London: Routledge and Kegan Paul.

Ferenczi, S. (1921) 'The further development of an active therapy in psychoanalysis', *Further Contributions to the Theory and Technique of Psychoanalysis*, London: Hogarth.

—— (1932) 'Confusion of tongues between adults and the child', in *Final Contributions*, p. 162.

Flanders, S. (ed.) (1993) *The Dream Discourse Today*, London: Routledge.

Fliess, R. (1942) 'The metapsychology of the analyst', *Psychoanal. Quart.*, 11: 211–27.

—— (1953) 'Countertransference and counter-identification', *J.Amer. Psychoanal. Ass.*, 1: 268–84.

Fonagy, P. (1989) 'On the integration of cognitive behaviour theory with psychoanalysis', *Brit. J. Psychother.*, 5: 557–63.

—— (1991) 'Thinking about thinking: some clinical and theoretical considerations in the treatment of a borderline patient', *Int. J. Psycho-Anal.*, 72: 639–56.

—— (1993) 'Psychoanalytic and empirical approaches to developmental psychopathology: can they be usefully integrated?', *J. Roy. Soc. Med.*, 86: 577–81.

Fonagy, P., Steele, M., Steele, H. Leigh, T. *et al.* (1995) 'The predictive specificity of Mary Main's Adult Attachment Interview: implications for psychodynamic theories of normal and pathological emotional development', in S. Goldberg, R. Muir and J. Kerr (eds) *John Bowlby's Attachment Theory: Historical, Clinical and Social Significance*, New York: Academic Press.

Fosshage, J. (1994) 'Towards reconceptualising transference: theoretical and clinical considerations', *Int. J. Psycho-Anal.*, 75: 265–80.

Fraiberg, P., Adelson, E. and Shapiro, V. (1975) 'Ghosts in the nursery: a psychoanalytic approach to the problem of impaired mother–infant relationships', *J. Amer. Acad. Child Psychiat.*, 14: 387–422.

Frank, J. (1986) 'Psychotherapy: the transformation of meanings', *J. Roy. Soc. Med.*, 79: 341–6.

Fretter, P., Bucci, W., Broitman, J. *et al.* (1994) 'How the patient's plan relates to the concept of transference', *Psychother. Res.*, 4: 58–72.

Freud, A. (1936) *The Ego and the Mechanisms of Defence* London: Hogarth.

—— (1965) *Normality and Pathology in Childhood*, New York: International Universities Press.

Freud, S. (1894) 'The neuro-psychoses of defence', *S.E. 3*, London: Hogarth.

—— (1896) 'Further remarks on the neuro-psychoses of defence', *S.E. 3*, London: Hogarth.

—— (1898) 'Sexuality in the aetiology of the neuroses', *S.E. 3*, London: Hogarth.

*—— (1900) 'The interpretation of dreams', *S.E. 4/5*, London: Hogarth.

—— (1904) 'Freud's psychoanalytic procedure', *S.E. 7*, London: Hogarth.

—— (1905a) 'Three essays on the theory of sexuality', *S.E. 7*, London: Hogarth.

—— (1905b) 'On psychotherapy', *S.E. 7*, London: Hogarth.

*—— (1905c) 'Fragment of an analysis of a case of hysteria', *S.E. 7*, London: Hogarth.

—— (1909) 'Note upon a case of obsessional neurosis', *S.E. 10*, London: Hogarth.

—— (1910) 'The future prospects of psychoanalysis', *S.E. 11*, London: Hogarth.

—— (1911a) 'Formulations of the two principles of mental functioning', *S.E. 12*, London: Hogarth.

—— (1911b) 'Psycho-analytic notes on an autobiographical account of a case of paranoia', *S.E. 12*, London: Hogarth.

*—— (1912a) 'Recommendations to physicians practising psychoanalysis', *S.E. 13*, London: Hogarth.

*—— (1912b) 'The dynamics of transference', *S.E. 12*, London: Hogarth.

*—— (1913) 'On beginning the treatment', *S.E. 12*, London: Hogarth.

—— (1914a) 'On Narcissism', *S.E. 14*, London: Hogarth.

—— (1914b) 'On the history of the psychoanalytic movement', *S.E. 14*, London: Hogarth.

—— (1914c) 'Remembering, repeating, and working through', *S.E. 12*, London: Hogarth.

—— (1915) 'Observations on transference love', *S.E. 12*, London: Hogarth.

—— (1916) 'Development and regression', in Introductory Lectures in Psychoanalysis, *S.E. 16*, London: Hogarth.

*—— (1916/17) 'Introductory lectures in psychoanalysis', *S.E. 15/16*, London: Hogarth.

—— (1917) 'Mourning and melancholia', *S.E. 14*, London: Hogarth.

—— (1918) 'From the history of an infantile neurosis', *S.E. 17*, London: Hogarth.

—— (1919) 'Lines of advance in psychoanalytic therapy', *S.E. 17*, London: Hogarth.

—— (1920) 'Beyond the pleasure principle', *S.E. 18*, London: Hogarth.

—— (1922) 'Two encyclopaedia articles', *S.E. 18*, London: Hogarth.

*—— (1923) 'The ego and the id', *S.E. 19*, London: Hogarth.

—— (1924) 'Neurosis and psychosis', *S.E. 19*. London: Hogarth.

—— (1925a) 'An autobiographical study', *S.E. 20*, London: Hogarth.

—— (1925b) 'Some additional notes on dream interpretation as a whole', *S.E. 19*, London: Hogarth.

—— (1926a) 'Inhibitions, symptoms and anxiety', *S.E. 20*, London: Hogarth.

—— (1926b) 'The question of lay analysis', *S.E. 20*, London: Hogarth.

—— (1927) 'Fetishism', *S.E. 21*, London: Hogarth.

—— (1930) 'Civilisation and its discontents', *S.E. 21*, London: Hogarth.

—— (1931) 'Female sexuality', *S.E. 21*, London: Hogarth

—— (1932) 'Revision of the Interpretation of Dreams', in 'New Introductory Lectures', *S.E. 22*, London; Hogarth.

—— (1933) 'Dissection of the personality', in 'New Introductory Lectures on Psychoanalysis', *S.E. 22*, London: Hogarth.

*—— (1937) 'Analysis terminable and interminable', *S.E. 23*, Hogarth: London.

—— (1940a) 'An outline of psychoanalysis', *S.E. 23*, London: Hogarth.

—— (1940b) 'Project for a scientific psychology', *S.E. 1*, London: Hogarth.

Freud, S. and Breuer, J. (1895) 'Studies on Hysteria', *S.E. 2*, London: Hogarth.

Friedman, L. (1978) 'Piaget and psychotherapy', *J. Amer. Acad. Psychoanal.*, 6: 175–92.

Fromm, E. (1973) *The Crisis of Psychoanalysis*, London: Penguin.

Fromm-Reichmann, F. (1959) *Psychoanalysis and Psychotherapy: Collected Papers of Freida Fromm-Reichmann*, Chicago: University of Chicago Press.

Frosh, S. (1991) *Identity Crisis: Modernity, Psychoanalysis and the Self*, London: Macmillan.

Gabbard, G. (1986) 'The treatment of the "special" patient in a psychiatric hospital', *Int. Rev. Psycho-Anal.*, 13: 333–47.

—— (1989) 'Splitting in hospital treatment', *Amer. J. Psychiat.*, 146: 444–51.

*—— (1990) *Psychodynamic Psychiatry in Clinical Practice*, Washington, DC: American Psychiatric Press.

—— (1992) 'Psychodynamic psychiatry in the "decade of the brain"', *Amer. J. Psychiat.*, 149: 991–8.

Galwey, P. (1994) *The Concept of a Person: Sanity and Insanity in Thinking and Feeling*, unpublished manuscript.

Gardner, M. (1981) *The Mind's New Science*, London: Penguin.

Garland, C. (1991) 'External disasters and the internal world: an approach to the psychotherapeutic understanding of survivors', in J. Holmes (ed.) *A Textbook of Psychotherapy in Psychiatric Practice*, Edinburgh: Churchill Livingstone.

Gedo, J. and Goldberg, A. (1973) *Models of the Mind*, Chicago: University of Chicago Press.

Gill, M.M. (1982) *Analysis of Transference. Vol. I, Theory and Technique*, Psychological Issues, Monogram, 53, New York: International Universities Press.

—— (1984) Transference: a change in conception or only in emphasis?, *Psychoanal Inquiry*, 4: 489–523.

Gill, M.M. and Hoffman, I.Z. (1982) *Analysis of Transference, Vol. II*, New York: International Universities Press.

Glasser, M. (1979) 'Some aspects of the role of aggression in the perversions', in I. Rosen (ed.) *Sexual Deviation*, 2nd edn, Oxford: OUP.

Glasser. M. (1986) 'Identification and its vicissitudes as observed in the perversions', *Int. J. Psycho-Anal.*, 67: 9–17.

Glover, E. (1931) 'The therapeutic effect of inexact interpretation: a contribution to the theory of suggestion', *Int. J. Psycho-Anal.*, 12: 397–411.

Goldberg, E. *et al.*, (1974) 'Some observations on three interracial analyses', *Int. J. Psycho-Anal.*, 55: 495–500.

Green, A. (1975) The analyst, symbolisation and absence in the analytic setting (on changes in analytic practice and analytic experience), *Int. J. Psycho-Anal.*, 56: 1–22.

—— (1977) 'Conceptions of affect', *Int. J. Psycho-Anal.*, 58: 129–56.

Greenacre, P. (1954) The role of transference: practical considerations in relation to psychoanalytic therapy, *J. Amer. Psychoanal. Ass.*, 2: 671–84

Greenberg, J.R. and Mitchell, S.A. (1982) *Object Relations in Psychoanalytic Theory*, Cambridge, Mass.: Harvard University Press.

Greer, S., Morris, T. and Pettingale, K.W. (1979) 'Psychological response to breast cancer: effect on outcome', *Lancet*, II: 785–7.

Grinberg, L. (1962) 'On a specific aspect of countertransference due to the patient's projective identification', *Int. J. Psycho-Anal.*, 43: 436–40.

Grosskurth, P. (1986) *Melanie Klein: Her World and her Work*, Cambridge MA: Harvard University Press.

Grossman, W. and Kaplan, M.D. (1989) 'Three commentaries on gender in Freud's thought: a prologue on the psychoanalytic theory of sexuality', *Psychoanal. Quart.*, 58: 179–81.

Grosz, S. (1993) 'A phantasy of infection', *Int. J. Psycho-Anal.*, 74, 965–74.

Grotstein, J. (1977a and 1977b) 'The psychoanalytic concept of schizophrenia, I', *Int. J. Psycho-Anal.*, 58: 403–25, 427–52.

—— (1981) *Splitting and Projective Identification*, New York: Jason Aronson.

Grunbaum, A. (1984) *The Foundations of Psychoanalysis*, Berkeley: University of California Press.

Gunderson, J. (1984) *Borderline Personality Disorder*, Washington, DC: American Psychiatric Press.

Gunderson, J. and Sabo, A. (1993) 'The phenomenal and conceptual interface between borderline personality disorder and PTSD', *Amer. J. Psychiat.*, **150**, 19–27.

Gunderson, J., Frank, A., Ronningstam, E. *et al.* (1989) 'Early discontinuance of borderline patients from psychotherapy', *J. Nerv. Ment. Dis.*, 177: 38–42.

Guntrip, H. (1961) *Personality Structure and Human Interaction: the Developing Synthesis of Psychodynamic Theory*, New York: International Universities Press.

Gustavson, D. (1964) (ed.) *Essays in Philosophical Psychology*, New York: Doubleday.

Haan, N. (1963) 'Proposed model of ego functioning: coping and defence mechanisms in relationship to IQ change', *Psychol. Monogr.*, 77: 1–23.

Habermas, J. (1968) *Knowledge and Human Interests*, trans. J. Shapiro, Boston: Beacon Press.

Hamilton, V. (1982) *Narcissus and Oedipus*, London: Routledge.

—— (1985) 'John Bowlby: an ethological basis for psychoanalysis', in J. Reppen (ed.) *Beyond Freud: a Study of Modern Psychoanalytic Theorists*, New York: Analytic Press.

—— (1993) 'Truth and reality in psychoanalytic discourse', *Int. J. Psycho-Anal.*, 74: 63–79.

Hartmann, H. (1939) *Ego Psychology and the Problem of Adaptation*, London: Imago.

—— (1964) *Essays in Ego Psychology: Selected Problems in Psychoanalytic Theory*, New York: International Universities Press.

Heimann, P. (1950) 'On countertransference', *Int. J. Psycho-Anal.*, 31: 81–4.

—— (1990) *About Children and Children No Longer*, London: Routledge.

Higgitt, A. and Fonagy, P. (1992) 'Psychotherapy in borderline and narcissistic personality disorder', *Brit. J. Psychiat.*, 161: 23–43.

Hildebrand, P. (1995) *Beyond the Mid-life Crisis*, London: Sheldon.

Hinshelwood, R.D. (1987) 'The psychotherapist's role in a large psychiatric institution', *Psychoanal. Psychother.* 2, 207–15.

*—— (1989) *A Dictionary of Kleinian Thought*, London: Free Association Books.

—— (1991) 'Psychodynamic formulation in assessment for psychotherapy', *Brit. J. Psychother.*, 8: 166–74.

—— (1993) 'Locked in a role: a psychotherapist within the social defence system of a prison', *J. Forensic Psychiat.*, 4: 427–40.

*—— (1994a) *Clinical Klein*, London: Free Association Books.
—— (1994b) 'The relevance of psychotherapy', *Psychoanal. Psychother.*, 8: 283–94.

Hobson, J. (1988) *The Dreaming Brain*, London: Penguin.

Hoffer, W. (1950) 'Three psychological criteria for the termination of treatment', *Int. J. Psycho-Anal.*, 31: 194–5.

Hoffman, I.Z. (1983) 'The patient as interpreter of the analyst's experience', *Contemp. Psychoanal.*, 19: 389–422.

Hoffman, M.L. (1978) 'Toward a theory of empathic arousal and development', in M. Lewis and L.A. Rosenblum (eds) *The Development of Affect*, New York: Plenum Press.

Hoggett, P. (1992) *Partisans in an Uncertain World: The Psychoanalysis of Engagement*, London; Free Association Books.

Holmes, D. (1992) 'Race and transference in psychoanalysis and psychotherapy', *Int. J. Psycho-Anal.*, 73: 1–11.

Holmes, J. (1992) *Between Art and Science: Essays in Psychotherapy and Psychiatry*, London: Routledge.

*—— (1993) *John Bowlby and Attachment Theory*, London: Routledge.
—— (1994a) 'Brief dynamic psychotherapy', *Adv. Psychiat. Treatment*, 1: 15–24.
—— (1994b) 'Clinical implications of attachment theory', *Brit. J. Psychother.*, 11: 62–76.
—— (1994c) 'Psychotherapy and its relationships', *Current Opin. Psychiat.* 7: 213–15.
—— (1995) 'How I assess for psychoanalytic psychotherapy', in C. Mace (ed.) *The Art and Science of Assessment in Psychotherapy*, London: Routledge.

Holmes, J. and Lindley, R. (1989) *The Values of Psychotherapy*, Oxford: Oxford University Press.
—— (1994) 'Ethics and psychotherapy', in R. Gillon (ed.) *Principles of Health Care Ethics*, Chichester: Wiley.

Holmes, J. and Mitcheson, S. (1995) 'A model for an integrated psychotherapy service', *Psychiatric Bulletin*, 19: 210–13.

Home, J. (1966) 'The concept of mind', *Int. J. Psycho-Anal.*, 47: 42–9.

Hooke, A. (1959) *Psychoanalysis, Scientific Method, and Philosophy*, New York; New York University Press.

Horney, K. (1939) *New Ways in Psychoanalysis*, New York: Norton.

Horowitz, M., Marmar, C., Weiss, D. *et al.* (1984) 'Brief psychotherapy of bereavement reactions: the relationship of process to outcome', *Arch. Gen. Psychiat*, 41, 438–48.

Horowitz, M.J., Markman, M.C., Stinson, C. *et al.* (1990) 'A classification theory of defense', in J.L. Singer (ed.) *Repression and Dissociation*, Chicago: University of Chicago Press.

Horrocks, R. (1994) *Masculinity in Crisis*, London: Macmillan.

Howard, K., Kopta, S., Krause, M. and Orlinsky, D. (1986) 'The dose-effect relationship in psychotherapy', *Amer. Psychol.*, 41: 159–64.

Isaacs, S. (1943) 'The nature and function of phantasy', In M. Klein, P. Heimann, S. Isaaca and J. Riviere (eds) *Developments in Psychoanalysis*, London: Hogarth, 1952.

Israel, P. (1994) 'Some specific features of the psychoanalytic training', *Psychoanalysis in Europe*, Bulletin 42 29–37.

Jackson, M. (1993) 'Manic-depressive psychosis: psychopathology and individual psychotherapy within a psychodynamic milieu', *Psychoanal. Psychother.*, 7, No. 2: 103–33.

Jacobson, E. (1964) *The Self and the Object World*, New York: International Universities Press.

Jaques, E. (1955) 'Social systems as a defence against persecutory and depressive anxiety', in M. Klein, P. Heimann, and R.E. Money-Kyrle (eds) *New Directions in Psychoanalysis*, London: Tavistock Publications pp. 478–98; paperback, Tavistock Publications, 1971; also reprinted by Maresfield Reprints, London: Karnac Books, 1985.

—— (1965) 'Death and the mid-life crisis', *Int. J. Psycho-Anal.*, 46: 502–14.

Jones, E. (1978) 'The effects of race on psychotherapy process and outcome: an exploratory investigation', *Psychotherapy: Theory, Res. Prac.*, 15: 226–36.

Jones, E. (1916) 'The theory of symbolism', in *Papers on Psychoanalysis* (5th edn 1948), London: Hogarth.

—— (1953) *Sigmund Freud: Life and Work*, London: Hogarth.

Joseph, B. (1986) 'Transference: the total situation', *Int. J. Psycho-Anal.*, 66: 447–54.

—— (1987) 'Projective identification: some clinical aspects', in J. Sandler (ed.) *Projection, Identification, Projective Identification*, New York: International Universities Press.

—— (1989) *Psychic Equilibrium and Psychic Change*, London: Routledge.

Joseph, E. (1984) 'Insight', in A. Richards and M. Willick (eds) *Psychoanalysis: the Science of Mental Conflict*, Hillsdale, NJ: The Analytic Press.

Jung, C.G. (1943) 'The psychology of the unconscious' (5th edn), in *The Collected Works of C.G. Jung*, Vol. 7, London: Routledge and Kegan Paul.

—— (1974) *Dreams*, New Jersey: Princeton University Press.

Kantrowitz, J., Katz, A. and Paolitto, F. (1990a, b and c) 'Follow-up of psychoanalysis five to ten years after termination', *J. Amer. Psychoanal. Ass.*, 38: 471–496, 637–654, 655–678.

Karasu, T. (1982) 'Psychotherapy and pharmacotherapy: toward an integrative model', *Amer. J. Psychiat.*, 139: 1102–13.

—— (1990) 'Towards a clinical model of psychotherapy for depression', *Amer. J. Psychiat.*, 147: 269–78.

Karme, L. (1979) 'The analysis of a male patient by a female analyst: the problem of the negative oedipal transference', *Int. J. Psycho-Anal.*, 60: 253–61.

Kastenbaum, R. (1964) 'The reluctant therapist', in *New Thoughts on Old Age*, New York: Springer.

Kemper, W. (1950) 'Die Honorarfrage in der Psychotherapie', *Psyche*, 4: 201–22.

Kernberg, O. (1975) *Borderline Conditions and Pathological Narcissism*, New York: Jason Aronson.

—— (1976) *Object Relations Theory and Clinical Psychoanalysis*, New York: Jason Aronson.

—— (1980) *Internal World and External Reality*, New York: Jason Aronson.

—— (1982) 'Self, ego, affects, and drives', *J. Amer. Psychoanal. Assn.*, 30: 893–917.

—— (1984) *Severe Personality Disorders: Psychotherapeutic Strategies*, New Haven, Conn.: Yale University Press.

—— (1987) 'Projection and projective identification; developmental and clinical aspects', in J. Sandler (ed.) *Projection, Identification, Projective Identification*, London: Karnac Books.

—— (1988) 'Object relations theory in clinical practice', *Psychoanal. Quart.*, 57: 481–504.

—— (1993) 'Convergences and divergences in contemporary psychoanalytic technique', *Int. J. Psycho-Anal.* 74: 659–73.

Kernberg, O.F, Selzer, M.A., Koenigsberg, H.W. *et al.* (1990) *Psychodynamic Psychotherapy of Borderline Patients*, New York: Basic Books.

King, P. (1980) 'The life cycle as indicated by the nature of transference in the psychoanalysis of the middle-aged and elderly', *Int. J. Psycho-Anal.*, 61: 153–60.

King, P. and Steiner, J. (1990) *The Freud–Klein Controversies 1941–1945*, London: Routledge.

Klauber, J. (1972) 'The relation of transference and interpretation', *Int. J. Psycho-Anal.*, 53: 385–91.

Klein, G. (1976) *Psychoanalytic Theory: An Exploration of Essentials*, New York: International Universities Press.

Klein, M. (1932) *The Psychoanalysis of Children*, London: Hogarth.

—— (1935) 'A contribution to the psychogenesis of manic-depressive states', in *The Writings of Melanie Klein*, Vol. 1, *Love, Guilt and Reparation*, London: Hogarth, pp. 262–89.

—— (1940) 'Mourning and its relation to manic depressive states', in *The Writings of Melanie Klein*, Vol. 1, *Love, Guilt and Reparation*, London, Hogarth, pp. 344–69.

—— (1946) 'Notes on some schizoid mechanisms', in M. Klein, P. Heimann, S. Isaacs and J. Riviere (eds) *Developments in Psychoanalysis*, London: Hogarth (reprinted London: Karnac Books, 1989).

—— (1950a) 'On the criteria for the termination of a psychoanalysis', in: *Writings*, Vol. 3: *Envy and Gratitude and Other works* (Chap. 3), 1975.

—— (1950b) 'On the criteria for the termination of psychoanalysis', *Int. J. Psycho-Anal.*, 31: 78–80; reprinted in *The Writings of Melanie Klein*, Vol. 3, London: Hogarth (1975).

—— (1952) 'Some theoretical conclusions regarding the emotional life of the infant', in J. Riviere (ed.) *Developments in Psychoanalysis*, reprinted in *The Writings of Melanie Klein*, Vol. 3, London: Hogarth.

—— (1955) 'On identification', in *New Directions in Psychoanalysis*, London: Hogarth; reprinted in *The Writings of Melanie Klein*, Vol. 3, London: Hogarth (1975).

—— (1957) 'Envy and Gratitude', in *Envy and Gratitude and Other Works, 1946–63*, London: Hogarth, 1975.

—— (1986) in J. Mitchell (ed.), *The Selected Melanie Klein*, London: Penguin.

Klerman, G. (1986) 'Drugs and psychotherapy', in (S.) Garfield and A. Bergin (eds) *Handbook of Psychotherapy and Behaviour Change*, Chichester: Wiley.

Klerman, G. and Weissman, E. (1984) *Interpersonal Psychotherapy: A Manual*, New York: Basic Books.

Knight, R. (1941) 'Evaluation of the results of psychoanalytic therapy', *Amer. J. Psychiat.*, 98: 434–46.

*Kohon, G. (1986) *The British School of Psychoanalysis – The Independent Tradition*, London: Free Association Books.

Kohut, H. (1971) *The Analysis of the Self*, New York: International Universities Press.

—— (1977) *The Restoration of the Self*, New York: International Universities Press.

—— (1983) in J. Litchtenberg and S. Kaplan (eds) *Reflections on Self Psychology*, Hillsdale, NJ: Analytic Press.

—— (1984) in A. Goldberg and P. Stepansky (eds), *How Does Analysis Cure?*, Chicago: University of Chicago Press.

Kris, E. (1952) *Psychoanalytic Explorations in Art*, New York: International Universities Press

—— (1956) 'On some vicissitudes of insight in psychoanalysis', *Int. J. Psycho-Anal.*, 37: 445–55.

Kuhn, T.S. (1962) *The Structure of Scientific Revolutions*, Chicago: The University of Chicago Press.

Lacan, J. (1966) *Ecrits*, trans. A. Sheridon, London: Tavistock.

—— (1977) *The Four Fundamental Concepts of Psychoanalysis*, London: Hogarth.

Laing, R. (1960) *The Divided Self*, London: Penguin.

Lambert, M., Shapiro, D. and Bergin, A. (1986) 'The effectiveness of psychotherapy', in S. Garfield and A. Bergin (eds), *Handbook of Psychotherapy and Behaviour Change*, Chichester: Wiley.

Langs, R. (1976) *The Bipersonal Field*, New York: Jason Aronson.

—— (1978a) 'Some communicative properties of the bipersonal field', *Int. J. Psycho-Anal. Psychother.*, 7: 87–135.

—— (1978b) *The Listening Process*, New York: Jason Aronson.

Laplanche, J. (1989) *New Foundations for Psychoanalysis*, Oxford: Blackwell.

*Laplanche, J. and Pontalis, J. (1973) *The Language of Psycho-Analysis*, trans. D. Nicholson-Smith, London: Hogarth.

Lasch, C. (1975) *The Culture of Narcissism*, New York: Basic Books.

—— (1979) *Haven in a Heartless World. The Family Besieged*, New York: Basic Books.

Laufer, E. (1987) 'Suicide in adolescence', *Psychoanal. Psychother.*, 3, No. 1: 1–10.

Laufer, M. and Laufer, E. (1984) *Adolescence and Developmental Breakdown*, New Haven: Yale University Press.

Lazarus, R.S., Averill, J.R. and Opton, E.M. (1974) 'The psychology of coping: issues of research and assessment', in E.G. Coehlo, D. Hamburg and J. Adams (eds) *Coping and Adaptation*, New York: Basic Books

Leiman, M. (1994) 'Projective identification as early joint action sequences: a Vygotskian addendum to the Procedural Sequence Object Relations Model', *Brit. J. Med. Psychol.*, 67: 97–106.

Lester, E. (1990) 'Gender and identity issues in the analytic process', *Int. J. Psycho-Anal.*, 71: 435–44.

Levenson, E. (1983) *The Ambiguity of Change*, New York, Basic Books.

Lewin, B. (1955) 'Dream psychology and the analytic situation', *Psychoanal Quart.*, 25: 169–99.

Limentani, A. (1966) 'A re-evaluation of acting out in relation to working through', *Int. J. Psycho-Anal.*, 47: 274–82.

—— (1972) 'The assessment of analysability: a major hazard in selection for psychoanalysis', *Int. J. Psycho-Anal.*, 53: 351–61.

Lipton, M.A. (1983) 'A letter from Anna Freud', *Amer. J. Psychiat.*, 140: 1583–4.

Little, M. (1951) 'Countertransference and the patient's response to it', *Int. J. Psycho-Anal.*, 32: 32–40.

Loeb, F.F. and Loeb, L.R. (1987) 'Pychoanalytic observations on the effect of lithium on manic attacks', *J. Amer. Psychoanal. Ass.*, 35: 877–902.

Loewenstein, R. (1969) 'Developments in the theory of transference in the last fifty years', *Int. J. Psycho-Anal.*, 50: 583–8.

Loewenstein, R., Newman, L., Schur, M. and Solnit, A. (eds) (1966) *Psychoanalysis: A General Psychology – Essays in Honour of Heinz Hartmann*, New York: International Universities Press.

Luborsky, L. and Crits-Cristoph, P. (1990) *Understanding Transference: the CCRT Method*, New York: Basic Books.

Luborsky, L., Crits-Cristoph, P., Mintz, J. and Auerbach, A. (1988) *Who will Benefit from Psychotherapy? Predicting Therapeutic Outcomes*, New York: Basic Books.

Luborsky, L. Popp, C. and Barber, J. (1994) 'Common and special factors in different transference-related measures', *Psychother. Res.*, 4: 277–86.

Luborsky, L., Singer, B. and Luborsky, L. (1975) 'Comparative studies of psychotherapies: is it true that "everyone has won and all must have prizes"?', *Arch. Gen. Psychiat.*, 37: 471–81.

Mahler, M., Pine, F. and Bergman, A. (1975) *The Psychological Birth of the Human Infant*, London: Hutchinson.

Main, M. (1991) 'Metacognitive knowledge, metacognitive monitoring, and singular vs multiple models of attachment', in C. Parkes *et al.* (eds) *Attachment Across the Life Cycle*, London: Routledge.

Main, T. (1957) 'The ailment', *Brit. J. Med. Psychol.*, 30: 129–45.

Malan, D. (1963) *A Study of Brief Psychotherapy*, London: Tavistock.

—— (1976) *The Frontier of Brief Psychotherapy*. New York: Plenum.

*—— (1979) *Individual Psychotherapy and the Science of Psychodynamics*, London: Butterworth.

Malin, A. and Grotstein, J.S. (1966) 'Projective identification in the therapeutic process', *Int. J. of Psycho-Anal.*, 47, 26–31.

Martindale, B. (1989) 'Becoming dependent again: the fears of some elderly persons and their younger therapists', *Psychoanal. Psychother.*, 4, No 1: 67–75.

Masterson, J. (1976) *Psychotherapy of the Borderline Adult: A Developmental Approach*, New York: Brunner.

Matte-Blanco, I. (1975) *The Unconscious as Infinite Sets*, London: Routledge.

—— (1988) *Thinking, Feeling and Being*, London: Routledge.

McDougall, J. (1990) *Plea for a Measure of Abnormality*, London: Free Association Books.

McLaughlin, J.T. (1981) Transference, psychic reality, and countertransference, *Psychoanal. Quart.*, 50: 639–64.

McNeilly C. and Howard, K. (1991) 'The effects of psychotherapy: a reevaluation based on dosage', *Psychother. Res.*, 1: 74–8.

Meares, R. and Coombes, T. (1994) 'A drive to play: evolution and psychotherapeutic theory', *Austral. and New Zeal. J. Psychiat.*, 28: 58–67.

Meltzer, D. (1967) *The Pychoanalytical Process*, London: Heinemann (reprinted Perthshire: Clunie Press).

—— (1968) 'Terror, persecution, dread – a dissection of paranoid anxieties', *Int. J. Psycho-Anal.*, 49: 396–400; also in *Sexual States of Mind*, Strathtay, Perthshire: Clunie Press, 1973, pp. 99–106.

—— (1991) Foreword to *The Chamber of Maiden Thought*, by M. Williams and M. Waddell, London: Routledge.

Menninger, K. (1958) *Theory of Psychoanalytic Technique*, New York: Basic Books.

Menzies, D., Dolan, B. and Norton, K. (1993) 'Are short term savings worth long term costs? Funding treatment for personality disorders', *Psychiatr. Bull.*, 17: 517–19.

Menzies-Lyth, I. (1988) 'A psychoanalytic perspective on social institutions', in *Melanie Klein Today, Vol. 2: Mainly Practice*, London: Routledge, pp. 284–99.

Mitchell, S. (1988) *Relational Concepts in Psychoanalysis: An Integration*, Cambridge, Mass.: Harvard University Press.

Money-Kyrle, R.E. (1956) 'Normal countertransference and some of its deviations', *Int. J. Psycho-Anal.*, 37: 360–6.

Moran, G. and Fonagy, P. (1987) 'Psychoanalysis and diabetic control: a single case study', *Brit. J. Med. Psychol.*, 60: 357–72.

Mullen, P. (1973) Personal communication.

Murphy, L.B. (1962) *The Widening World of Childhood: Paths towards Mastery*, New York: Basic Books.

Myers, W.A. (1984) *Dynamic Therapy of the Older Patient*, New York: Aronson.

—— (1986) Transference and countertransference issues in treatments involving older patients and younger therapists, *J. Geriat. Psychiat.*, 19, 221–39.

Nemiah, J. (1977) 'Alexithymia: theoretical considerations', *Psychother. Psychosomat.*, 28: 199–206.

Nemiroff, R. and Colarusso, C. (eds) (1985) *The Race Against Time*, New York: Plenum.

Nobel, L. (1989) 'When it is not the patient who pays', *Psychoanal. Psychother.*, 4: 1–12.

O'Shaughnessy, E. (1981) 'A clinical study of a defensive organisation', *Int. J. Psycho-Anal..*, 62: 359–69.
—— (1992) 'Enclaves and excursions', *Int. J. Psycho-Anal.*, 73: 603–11.
Ogden, T.H. (1979) 'On projective identification', *Int. J. Psycho-Anal*, 60: 357–73.
Orlinsky, D. and Howard, K. (1986) 'Process and outcome in psychotherapy', in S. Garfield and A. Bergin (eds) *Handbook of Psychotherapy and Behaviour Change*, London: Wiley.
Ortmeyer, D. (1988) Reporter, Panel: Gender of the psychoanalyst: central or peripheral, *Contemp. Psychoanal.*, 24: 667–97.
Ostow, M. (1990) 'On beginning with patients who require medication', in T. Jacobs and A. Rothstein (eds) *On Beginning an Analysis*, Madison, Conn.: International Universities Press.
Padel, J. (1991) 'Fairbairn's thought of the relationship of inner and outer worlds', *Free Associations*, 24: 589–616.
Parkes, C., Stevenson-Hinde, J. and Marris, P. (1991) *Attachment Across the Life Cycle*, London: Routledge.
Payne, S. (1950) Short communication on criteria for terminating analysis, *Int. J. Psycho-Anal.*, 31: 205.
Pedder, J. (1982) 'Failure to mourn and melancholia', *Brit, J. Psychiat.*, 41: 327–37.
—— (1986) 'Attachment and new beginning', in G. Kohon, (ed.) *The British School of Psychoanalysis: the Independent Tradition*, London: Free Association Books.
—— (1988) 'Termination reconsidered', *Int. J. Psycho-Anal.*, 69: 495–505.
Perry, J.C. and Cooper, S. (1989) 'An empirical study of defence mechanisms, I: Clinical interviews and life vignette ratings,' *Arch. Gen. Psychiat.* 46: 444–52.
Perry, J., Cooper, A. and Michels, R. (1987) 'The psychodynamic formulation', *Amer. J. Psychiat.*, 144: 543–50.
Perry, J., Luborsky, L., Silberschatz, G. and Popp, C. (1989) 'An examination of three methods of psychodynamic formulation based on the same videotaped interview', *Psychiatry*, 52: 302–23.
Person, E. (1985) The erotic transference in women and men: differences and consequences, *J. Amer. Acad. Psychoanal.*, 13: 159–80.
Pfeffer, A. (1961) 'Follow-up study of a satisfactory analysis', *J. Amer. Psychoanal. Ass.*, 9: 698–718.
—— (1963) 'The meaning of the analyst after analysis', *J. Amer. Psychoanal. Ass.*, 11: 229–44.
Phillips, A. (1988) *Winnicott*, London: Fontana.
Piaget, J. (1954) *The Construction of Reality in the Child*, New York: Basic Books.
Pine, F. (1981) 'In the beginning: contributions to a psychoanalytic developmental psychology', *Int. Rev. Psycho-Anal..*, 8: 15–33.
—— (1990) *Drive, Ego, Object, Self: A Synthesis for Clinical Work*, New York: Basic Books.
Pines, M. (ed.) (1985) *Bion and Group Psychotherapy*, London: Routledge & Kegan Paul.

—— (1991) 'A history of psychodynamic psychiatry in Britain', in J. Holmes (ed.) *A Textbook of Psychotherapy in Psychiatric Practice*, Edinburgh: Churchill Livingstone.

Piper, W., Azim, H., Joyce, A. and McCallum, M. (1991) 'Transference interpretations, therapeutic alliance, and outcome in short-term individual therapy', *Arch. Gen. Psychiat.*, 48: 946–53.

Porter R. (1991) 'Psychotherapy with the elderly', in J. Holmes (ed.) *A Textbook of Psychotherapy in Psychiatric Practice*, Edinburgh: Churchill Livingstone.

Quinodoz, J.M. (1992) 'The displacement of transference in the supervision; or how transference and countertransference between candidate and analysand can sometimes be acted out in supervision', *Psychoanal. in Europe*, Bull. 38, 46–50.

Racker, H. (1953) 'A contribution to the problem of countertransference', *Int. J. Psycho-Anal.*, 34: 313–24.

—— (1957) 'The meanings and uses of countertransference', *Psychoanal. Quart.*, 26: 303–57.

—— (1968) *Transference and Countertransference*, London: Karnac (reprinted 1985).

Rapaport, D. (1951) *Organisation and Pathology of Thought*, New York: Colombia University Press.

—— (1967) in M. Gill (ed.) *The Collected Papers of David Rapaport*, New York: Basic Books.

Rappaport, E. (1956) 'The management of an erotised transference', *Psychoanal. Quart.*, 25: 515–29.

Rayner, E. (1991) *The Independent Mind in British Psychoanalysis'*, London: Free Association Books.

Reich, A. (1951) 'On countertransference', *Int. J. Psycho-Anal.*, 32: 25–31.

Reich, W. (1928) 'On character analysis', in R. Fliess (ed.) *The Psychoanalytic Reader*, London: Hogarth.

—— (1933) *Charakteranalyse*, Vienna: Private Publication.

Reid, J.R. and Finesinger, J.E. (1952) 'The role of insight in psychotherapy', *Amer. J. Psychiat.*, 18: 726–34.

Reik, T. (1922) *The Inner Eye of a Psychoanalyst*, London: Allen & Unwin.

Rey, H. (1994) *Schizoid Modes of Being*, London: Free Association Books.

Rickman, J. (1950) 'On the criteria for the termination of analysis', *Int. J. Psycho-Anal.*, 31: 200–1

Ricoeur, P. (1970) *Freud and Philosophy: An Essay on Interpretation*, New York: Yale University Press.

Rieff, P. (1960) *Freud: The Mind of the Moralist*. London: Gollancz.

Rinsley, D. (1989) *Developmental Psychodynamics of Borderline and Narcissistic Personalities*, New York: Jason Aronson.

Roazen, P. (1979) *Freud and his Followers*, London: Peregrine.

Robbins, M. (1992) Psychoanalytic and biological approaches to mental illness, *J. Amer. Psychoanal. Ass.*, 40: 425–54.

Roberts, G. (1992) 'The origins of delusion', *Brit. J. Psychiat.* 161: 298–308.

Rorty, R. (1989) *Contingency, Irony, and Solidarity*, Cambridge: Cambridge University Press.

Rosenfeld, H. (1952) 'Transference phenomena and transference analysis in an acute catatonic schizophrenic patient', *Int. J. Psycho-Anal.*, 33: 457–64.

—— (1964) 'On the psychopathology of narcissism: a clinical approach', *Int. J. Psycho-Anal.*, 45: 332–7; also in *Psychotic States*, London: Hogarth, 1965.

—— (1971) 'A clinical approach to the psychoanalytical theory of the life and death instincts: an investigation into the aggressive aspects of narcissism', *Int. J. Psycho-Anal.*, 52: 169–78.

—— (1975) 'Negative therapeutic reaction', in P.L. Giovacchini, (ed.) *Tactics and Techniques in Psychoanalytic Therapy*, Vol. 2, London: Hogarth.

—— (1987) *Impasse and Interpretation: Therapeutic and Anti-Therapeutic Factors in Psychoanalytic Treatment of Psychotic, Borderline and Neurotic Patients*, London: Routledge.

Rosser, R., Birch, S., Bond, H., Denford, J. and Schachter, J. (1987) 'Five year follow-up of patients treated with in-patient psychotherapy at the Cassel Hospital for Nervous Diseases', *J. Roy. Soc. Med.*, 80: 549–55.

Rustin, M. (1992) *The Good Society and the Inner World*, London: Verso.

Ruszczynski, S. (1993) *Psychotherapy with Couples. Theory and Practice at the T.I.M.S.*, London: Karnac.

Rycroft, C. (1958) *Illusion and Reality*, London: Hogarth.

—— (1968) *Imagination and Reality*, London: Hogarth.

*—— (1972) *A Critical Dictionary of Psychoanalysis*, Harmondsworth: Penguin.

—— (1979a) Personal communication.

—— (1979b) *The Innocence of Dreams*, London: Hogarth.

—— (1985) *Psychoanalysis and Beyond*, London: Chatto.

Ryle, A. (1990) *Cognitive Analytic Therapy: Active Participation in Change*, Chichester: Wiley.

Ryle, A. (1994) 'Psychoanalysis and cognitive analytic therapy', *Brit. J. Psychother.*, 10: 404–5.

Sager *et al.* (1972) 'Black patient – white therapist', *Amer. J. Orthopsychiat.*, 42: 415–23.

Sandler, A.M. (1978) 'Psychoanalysis in later life. Problems in the psychoanalysis of an ageing narcissistic patient', *J. Geriat. Psychiat.*, 11: 5–36.

Sandler, J (1968) 'Psychoanalysis: an introductory survey', In W.G. Joffe (ed.) *What is Psychoanalysis?* London: Bailliere, Tindall and Cassell.

—— (1976a) 'Dreams, unconscious fantasies and "identity of perception"', *Int. Rev. Psychoanal.*, 3: 33–42.

—— (1976b) 'Countertransference and role-responsiveness, *Int. Rev. Psycho-Anal.*, 3: 43–7.

—— (1981) 'Unconscious wishes and human relationships', *Contemp. Psychoanal.*, 17, 180–96.

—— (1983) 'Reflections on some relations between psychoanalytic concepts and psychoanalytic practice', *Int. J. Psycho-Anal.*, 64: 35–45.

*—— (1987) 'The concept of projective identification', in *Projection, Identification, Projective Identification*, London: Karnac Books.

—— (1992) 'Reflections on developments in the theory of psychoanalytic technique', *Int. J. Psycho-Anal.*, 73: 189–98.

—— (1993) 'On communication from patient to analyst; not everything is projective identification', *Int. J. Psycho-Anal.*, 74: 1097–1107.

Sandler, J. and Rosenblatt, B. (1962) 'The concept of the representational world', *Psychoanal. Study of the Child*, 17: 128–45.

Sandler, J. and Sandler, A.M. (1978) 'On the development of object relationships and affects', *Int. J. Psycho-Anal.*, 59: 285–96.

—— (1984) 'The past unconscious, the present unconscious, and interpretation of the transference', *Psychoanal. Inquiry*, 4: 367–99.

—— (1994a) 'Theoretical and technical comments on regression and anti-regression', *Int. J. Psycho-Anal.*, 75: 431–39.

—— (1994b) 'The past unconscious and the present unconscious: a contribution to a technical frame of reference', *Psychoanal. Study of the Child* (in press).

*Sandler J., Dare, C. and Holder, A. (1992) *The Patient and the Analyst*, (2nd edn), London: Karnac.

Sandler, J., Holder, A. and Dare, C. (1972) 'Frames of reference in psychoanalytic psychology', *Brit. J. Med. Psychol..*, 45: 265–72.

Sandler, J., Holder, A., Kawenoka, M., Kennedy, H. E., and Neurath, L. (1969) 'Notes on some theoretical and clinical aspects of transference', *Int. J. Psycho-Anal.*, 50: 633–45.

Sartorius, N., Jablensky, A. and Regier, D.A. (eds) (1990) *Sources and Traditions of Classification in Psychiatry*, Toronto: Hogrefe and Huber.

Sartre, J. (1957) *Being and Nothingness*, trans. H. Barnes, London; Methuen.

Sashin, J., Eldred, S. and Van Amerogen, S. (1975) 'A search for predictive factors in institute supervised cases: a retrospective study of 183 cases from 1959–1966 at the Boston Psychoanalytic Society and Institute', *Int. J. Psycho-Anal.*, 56: 343–59.

Sayers, J. (1992) *Mothering Psychoanalysis*, London: Penguin.

—— (1995) 'Consuming male fantasy: feminist psychoanalysis retold', in *Psychoanalysis in Contexts*, London: Routledge.

Schafer, R. (1976) *A New Language for Psychoanalysis*, New Haven; Yale University Press.

—— (1977) 'The interpretation of transference and the conditions of loving', *J. Amer. Psychoanal. Ass.*, 25: 335–62.

—— (1981) *Narrative Actions in Psychoanalysis*, Worcester, Mass.: Clark University Press.

—— (1982) 'The relevance of the "here and now" transference interpretation to the reconstruction of early development', *Int. J. Psycho-Anal.*, 63: 77–82.

—— (1983) *The Analytic Attitude*, New York: Basic Books.

—— (1990) 'The search for common ground', *Int. J. Psycho-Anal.*, 71: 49–52.

Schatzman, M. (1973) *Soul Murder*, London: Penguin.

Schur, M. (1966) in M. Schur *Psychoanalysis: a General Psychology – Essays in Honor of Heinz Hartmann*, New York: R. Loewenstein, L. Newman, M. Schur, and A. Sonit, (eds) International Universities Press.

Searles, H. (1963) Transference psychosis in the psychotherapy of chronic schizophrenia, *Int. J. Psycho-Anal.*, 44: 249–81.

—— (1965) *Collected Papers on Schizophrenia and Related Subjects*, London: Hogarth.

Segal, H. (1958) 'Fear of death: notes on the analysis of an old man', *Int. J. Psycho-Anal.*, 39: 178–81.

*—— (1973) *Introduction to the Work of Melanie Klein*. London: Hogarth.

—— (1981) *The Work of Hannah Segal*, New York; Jason Aronson.

—— (1991) *Dream, Phantasy, and Art*, London: Routledge.

—— (1986) *The Work of Hannah Segal*, London: Free Association Books.

—— (1993) 'The clinical usefulness of the concept of the death instinct', *Int. J. Psycho-Anal.*, 74: 55–61.

—— (1994) 'Phantasy and reality', *Int. J. Psycho-Anal.*, 75: 395–402.

Selzer, M.A., Koenigsberg, H.W. and Kernberg, O.F. (1987) 'The initial contract in the treatment of borderline patients', *Amer. J. Psychiat*, 144: 927–30.

Shane, M. and Shane, E. (1986) 'Self change and development in the analysis of an adolescent patient', in A. Goldberg (ed.) *Progress in Self Psychology*, Vol. 2, New York: Guilford Press.

Sharpe, E. (1937) *Dream Analysis*, London: Karnac (reprinted 1988).

Simburg, E.J. (1985) 'Psychoanalysis of the older patient', *J. Amer. Psychoanal. Ass.*, 33: 117–32.

Sinason, M. (1993) 'Who is the mad voice inside?', *Psychoanal. Psychother.*, 7: 207–21.

Skynner, R. (1976) *One Flesh, Separate Persons*, London: Constable.

Slavin, B. and Kriegman, M. (1992) *The Adaptive Design of the Human Psyche*, New York: Academic Press.

Smith, M., Glass G. and Miller, T. (1980) *The Benefits of Psychotherapy*, Baltimore: Johns Hopkins University Press.

Sohn, L. (1985) 'Narcissistic organisation, projective identification, and the formation of the identificate', *Int. J. Psycho-Anal.*, 66: 201–13.

Solms, D. (1995) *The Neuropsychology of Dreams. A Clinico-anatomical Study*, Hillsdale, NJ: Lawrence Erlbaum Associates.

Spence, D. (1982) *Narrative Truth and Historical Truth: Meaning and Interpretation in Psychoanalysis*, New York; Norton.

—— (1986) 'When interpretation masquerades as explanation', *J. Amer. Psychoanal. Ass.*, 34: 3–22.

—— (1987) *The Freudian Metaphor: Towards Paradigm Change in Psychoanalysis*, New York: Norton.

Spence, D., Dahl, H. and Jones, E. (1993) 'Impact of interpretation on associative freedom', *J. Consult. Clinc. Psychol.*, 61: 395–402.

*Spillius, E. (ed.) (1988) *Melanie Klein Today*, London: Routledge.

—— (1994) 'Developments on Kleinian thought: overview and personal view', in *Contemporary Kleinian Psychoanalysis, Psychoanalytic Inquiry*, Vol. 14, pp. 324–64

Steiner, J. (1982) 'Perverse relationships between parts of the self: a clinical illustration', *Int. J. Psycho-Anal.*, 63: 241–51.

—— (1985) 'Psychotherapy under attack', *Lancet*, 1: 266–7.

—— (1989) 'The aim of psychoanalysis', *Psychoanal. Psychother.*, 4: 109–20.

—— (1993) *Psychic Retreats*, London: Routledge.

*Stern, D. (1985) *The Interpersonal World of the Infant*, New York: Basic Books.

Stevenson, J. and Meares, R. (1992) An outcome study of psychotherapy for patients with borderline personality disorder. *Amer. J. Psychiat.*, 149: 358–62.

Stewart, H. (1977) 'Problems of management in the analysis of a hallucinating hysteric', in G. Kohon (ed.) *The British School of Psychoanalysis: the Independent Tradition*, London: Free Association Books.

—— (1989) 'Technique at the basic fault: regression', *Int. J. Psycho-Anal.*, 70: 221–30.

—— (1992) *Psychic Experience and the Problems of Technique*, London: Routledge.

Stiles, W., Shapiro, D., Harper, H. and Morrison, L. (1995) 'Therapist contributions to psychotherapeutic assimilation: an alternative to the drug metaphor', *Brit. J. Med. Psychol.*, 68: 1–13.

Stoller, R.J. (1985) *Presentation of Gender*, New Haven: Yale University Press.

Stolorow, R., Brandchaft, B. and Atwood, G. (1987) *Psychoanalytic Treatment: an Intersubjective Approach*, Hillsdale, NJ: Analytic Press.

Stone, L. (1973) 'On resistance to the psychoanalytic process: some thoughts on its nature and motivations', in B.B. Rubenstein (ed.) *Psychoanalysis and Contemporary Science*, Vol. 2, New York: Macmillan.

Stone, M. (1993) 'Long-term outcome in personality disorders', *Brit. J. Psychiat.*, 162: 299–313.

Strachey, J. (1934) 'The nature of the therapeutic action of psychoanalysis', *Int. J. Psycho-Anal.*, 15: 127–59.

—— (1937) 'Symposium on the theory of the therapeutic results of psychoanalysis', *Int. J. Psycho-Anal.*, 18: 139–45.

Sullivan, H. (1953) *The Interpersonal Theory of Psychiatry*, New York: Norton.

—— (1962) *Schizophrenia as a Human Process*, New York: Norton.

—— (1964) *The Fusion of Psychiatry and Social Science*, New York: Norton.

Sulloway, F.J. (1980) *Freud, Biologist of the Mind*, London: Fontana.

Sutherland, J. (1980) 'The British object relations theorists: Balint, Winnicott, Fairbairn, Guntrip', *J. Amer. Psychoanal. Ass.*, 28: 829–60.

—— (1989) *Fairbairn's Journey to the Interior*, London: Free Association Books.

Symington, N. (1983) 'The analyst's act of freedom as agent of therapeutic change', *Int. Rev. Psycho-Anal.*, 10: 783–92.

*—— (1986) *The Analytic Experience: Lectures from the Tavistock*, London: Free Association Books.

—— (1993) *Narcissism: A New Theory*, London: Karnac.

Teesdale, J. (1993) 'Emotion and two kinds of meaning; cognitive therapy and applied cognitive science', *Behav. Res. Ther.*, 31: 339–54.

Temperley, J. (1993) 'Is the oedipus complex bad news for women?', *Free Associations*, 30: 265–76.

*Thoma, H. and Kachele, H. (1987 and 1992) *Psychoanalytic Practice*, Vol. 1: *Principles*, Vol. 2: *Clinical Studies*, London: Springer-Verlag.

Treliving, L.R. (1988) 'The use of pychodynamics in understanding elderly in-patients', *Psychoanal. Psychother.*, 3, No. 3: 225–33

Trist, E.L. and Bamforth, K.W. (1951) 'Some social and psychological consequences of the Longwell method of coal-getting', *Human Relations*, 4.

Tuckett, D. (1994) 'The conceptualisation and communication of clinical facts in psychoanalysis', *Int. J. Psycho-Anal.*, 75: 865–71.

Tulving, E. (1985) 'How many memory systems are there?', *Amer. Psychol.*, 40: 385–98.

Turkle, S. (1978) *Psychoanalytic Politics; Freud's French Revolution*, New York: Basic Books.

Tustin, F. (1986) *Autistic Barriers in Neurotic Patients*, London: Karnac.

—— (1994) 'The perpetration of an error', *J. Child Psychother.*, 20, No. 1.

Tyson, R. and Sandler, J. (1971) 'Problems in the selection of patients for psychoanalysis. Comments on the the application of the concepts of "indications", "suitability", and "analysability"', *Brit. J. Med. Psychol.*, 44: 211–28.

Vaillant, G.E. (1971) 'Theoretical hierarchy of adaptive ego mechanisms', *Arch. Gen. Psychiat.*, 24: 107–18.

Vaillant, G.E. (1977) *Adaptation to Life*, Boston: Little & Brown.

—— (1992) *Ego Mechanisms of Defense: A Guide for Clinicians and Researchers*, Washington, DC: American Psychiatric Press.

Vaillant G.E. and Drake, R.E., (1985) 'Maturity of ego defences in relation to DSM-III Axis II personality disorder', *Arch. Gen. Psychiat.*, 42: 597–601.

Vaillant, G.E., Bond, M. and Vaillant, C.O. (1986) 'An empirically validated hierarchy of defence mechanisms', *Arch. Gen. Psychiat.*, 43: 786–94.

Van de Kolk, B. (1987) *Psychological Trauma*, Washington, DC: American Psychiatric Press.

Vygotsky, L. (1962) *Thought and Language*, Cambridge, MA: MIT Press.

Waelder, R (1956) 'Introduction to the discussion on problems of transference', *Int. J. Psycho-Anal.*, 37: 367–8.

—— (1962) 'Psychoanalysis, scientific method, and philosophy', *J. Amer. Psychoanal. Ass.*, 10: 617–37.

Waldinger, R. (1987) 'Intensive psychodynamic therapy with borderline patients', *Amer. J. Psychiat.*, 144: 267–74.

Wallerstein R. (1992) (ed.) *The Common Ground of Psychoanalysis*, New Jersey: Jason Aronson.

—— (1967) 'Reconstruction and mastery in the transference psychosis', *J. Amer. Psychoanal. Ass.*, 15: 551–83.

—— (1986) *Forty-Two Lives in Treatment: A Study of Psychoanalysis and Psychotherapy*, New York: Guilford.

—— (1994) 'Borderline disorders: report on the 4th IPA research conference', *Int J. Psycho-Anal.*, 75: 763–74.

Weber, J., Bachrach, H. and Solomon, M. (1985a and 1985b) 'Factors associated with the outcome of psychoanalysis', *Int. Rev. Psycho-Anal.*, 12: 127–41, 251–62.

Weiss, J. Sampson, H. and The Mount Zion Psychotherapy Research Group (1986) *The Psychoanalytic Process: Theory, Clinical Observation, and Empirical Research*, New York: Guilford Press.

Westen, D. (1990) 'Towards a revised theory of borderline object relations: contributions of empirical research', *Int. J. Psycho-Anal.*, 71: 661–93.

Winnicott, D. (1949) 'Hate in the countertransference', *Int. J. Psycho-Anal.*, 30: 69–74.

—— (1958) *Collected Papers: Through Paediatrics to Psychoanalysis*, London: Tavistock.

—— (1965) *The Maturational Processes and the Facilitating Environment*, London: Hogarth.

—— (1971) *Playing and Reality*, London: Penguin.

—— (1977) *The Piggle: An Account of the Psychoanalytic Treatment of a Little Girl*, London: Hogarth.

Wittgenstein, L. (1982) 'Conversations on Freud; excerpt from 1932–3 lectures', in R. Wollheim and J. Hopkins (eds), *Philosophical Essays on Freud*, Cambridge: Cambridge University Press.

Wolff, H.H. (1971) 'The therapeutic and developmental functions of psychotherapy', *Brit. J. Med. Psychol.*, 44 117–30.

Wollheim, R. and Hopkins, J. (1982) *Philosophical Essays on Freud*, Cambridge: Cambridge University Press.

Wolpert, L. (1992) *The Unnatural Nature of Science*, London: Faber.

Wright, K. (1991) *Vision and Separation*, London: Free Association Books.

Wrye. H.K. and Welles, J.K. (1989) The maternal erotic transference, *Int. J. Psycho-Anal.*, 70: 673–84.

Wylie, H.W. Jr and Wylie, M.L. (1987) 'An effect of pharmacotherapy on the psychoanalytic process: case report of a modified analysis', *Amer. J. Psychiat*, 144: 489–92.

Young R. (1994) *Mental Space*, London: Plenum.

Zetzel, E. (1968) 'The so-called good hysteric', *Int. J. Psycho-Anal.*, 49: 250–60.

Zilboorg, G. (1952) 'The emotional problem and the therapeutic role of insight', *Psychoanal. Quart.*, 21: 1–24.

Index